D1546492

Insurance Reform

CONSUMER ACTION IN THE PROGRESSIVE ERA

Insurance Reform

CONSUMER ACTION
IN THE PROGRESSIVE ERA

H. Roger Grant

THE IOWA STATE UNIVERSITY PRESS, AMES, IOWA

For my mother

and in memory of my father
Harry R. Grant (1900–1944)
and my stepfather
Thomas H. Dearinger (1900–1968)

H. ROGER GRANT is Associate Professor of History at The University of Akron, Akron, Ohio. He holds the B.A. degree from Simpson College and the M.A. and Ph.D. degrees from the University of Missouri-Columbia. Grant specializes in American Western History and in American Political and Social History of the late nineteenth and early twentieth centuries. He is coeditor of *Years of Struggle: The Farm Diary of Elmer G. Powers, 1931–1936* and coauthor of *The Country Railroad Station in America.* Grant also has contributed numerous articles to both state and national historical publications.

© 1979 The Iowa State University Press. All rights reserved

Composed and printed by The Iowa State University Press, Ames, Iowa 50010

No part of this publication may be reproduced, stored in a retrieval system, or transmitted in any form or by any means—electronic, mechanical, photocopying, recording, or otherwise—without the prior written permission of the publisher.

First edition, 1979

Library of Congress Cataloging in Publication Data

Grant, H   Roger, 1943–
    Insurance reform.

    Bibliography: p.
    Includes index.
    1. Insurance, Life—United States—History. 2. Insurance, Life—United States—State supervision—History. 3. Insurance, Fire—United States—History. 4. Insurance, Fire—United States—State supervision—History.
I. Title.
HG8531.G7   368.3′2′00973   79-11795
ISBN 0-8138-0935-5
ISBN 0-8138-1210-0 (pbk)

Contents

Preface

I HAVE two aims in mind in writing this book. Both relate to my efforts at explaining the origin, development, and overall impact of an important, historic reform movement. Since the action was most of all a consumer crusade, ideally this work will inform, perhaps inspire, individuals presently engaged in similar drives or those interested in the roots of consumerism. I am also seeking an academic audience. It is my contention that an understanding of insurance reform during this period makes it easier to grasp the true nature of that great housecleaning escapade, the progressive era.

Reflecting in the 1920s on the previous three decades, William R. Baker, a perceptive insurance commissioner in Kansas, commented, "When historians look at the time from the rise of populism to the World War, they will say that reforms made in the insurance industry were a major accomplishment of the times."[1] Unfortunately, scholars have only partially examined changes in insurance in what may be called the progressive era, the years from the 1890s through the First World War. Two historians, Robert S. Maxwell and James A. Tinsley, for instance, in their respective studies of progressivism in Wisconsin and Texas, while concluding that the regulation of the insurance industry was an important reform accomplishment, failed to explain fully the forces that produced change.[2] They and others, in investigating late nineteenth-century and early twentieth-century insurance regulation, have either neglected or inadequately treated the sources of support for such reform, the effects of the depression of the 1890s on it, and the role of the insurance commissioner.

This study examines reform in life and fire insurance for the years 1885 to 1915 in five states: New York, Wisconsin, Missouri, Kansas, and Texas. Reasons for these limitations as to the types, time period, and geographic area covered should be noted. While it is true that reformers also sought to remedy abuses in the fields of accident, marine, and other types of insurance, they concentrated on the life and fire companies. These were the giants in the industry, receiving approximately ninety cents out of every dollar spent on protection. Moreover, an analysis of reform movements in these two fields illustrates the differences in the kinds of insurance corrections sought, the problems reformers faced, and their ultimate achievements, all facets that have received little or no attention in previous studies.

The period 1885 to 1915 covers those years in which the life and fire insurance firms grew to their current degree of importance in American life—years when political, economic, and social reform activities reached major proportions in the form of the populist and progressive movements. While historians commonly date the end of progressivism at the conclusion of World War I, for the purpose of this study 1915 makes a more logical stopping point, since by then nearly all the major reform legislation had been passed.

Although additional states could be examined fruitfully, those chosen all experienced a mixture of trend-setting life and fire insurance reform; no others sustained more activity than the five selected. Developments were continuously discussed in the trade press; at meetings of industry officials, agents, and state commissioners; and among those interested in all facets of uplift.

A review of the states reveals their varied accomplishments. No study of late nineteenth-century and early twentieth-century insurance would be complete without an analysis of New York. The Empire State, in addition to being the home of the nation's "Big Three" life insurance firms and of a host of fire companies, led the country with a plethora of corrective measures following the internationally famous Armstrong legislative investigation of 1905. Wisconsin, the state some historians consider to have produced "model" progressive legislation, experienced a long period of activity. Beginning in the 1870s the state pioneered in fire insurance policy reform and went on in the early twentieth century to launch the nation's first systems of publicly operated fire and life insurance. Missouri continually battled industry abuses during this period and gained national attention with experiments in state-made fire-insurance rates between 1909 and 1915. Kansas also experimented with the same concept; the first widely publicized suggestion for this type of regulation came from there in the early nineties. Kansas, too, was the home base of Webb McNall, a nationally recognized consumer champion who served as insurance superintendent during the late 1890s. In the vanguard of the crusade for state-made fire rates, Texas also became famous for passage of the Robertson Investment Act of 1907, which required out-of-state life companies to invest seventy-five percent of their Texas policy reserves in local securities.

Throughout this book I repeatedly relate my findings to three well-known, yet diverse analyses of political progressivism, studies made by Gabriel Kolko, Robert H. Wiebe, and David P. Thelen.

Because these historians' views are so vital to my study, a brief review of their scholarship is in order.

Gabriel Kolko in the early 1960s wrote the classic New Left view of progressivism. In *The Triumph of Conservatism: A Reinterpretation of American History, 1900–1916* (New York, 1963) he suggested that "it was business control over politics rather than political regulation of the economy that is the significant phenomenon of the Progressive Era" (p. 3). Kolko concluded that this era of reform was a fraud; the nation's dominant businessmen—for example, railroad officials and meat packers—wrote major pieces of regulatory legislation to suit their own needs. The Supreme Court's 1869 ruling in *Paul* vs. *Virginia* that insurance was a contract and hence not interstate commerce limited the possibilities for national control; but insurance men, nonetheless, actively sought federal regulation. Kolko felt insurance leaders like other businessmen wanted to replace radical state control by federal supervision, which they thought would be more favorable to their interests.

Another view of late nineteenth-century and early twentieth-century American reform came four years after the Kolko work. In *The Search for Order, 1877–1920* (New York, 1967) Robert H. Wiebe described the transformation of America from a preurban, preindustrial social organization based on the values of an interpersonal community to a new urban industrial state that transcended the institutional and geographical bounds of the older groups. The populist and progressive movements, according to Wiebe, came as responses to the shattering of the community. While populism was rooted in the defense of the old system, progressivism involved attempts to remedy the chaos caused by the new urban-industrial society. The solutions the progressives proposed involved "bureaucratization." Spearheaded by the new middle class, a producer-oriented group consisting largely of professional men and women, these reformers sought to bring about a modern orderly society through bureaucratic means. For example, they believed that independent regulatory commissions staffed by bureaucratic-minded professionals could best solve the problems posed by the new industrial disorder. Progressive era reform did not fail in Wiebe's mind, for his new middle class frequently succeeded in imposing its world view onto government. While Wiebe did not specifically discuss insurance regulation, his conclusion that the progressive movement consisted of the triumph of the bureaucratic mind-set provides a valuable framework in which to examine insurance reform.

In 1972 David P. Thelen's *The New Citizenship: Origins of Progressivism in Wisconsin, 1885–1900* (Columbia, Mo., 1972) appeared.

Rather than assuming a producer orientation as did Kolko and Wiebe, Thelen emphasized the consumer thrust of emerging progressivism. The cataclysmic depression of 1893 to 1897 caused badly fragmented reform efforts in Gilded Age Wisconsin to coalesce into a new crusade that, except for the business elite, crossed class lines. He described the outlook of movement members: "They saw politics as a never-ending struggle between the aroused consumers and taxpayers ('the people') and a producer-oriented establishment that constantly thwarted the will of the majority" (p. 2). Admittedly, the book deals with only a single state, but this widely acclaimed case study is suggestive of the nature of progressive reform elsewhere.

Although a rich literature on progressive era reform exists, the conclusions reached by Kolko, Wiebe, and Thelen help to relate insurance uplift to the broader picture. These interpretations have become a framework on which the insurance story has been fixed.

In an attempt to understand insurance regulation and relate it to the larger question of reform during the era of progressivism, this study first discusses life insurance, then fire insurance. Two reasons prompted this division. The earliest activities tended to center in the area of life rather than fire, making this a logical separation. Reformers succeeded in regulating the life industry, on the whole, sooner than they were able to do so in fire insurance. The Armstrong Investigation and the subsequent laws passed in New York and other states came during the years 1905 to 1907, while the most successful reform movement in the fire business—the drive to establish state-made rates—fell roughly in the period 1909 to 1915. The last chapters discuss the role state insurance commissioners played and the agitation for federal supervision. The latter topic serves as a means of assessing the overall success of the movement. Finally, a brief Afterword carries the chronicle to the 1970s.

Acknowledgments

I AM deeply grateful to the various individuals who aided me in the preparation of this work. I wish to thank the staffs of the State Historical Society of Missouri and the University of Missouri Library, Columbia; the Missouri Historical Society, St. Louis; the Office of the Missouri Secretary of State, Jefferson City; the University of Kansas Library, Lawrence; the Kansas State Historical Society, Topeka; the Texas State Historical Association and the University of Texas Library, Austin; the Dallas Historical Society, Dallas; the State Historical Society of Wisconsin and the University of Wisconsin Library, Madison; and the New York State Library and the New York State Department of Insurance, Albany. A Woodrow Wilson Dissertation Fellowship, in addition to providing me with a generous living stipend, helped pay a large part of my initial research costs. I also want to thank the Faculty Research Committee of The University of Akron for its financial assistance.

I am also grateful to the editors of the Kansas State Historical Society and the Missouri Historical Society for granting me permission to use portions of articles that originally appeared in their publications: "Insurance Reform: The Case of Webb McNall in Kansas," *Kansas Historical Quarterly* 36:62–73 (Spring 1970); and "W. D. Vandiver and the 1905 Life Insurance Scandals," *Missouri Historical Society Bulletin* 29:5–19 (October 1972). This material is included in Chapter 6.

Above all I should like to acknowledge my gratitude to Professors Lewis Atherton and David P. Thelen of the University of Missouri-Columbia, Professor George McJimsey of Iowa State University, and Professor Warren F. Kuehl of The University of Akron. These men gave encouragement and constructive criticism. University secretaries, particularly Garnette Dorsey, typed drafts of the manuscript with great skill and care. I alone, of course, am responsible for any errors that may remain. Finally, my wife Martha Farrington Grant proved to be my best critic, patiently rereading the many versions of this book.

Insurance Reform
CONSUMER ACTION IN THE PROGRESSIVE ERA

1

Life Insurance Reform before 1905

PUBLIC SUPERVISION of insurance in the United States is not a recent phenomenon. Duplicating much of the story of pioneer railroad and banking regulation, most states lacked major regulatory laws and agencies until after the Civil War. Yet several eastern states, led by New York and Massachusetts, sought to control corporate practices early in the nineteenth century. These initial attempts, particularly in banking and insurance, centered largely on dishonest and insolvent companies.

Get-rich-quick schemers soiled the image of the life insurance enterprise during its formative years. Unscrupulous businessmen took advantage of easily obtained state franchises and established supposedly "state-approved" firms. Carriers frequently considered premium payments their own and often contested or totally refused to pay policyholders' claims. Some promoters did not even bother to establish legal companies. They simply occupied an office, printed policy forms, and wrote insurance. Such "wildcatters" hoped to make their ventures profitable before the public discovered their unsavory activities.[1]

Even with reputable firms policyholders faced problems, the chief one being insolvency. Few life and fire insurance companies operating in the first decade of the 1800s existed by midcentury. Managerial ineptness led to insolvency, especially in the life field. While this factor played a significant role in a large number of fire insurance bankruptcies, small fires that became major conflagrations because of inadequate fire-fighting equipment and highly combustible buildings spelled ruin to still more insurance firms.

Desiring protection for life and property, policyholders bitterly protested the actions of dishonest fly-by-night and wildcat companies, and continuing problems posed by insolvencies troubled them. Moreover, there were those in the insurance world who longed for an orderly and sound industry. These individuals correctly realized they could generate business if they drove out dishonest promoters. "Insurance is getting a bad name," observed one New York City company manager in 1848. "The public demands a safe care-free business. Therefore, business expansion and general prosperity will not take place until we see that safeguards are provided for."[2] Such cautious and conservative men helped trigger drives aimed at curbing dishonest and insolvent firms, just as counterparts sought more businesslike railroad development and respectable banking operations. Throughout the nation these gentle reformers succeeded in having a variety of changes adopted, mainly in the period from the late 1840s to the early 1890s.[3]

New York made several attempts at meeting the challenges posed by fraudulent and insolvent companies. In 1849, nearly two decades after the state's intitial effort at preventing abuses and with strong industry backing, the legislature passed the nation's first truly comprehensive state insurance code, making incorporation of both life and fire firms more rigorous. In another attempt at preventing shortcomings, lawmakers in 1851 enacted what was called the "New York Deposit Law." This measure required each life company operating locally to place with the state comptroller by February 1, 1852, securities valued at $100,000. These would be held as protection for policyholders, although firms were permitted to collect interest. This deposit law sought to safeguard consumers from companies of questionable financial stability and to discourage the formation of new ones with insufficient reserves.[4]

Even with these legislative measures New York still lacked an arm of government to supervise the industry. The state needed an agency to cope with firms operating entirely outside the law, since it seemed impossible to legislate the wildcatters out of business. In 1856 a group of New York–based life companies successfully petitioned lawmakers to establish a special commission to examine the problems of regulation. Its conclusions were reported in December: "The only sure method . . . we can discover to prevent the organization of fraudulent institutions, and at the same time give the public an opportunity to know at all times the condition of the companies, is to have a system, sanctioned by law, requiring a rigid supervision on the part of the State, which can be accomplished by annual investigation and public registry of their securities."[5] Three years after the commission's report the New York legislature created an insurance department.[6]

Massachusetts, like New York, led in insurance regulation. In 1855 the more cautious life and fire managers, endorsed by concerned policyholders, forced the General Court (legislative assembly) to establish the country's first truly independent insurance department.

These crusaders believed that this would solve problems posed by fly-by-night and insolvent firms and that soundly managed businesses would flourish. Massachusetts went on to enact additional laws in the sixties, which included the requirement that annual dividend payments be made on life policies.[7]

In the post–Civil War years most states (including the others of this study) faced the question of dishonest and insolvent companies and followed the pattern of regulation set by New York and Massachusetts. While legislatures passed different corrective measures, creation of state departments of insurance was common to all. In 1867 Wisconsin authorized its secretary of state to supervise firms operating within its borders. Eleven years later Badger State lawmakers formed a separate agency to meet increasing demands from companies and consumers for regulation. Missouri created its insurance department in 1869, Kansas followed suit in 1871, and Texas acted in 1876. The specific statutes and regulatory practices formulated by departments in the East served as blueprints for regulation outside that region. Missouri's 1869 insurance code, for example, was virtually a carbon copy of the New York laws.[8]

By the last quarter of the nineteenth century the machinery for reform had been firmly established, and steps had been taken to solve the immediate problems of instability and insolvency. Indeed, adjustments to unruly, even chaotic, conditions became commonplace. While various insurance officers—often joined by the new state commissioners—were combating these evils, additional problems appeared. The policyholder, particularly the owner of life insurance, faced a mushrooming industry full of new abusive practices such as rebating and twisting.[9]

I

MOST AMERICAN INDUSTRIES experienced unparalleled growth after the Civil War. The life insurance enterprise was no exception. One scholar estimates that between 1865 and the New York Armstrong Investigation of 1905 the total income of all reporting companies soared from $25 million to $642 million annually, and the yearly excess of income over expenditures jumped from $14 million to $230 million. "The period from 1881 to the present time has been one of uninterrupted progress," reflected John A. McCall, president of New York Life, in 1898. "There has been but one failure of importance. . . . While it required fourteen years to regain the volume of insurance and income reached in 1872 and 1873, it only required seven years more to double it." And in 1904 an informed observer commented, "In a word their [life insurance companies] total income is a little larger than the income of all the railroads in this country, and their receipts for eighteen months would pay the United States national debt. This vast stream of money was barely a trickle 60 years ago, and it has increased nearly a hundredfold since the beginning of the Civil War." On the eve of the Armstrong Investigation the nation's largest life concerns, known popularly as the "Big Three,"—Mutual, Equitable, and New York Life—claimed nearly $5 billion worth of insurance in force compared to only $150 million forty years earlier. In 1905 their respective assets totaled $440, $412, and $391 million. The two principal life companies writing industrial insurance, Prudential and Metropolitan, enjoyed resources in excess of $100 million each.[10]

A variety of factors were involved in the gargantuan growth of the life insurance enterprise following the Civil War. These years witnessed the emergence of America as an urban-industrial society. Rapid, large-scale industrialization resulted in city workers becoming dependent upon the wage system. No longer did the self-sufficiency of the agrarian-based extended-family unit protect them from financial hardships. Thus, under these changed conditions the death of the breadwinner could mean immediate destitution for those who survived. It is understandable that wage earners eagerly sought the financial security offered by new and expanding life insurance firms. Even farmers expressed a strong desire to obtain protection, for they too faced uncertainties.[11]

Coupled with these economic considerations, attitudinal changes help explain the explosion of sales during the postwar era. Earlier, considerable cultural resistance existed to the concept of life insurance. Fundamentalist religions identified life protection policies with gambling and even sacrilege. Americans, moreover, seemed reluctant to shift the social practice of protecting widows and children from what one sociologist terms "an altruistic type of exchange" to a market one. However, life insurance triumphed when the fundamentalist religious outlook diminished; the notion of economic risk and rational speculation grew progressively more acceptable; and impersonal institutional figures such as professional morticians came increasingly to handle what once were family responsibilities after a death.[12]

Aggressive life insurance leaders, realizing the relative ease with which policies could now be sold, launched an all-out effort to reach every potential customer. New insurance plans and marketing techniques, developed by these highly optimistic businessmen, accelerated industry growth. Certainly one impetus to expansion came with the establishment of the Equitable Life Assurance Society of the United States in 1859. The company's founder, onetime Mutual Life agent Henry Baldwin Hyde, worked from the first to produce a high volume of policy sales. The Hyde years saw adoption of tontine insurance (deferred dividend policies) and formation of an enterprising agency force. The former revolutionized the industry. Based on a plan devised in the seventeenth century by Lorenzo Tonti for King Louis XIV, it offered policies on which dividends were paid only if the insured survived the time period specified in the contract. Thus survivors supposedly would receive handsome returns, while those who died before the specified date of distribution or who allowed their coverage to lapse would forfeit all rights to accrued dividends.[13]

Tontine insurance held certain appeals. The policyholder was offered the possibility of munificent returns on his investment if he adhered to his contractual agreement. Management, on the other hand, accumulated large amounts of capital since, unlike annual-dividend insurance, it did not have to disperse yearly payments. Furthermore, since the company did not pay a cash surrender value on tontine policies, lapsed money was not returned. This amount proved sizable; a twenty-five percent or higher lapse rate was common.[14]

Shortly after Henry Hyde began to market tontine policies successfully, other prominent American companies followed Equitable's energetic lead. New York Life offered its clients tontine policies beginning in 1871; Mutual Life began writing them fourteen years later, although it first opposed the plan. Firms that adopted tontine insurance soon discovered it constituted a sizable, if not the largest, portion of their annual sales. Several key companies, however, refused or hesitated. Colonel Jacob L. Greene of Connecticut Mutual firmly believed this new form to be too speculative. He argued that the function of life insurance was to supply family protection at a mathematically prearranged cost and that annual-dividend insurance seemed the best way to do so. Greene's dedication to "old ways" caused Connecticut Mutual to lose out in the rush for business in the late nineteenth century when the American consumer clearly preferred "something for nothing."[15]

This split within the ranks of the life industry merely mirrors the divisions among the world views of other business leaders, most noticeably railroaders. Just as contemporary "robber barons"—for instance, Jay Gould, Daniel Drew, and Collis P. Huntington—converted their properties into quick money-making machines with little regard for their obligations as public carriers, other railroad executives—Stuyvesant Fish, Robert Harris, and Charles Elliott Perkins, to name a few—preferred tradition to innovation and exhibited high moral standards. They were not part of the irresponsible type of operator so commonly associated with their industry. Although parallels are imperfect, Henry Hyde shares more in common with a Gould or a Drew, while Jacob Greene seems more akin to a Fish or a Harris.

Henry B. Hyde's other new marketing technique was a large and aggressive agency sales force. He encouraged high-pressure techniques by granting agents lucrative commissions. In some instances an Equitable representative received up to three-quarters of the first year's premium as his reward for a sale. Seeing the success with which Equitable attracted new customers, other companies offered their agents similar incentives. Wholesale looting of a firm's personnel sometimes resulted from this increased competition. In the seventies and eighties it was not unusual for a company simply to offer more in the way of commissions and fringe benefits to the sales representatives of a competitor and hence bring these men over to the bidder's side.[16]

While tontine policies and mighty sales forces enabled the Big Three to grow rapidly, other companies found another way to tap millions of potential customers—members of the working class. In 1875 John F. Dryden, president of the New Jersey–based Prudential Insurance Company of America, introduced industrial insurance to the American public. Patterned after a British plan, it called for the weekly payment of premiums averaging only a dime, collected by a door-to-door call. Usually the amount of the policy was small, the face value averaging about $150, and such insurance usually required no medical examination.[17]

Shortly after Prudential offered working-class insurance, the John Hancock Company entered the field; the Metropolitan began its coverage in 1879. The most striking feature of this type of operation was its high lapse rate. In 1904, for example, fifty-one percent of Metropolitan's policies lapsed within a single year. As a result, companies built huge cash reserves. Their financial strength increased still further, for policyholders often were not entitled to dividends.[18]

II

NOT SURPRISINGLY, a series of new consumer abuses accompanied this expansion of the life insurance industry. While policyholders initially worried about dishonest and insolvent firms, they later fretted over the problems stemming from cutthroat competition—rebating, twisting, unfulfilled dividend promises, lapsing, and unscrupulous agents.

Although these abuses continued from the late sixties to the time of the Armstrong Investigation and after, they seemed most pronounced before the depression years of the 1890s.

The fierce competition that marked the life insurance enterprise following the Civil War prompted numerous agents, at times with their company's blessing, to seek increased annual sales by offering clients attractive rebates, usually a division of their commissions. One insurance trade journal in the eighties estimated that rebating had become "so general that it may almost be said to be common to all companies and a majority of agents."[19] While some of the insured may have appreciated rebates, policyholders and industry representatives typically attacked the practice.

A variety of reasons produced these strong antirebate feelings. Most of all, because policyholders knew rebating was common, they felt discriminated against by a company that did not favor them. A New York City shopkeeper reflected this widespread complaint when he wrote, "I know of others here in the city who have been receiving from life agents a substantial rebate or drawback, if you will, on their policies. . . . It is infuriating not to receive equal treatment." Since insurance was sold at a discount, consumers correctly sensed that their policies were worth less than their supposed value. The rebate was also heartily disliked because the public knew that the titans of finance used this device to destroy competition and to form hated monopolies.[20] Finally, numerous industry officials and agents found the practice to be both disruptive and costly. For example, the Missouri agency superintendent for New York Life observed in 1882 that "this rebate business continually causes chaos." And he asked, "How much does an agent rebate? Who gets a rebate? I do not know." The official concluded that his own firm was "losing thousands of dollars annually on this unnecessary practice in the St. Louis and Hannibal areas alone. Every dollar's worth of insurance has to be bought."[21] However, an Ottawa, Kansas, underwriter charged that "the companies are not hurt nearly as much as the agent, for his customers will sooner or later find out that he has not used them all alike."[22]

Another marketing abuse was "twisting." Defined by an industry spokesman as "the inducing of a man who has a policy to surrender it and buy another policy from another company to take its place,"[23] twisting, like rebating, stemmed from intense competition. In their hunger for sales, agents used any means possible to convince prospective clients that they had mistakenly purchased the wrong policy from the wrong firm. Misrepresentation and slander of rival companies were common. Policyholders, often in complete ignorance of their own insurance contracts, became easy prey for twisters. The real evil was that consumers sacrificed valuable assets built up in prior years so that unscrupulous agents might collect commissions.[24]

Public complaints about twisting, while less numerous than those protesting rebating, were universal. Policyholders naturally became embittered when they learned how twisters had abused them. Various insurance leaders also attacked the practice. With great conviction Equitable president James A. Alexander blasted it in a 1904 speech: "This 'twisting' business is a crime, and it must be stopped. Lying about other companies is pernicious, and that must be stopped."[25] Like rebating, twisting disrupted sales and tarnished the insurance image.

Deceitful dividend promises constituted still another abusive marketing practice during this era of rapid insurance growth. To increase sales, life companies and their agents regularly exaggerated claims about future earnings. Sellers of tontine policies often estimated that their holders would double or even triple their initial investment! In an 1869 advertisement, Phoenix Mutual Life "guaranteed" a regular annual dividend of fifty percent on all its life plans, with premiums to be paid half in cash and half in company notes. Such extravagant promises never materialized, and they thus served to heighten public resentment toward the industry.[26]

Perhaps more discouraging to the average policyholder than his failure to realize high dividends were the provisions on forfeiture. If a tontine owner failed to meet his payments, he would lose everything. Tontine, semitontine, and annual dividend policies usually contained the stipulation that no matter how many years the contract had been in force, a missed payment meant immediate insurance cancellation, and in some cases no cash surrender value at all. Marketers of industrial insurance also did not generally pay a cash surrender value on lapsed policies that had been in force for less than three years. Such practices were hardly conducive to good company-client relations.[27]

Along with rebating, twisting, unfulfilled dividend promises, and harsh forfeiture practices, one more problem confronting the post–Civil War insurance consumer was the "lightning agent." This term, or "lightning solicitor," became a synonym for deceit, dishonesty, and duplicity. In the tradition of wildcat and fly-by-night operators, the lightning agent deliberately hoodwinked the public. He used rebating, twisting, or any other technique to sell policies in order to receive commissions. This unsavory character showed absolutely no concern for the financial well-being of his clients and frequently sold them too much insurance at too high a cost. Duped policyholders complained to companies, insurance departments, and lawmakers about such tactics. Respectable firms and their representatives similarly voiced their unhappiness, for these agents made the public more distrustful of all industry personnel.[28] Appearing before a group of Milwaukee insurance men, a representative of the Wisconsin Life Insurance Company excoriated the lightning agent: "He is ruining our business! If a stranger is seen upon the streets of a town, and upon inquiry it is learned that he is a lawyer or a doctor or a banker or a preacher or a professor in some college or a merchant from somewhere, a feeling of respect toward him is established; but if it be said that he is a life insurance agent, every man instinctively gets away from him—thanks to the lightning solicitor."[29]

III

POLICYHOLDER CONDEMNATION of ruthless marketing tactics, similar to earlier protests against company dishonesty and insolvency, helped to prompt the life insurance enterprise once again to respond sympathetically. Considerable support came from the consumer-sensitive National Association of Life Underwriters (NALU), typical of the era's emerging broad-based interest groups and professional organizations. Although not nationally established until 1890, local life underwriters had banded together in Cincinnati, Cleveland, Pittsburgh, and several other cities as early as the seventies to battle rebating, twisting, and lightning agents.

Underwriters had good reasons for supporting market reforms. Daily contacts with disgruntled customers made them extremely sensitive to grievances and naturally encouraged them to seek change. A Kansas City, Missouri, agent gave the common response: "Frankly my clients' anger with the present rebate situation and twisting by competitors frightens me. Some morning I expect so see a mob with clubs outside the office. Reforms must come . . . either self-regulation or enactment of our various reform proposals by the state government is the answer to these momentous problems." This interest in controlling abuse also stemmed from underwriters' fear of stiffer state supervision. "If we do not shortly start to mend our ways, the powers that be will bend us into a most confining mold," warned New York Life agent William Lucus Benton. "Policyholder opposition to the present marketing situation might well force the various state legislatures to take hasty and undesirable actions." Benton's fellow underwriters apparently agreed.[30]

Closely related to these urgings for marketing reforms was the deep-seated desire to establish respectable and orderly business conditions. From the 1870s on, a corps of agents voiced approval of attempts to professionalize their work. They eagerly endorsed codes of ethics for those joining their ranks, believing that professional standards would produce a class of underwriters "who are upright individuals . . . and who will make the selling of insurance protection a respected calling." A life insurance "professional" had no use for the lightning agent or anyone else who rebated, twisted, or intentionally deceived the customer.[31]

The principal concern of local underwriters' affiliates and the national society centered on abolishing rebates. In New York City, the Life Underwriters' Association, one of the largest and most powerful of such groups in the country, adopted at its May 1888 annual meeting a memorial to all firms urging them to suppress the practice of rebating. At the insistence of the New York organization John A. McCall, president of New York Life and that state's former superintendent of insurance, drafted an antirebate bill, which the legislature adopted a year later. Yet the New York Underwriters' Association did not stop there. At a subsequent annual meeting the organization offered a $200 reward to anyone presenting evidence of the law's violation. Furthermore, it actively backed the state insurance department in its efforts to enforce the antirebate statute. Members rejoiced when their agitation prompted Superintendent James F. Pierce to rule in 1895 that acceptance of rebates by policyholders would automatically invalidate their contracts.[32]

The story of the antirebate crusade in other sections of the country differs little from that of New York. During the late eighties the Milwaukee-based Wisconsin Life Insurance Agents Association, a later affiliate of the NALU, considered the question. After several failures it succeeded in 1891 in pushing an antirebate measure through the legislature. The Wisconsin association continued to call attention to this evil. As one member remarked in an 1896 Milwaukee address, "Rebating makes the insurance business a disreputable and beggarly makeshift, instead of an honorable and profitable calling."[33]

At the second annual meeting of the newly formed National Association of Life Underwriters held in Detroit in 1891, the organization endorsed the proposal by its Committee on Anti-Rebate Legislation for a model bill designed for the guidance of those states without such laws. By 1895 twenty-one states had antirebate statutes, some patterned after the NALU model proposal. Association members played an active role in the adoption of virtually all such legislation.[34]

The NALU continued to battle against the abuse by taking such extralegal action as pressuring major life insurance firms to form an antirebate compact. Signed by thirty companies on October 12, 1895, the document called for the discharge of any agent found guilty of violating its terms. Each of the signatories pledged not to hire such a person, no matter what his ability, for one year. To make the compact more workable, Thomas B. Reed, former Speaker of the House of Representatives, was employed as referee. But in 1898 increased competition caused the agreement to crumble, and within a year it became moribund. "We are reluctantly compelled to admit that neither legislation nor the compact between the companies has been effective to do anything like the extent hoped for," announced Equitable in late 1899, one of the last companies to withdraw.[35] Although the antirebate agreement died prematurely, support given by the NALU further demonstrates its commitment to eliminate the rebate.

The NALU had other reform goals, notably the establishment of professional standards. At its 1891 convention, delegates backed the recommendation of their Committee on the Bureau of Information, which suggested creation of an information department designed to protect both NALU members and policyholders from dishonest salesmen. This agency would maintain a "blacklist" of the names of all underwriters convicted by a local association of "any crime, misdemeanor or gross misconduct, calculated to bring disgrace and reproach to the noble cause of life insurance." The committee further asked that "any person blacklisted . . . shall not thereafter be employed by or allowed, directly or indirectly, to solicit or do any life insurance business for any member of any association connected with the National Association of Life Underwriters." The NALU hoped that such a tactic would purge the industry of lightning agents and forever end rebating and twisting.[36]

The final reform effort of the NALU prior to the Armstrong Investigation came in 1903 when it supported an anti–competitive–literature compact. This agreement, signed by the Big Three on April 23, 1903, went into effect two months later. It called for the use only of advertising literature containing information that companies had already agreed to be fair and prohibited agents from doing anything that would "encourage, aid or abet, directly or indirectly, any hostile criticism or attack of any kind in the press upon any American Life Insurance Company."[37]

While agents' associations, spearheaded by the NALU, were in the vanguard of marketing reform, some companies also joined the crusade. Predictably, support came from firms managed by basically conservative individuals. For instance, Henry L. Palmer, the cautious president of the Northwestern Mutual Life Insurance Company of Milwaukee, threw his energy and the resources of his firm behind passage of the 1891 Wisconsin antirebate law. Another Northwestern official, Willard Merrill, early in 1893 notified the company's field force in those states having antirebate laws that any employee found guilty of violations would be dismissed. In the same year Northwestern Mutual made its position clear and added an antirebate clause as a provision of the standard sales contract with its agents. Companies like Equitable, New York Life, Mutual Life, Penn Mutual, Equitable of Iowa, and Union Central Life tried to put the damper on rebating, twisting, and lightning agents. They met with only limited success; abuses seemed too deeply rooted.[38] "No agency could singularly refuse to grant rebates and long remain in a competitive position," explained one insurance commissioner in 1905, "no matter if they have the best of intentions."[39]

Another industry-initiated reform during the pre-Armstrong era occurred when various life firms modified their tontine policy plans. Connecticut Mutual's Jacob L. Greene led the fight. Throughout the seventies and eighties in letters to the public and trade press, lawmakers, and others Greene bitterly denounced speculative features of the tontine contract. Due in part to his efforts and the threat of a New York legislative investigation, Equitable and other tontine-oriented companies began to convert to semitontine policy sales in the mid-1880s. Under the new arrangement the policyholder received a cash surrender amount if he terminated the contract prior to the date of dividend distribution. Dividends on semitontine policies, however, were much smaller than those granted under the full plan. During the decades between the introduction of semitontines and the Armstrong hearings most firms made additional policy reforms, including liberalization of loan provisions, insurance of females at rates comparable to males, and extension of grace periods.[40]

The willingness of certain industry officials to control various marketing abuses reflects the same desire demonstrated by underwriters for a more orderly and rational business enterprise. The leader most likely to back marketing changes was the cautious manager, like Connecticut Mutual's Greene, who demanded honesty in his business transactions. Even the flamboyant insurance official, Equitable's Henry B. Hyde in particular, generally supported such changes, although this type of person could hardly be considered as leading the movement.

While corrections of life insurance marketing abuses can be attributed largely to industry sources, the public also participated. Wisconsin's 1891 Anti-Rebate Act, for instance, received the endorsement of a large and diverse section of that state's populace. Although the Wisconsin Life Insurance Agent's Association pushed hard for the bill's enactment, the local press—both urban and rural, Republican and Democrat—also gave its blessing. In the legislature the proposal received similar bipartisan support.[41]

One important group outside the immediate life insurance family that joined the public in seeking an end to marketing abuses was the National Convention of Insurance Commissioners (NCIC). Founded in 1871 and composed of state insurance regulators and other government officials delegated to supervise insurance, the NCIC exhibited a strong desire to ameliorate abuses caused by the life industry's rapid growth, particularly rebating. At its 1891 convention held in St. Louis, the general body overwhelmingly endorsed a resolution prepared by its Committee on Legislation, which called for "the absolute suppression of the vicious practice of rebating commissions." It further urged "the enactment of a stringent anti-rebate law in all States which have not already such a statute, the amendment of such as have proved insufficient to remedy the evil, and the rigid enforcement of the penalties provided whenever and wherever the law is violated." The organization's interest in that reform did not flag. On the eve of the Armstrong Investigation, it seemed just as eager to abolish the rebate. The NCIC, furthermore, sought to correct such injustices as twisting and lapsing by suggesting model legislation and discussing techniques that member commissioners could effectively use to remedy these problems.[42]

IV

IT WOULD BE WRONG to assume that life insurance personnel always enthusiastically backed all forms of regulation. Like businessmen generally, they objected to most legislative controls. Such issues as taxation, premium investment, salaries and operating expenses, and claims settlement practices (especially from the time of the cataclysmic depression of the 1890s) created serious tensions between industry and consumer.

Hard times gripped the country during the closing years of the nineteenth century. The Panic of 1893 triggered a deep economic slide that bore every mark of permanence. Workers by the hundreds of thousands suddenly joined the ranks of the unemployed and underemployed, and strikes became endemic. Businesses by the thousands went bankrupt. As money became tight, government units found themselves strapped to meet demands posed by the nation's first full-scale industrial depression.

The states of this study were hard hit, but Kansas and Texas were in the greatest economic difficulty. Both had been in the throes of a major agricultural depression since the late eighties. The droughts of 1889 and 1890 caused complete crop failures throughout much of the Great Plains, and most farmers found it impossible to pay their debts, which were probably accumulated during the boom years of the late seventies and early eighties. Slogans of "In God We Trusted! In Kansas We Busted!" and "Twenty Miles to Water and Forty Miles to Wood! We're Leaving Texas and We're Leaving Her for Good!" became grim reminders of the fate of the typical plains agrarian.[43] One northern Texas newspaper in 1894 described local financial conditions: "The money in the state treasury is at a low ebb. The revenues for the past year have been insufficient to meet the appropriations. The comptroller so informed the governor and the legislature, but no provision was made, and now state and school warrants must be hawked around in the market at a discount."[44]

To raise desperately needed revenue, lawmakers debated different tax proposals, including bills to force insurance firms to help support the community financially. Hard times also provided an opportunity to regulate the life industry through taxing devices. During the pre-Armstrong years life insurance taxation emerged as a frequent public objective as well as a source of conflict between companies and policyholders. The concept of taxing insurance was not new. As early as the 1840s some eastern states imposed a levy on both life and fire insurance firms. From the first the industry bitterly objected to taxes of any kind. Typical of their arguments was one made by the *Spectator,* a leading insurance publication. It would be "a tax on . . . policyholders, thus discriminating against those thrifty and prudent citizens who take this method of providing for those dependent upon them and who, otherwise, might become a charge upon the State, or at least upon private charity."[45]

Policyholders generally held other notions. Tax dodging, whether by individuals or by corporations, developed into a serious national problem during the depression. Therefore it seemed logical to many citizens that companies, as members of the community, should share in its financial support. And there were those among proponents of life insurance taxation who argued cogently that a sizable surcharge on the industry's rapidly mounting surpluses could effectively discourage sales of troublesome tontine and semitontine policies.

New York, one of the first states to tax the life insurance enterprise, had launched a notable drive during an earlier depression. The effort following the Panic of 1873 met with initial failure when confronted by a well-organized and lavishly financed insurance lobby.

Yet a token victory came in 1880 when legislators approved a small franchise tax on all life companies operating within New York City. This special act soon encountered trouble. State officials, believing the law to be unconstitutional, made no attempt to collect the tax. Once again the industry triumphed. (More than a score of years later one lobbyist admitted that "friendly" politicians had used the question of the act's constitutionality to squelch the tax.) But by 1886 local courts found the law to be constitutional, and the state comptroller sought to collect all back payments due. In a legislative bill he suggested that because the amount was large, a compromise should be made on the basis of a fifty percent payment. Under such an agreement companies owed New York over $1,600,000. They opposed a settlement, and within a year their Albany agents were able to have the original tax law repealed.[46]

The press, apparently free of insurance company control, blasted the industry's victory. New York City newspapers denounced the companies as "grasping monopolies" seeking to evade their just share of taxation. Editors also charged that firms were being operated for the "individual profit of their managers" rather than in the policyholder's best interest. And they attacked Governor David B. Hill for signing what they called the "life insurance grab bill."[47]

Undaunted, the industry's lobby continued to wield great power in matters of taxation in New York. Thus, depressed conditions of the nineties, while injuring the state's financial health, did not produce a major life insurance revenue measure, although the legislature considered several. In addition, tax bills designed principally as reform measures died during the period. The industry did experience a mild setback in 1901 when lawmakers, at Governor Benjamin Odell's prodding, enacted a franchise tax of one percent on life insurance premiums.[48]

During the 1890s Wisconsinites exhibited a keen interest in life insurance tax measures. Efforts were made to use the state's power to tax in order to achieve reform and also to require Northwestern Mutual Life, the dominant local underwriter, to bear its fair share of the financial load. Wisconsin also desperately needed increased revenues because of the problems stemming from hard times. The movement began in earnest in 1897. During that year's legislative session and the following one in 1899, lawmakers debated bills designed to reduce the large capital reserves that deferred-dividend policies produced. One proposal called for a tax on a company's general surplus, beyond the legal reserve, to curtail excessive accumulations. This bill and a similar one in the 1899 legislature met defeat. The latter would have taxed all tontine policies at two percent and semitontine ones at one percent, but it would have exempted straight life policies. The powerful insurance lobby "with its pockets full of gold" once again demonstrated its ability to stymie such legislation.[49]

While tax reform bills were defeated, a measure designed principally to raise revenue became law in 1899. This bill—later known as the Orton Law after its sponsor, Assemblyman Philo A. Orton, who was a Northwestern Mutual agent and a member of the state's emerging progressive movement—taxed non-Wisconsin companies one percent of their Wisconsin premiums and taxed domestic companies one percent of gross income from all sources except income derived from tax-exempt bonds and taxed real estate. The act exempted the popular and largely problem-free fraternal type of life insurance, which operated on a mutual plan.[50]

Although Orton had obvious connections with the measure's principal target, Northwestern Mutual, the act in no way can be labeled a "company bill." Orton quickly found the tax reform issue popular "beyond my wildest expectations," and made it a campaign issue during the 1898 election. The doughty lawmaker told a hallful of farmers in his hometown of Darlington that if they sent him to Madison he would make Northwestern Mutual pay its way. Orton pointed out that the company had paid little, yet it had a valuation equal to that of the entire city of Milwaukee. On a cross-class basis, Wisconsinites responded to the Orton proposal, agreeing that all corporations should pay an equitable share of taxes. As one citizen asked, "Why should I have to pay my property tax bill, especially during hard times, when a big outfit like the Mutual dodges thereas [sic]?"[51]

In the legislature Orton's proposal received support from both ends of the political spectrum. For instance, both the radical agrarian reformer Albert R. Hall and the conservative editor of the *Beloit Free Press* Chalmers Ingersoll gave the measure their blessings. The bill, moreover, received support because of an earlier defeat of a railroad tax measure. Railroad lobbyists reportedly pressed for Orton's legislation as a substitute for increased rail levies.[52]

During the first years of the Orton Law, Northwestern Mutual Life's tax bill jumped from $33,357 to $186,396. In 1901 the company paid nearly $250,000. Northwestern Mutual opposed the Orton Law from the beginning. It petitioned the legislature in 1901 for a change, arguing that it was paying approximately two dollars to other states in retaliatory taxes for every dollar out-of-state firms paid Wisconsin.[53] Lawmakers agreed to modify the 1899 law. They reduced the levy on non-Wisconsin companies to a $300 license fee and set a rate on Northwestern Mutual's Wisconsin premiums at three percent of gross income, minus revenue received from out-of-state premiums and taxed real estate. The 1901 law remained in force until 1905 when the Robert M. La Follette administration persuaded the legislature to impose a three percent gross premium tax on "foreign" life firms, despite the competitive interests of Northwestern Mutual and over its emphatic objections.[54]

Life insurance taxation in Missouri, Kansas, and Texas in the pre-1905 period followed the Wisconsin pattern. In 1889 Missouri passed a basic revenue-producing law, imposing a moderate two percent tax on all premiums collected in the state. As in Wisconsin, bills proposed in the pre-Armstrong era to attack tontine insurance failed. Insurance lobbyists in Jefferson City, the state capital, thoroughly understood the political process. They consistently squelched "drastic" proposals in committee, relying "on the long-time and trusted friends of life insurance." However, one revenue measure, which was also formulated as a reform, became law in 1895. It permitted municipalities to impose levies and fees upon life insurance firms for the privilege of transacting business within their corporate limits. The act raised much needed revenue for Missouri communities, while at the same time allowing them to control undesirable wildcat operations.[55]

Kansas life insurance taxation began in the 1880s when lawmakers approved an act similar to the 1889 Missouri measure. Reflecting popular sentiment, depressed conditions of the nineties produced a flurry of revenue-oriented proposals. The most significant came during an 1889 special legislative session when lawmakers approved a levy of two percent upon the gross earnings of home companies and four percent on the total income of "foreign" firms doing business in the state.[56]

Although Texas set an annual fee of fifty dollars on life insurance companies in 1862 (increased to $300 in 1880), the decade of the nineties witnessed a host of bills designed to force the industry to pay its fair share. The movement to tax life companies began in 1893 when the legislature placed a one and one-quarter percent tax on gross premium receipts collected within the state. Companies also were charged an ad valorem rate on their Texas property. The Austin correspondent for the *Galveston Daily News* caught the popular mood when he commented on the new statute: "It salts the life companies, and they have few enthusiastic friends." Two years later the legislature tried to increase the amount, but the result was an occupation tax of fifty dollars on general-life agents, seven dollars on local-life solicitors, and two dollars on industrial-life underwriters. In 1897 the gross receipts levy was increased to two percent and the one on local agents was reduced to five dollars.[57]

Along with widespread public encouragement for passage of insurance tax measures came support in Kansas and Texas for proposals to have life companies invest locally. A decade of public dissatisfaction with both the outflow of capital and overall industry investment practices bubbled to the surface in the mid-1890s. In Kansas the Farmers' Alliance, especially, pointed out that for approximately every three dollars residents spent on all types of life insurance they received less than one dollar in return. "The excess of premiums over losses incurred, not paid merely, would entirely pay for the construction of the State house as it now stands in a little less than one year and two months," said Populist governor Lorenzo D. Lewelling. "It exceeds by more than $2,000,000 the aggregate of appropriations for the fiscal year 1894. It exceeds by more than $100,000 double the amount of the entire bonded debt of the State at this time."[58]

In addition to taking large amounts of money from the state, the life insurance companies almost without exception became reluctant to invest in Kansas mortgages, especially on farms, after the rise of the People's party. A Holton, Kansas, farmer in an 1894 letter to the Kansas Insurance Department reported on the farm mortgage situation. "The [Connecticut Mutual] holds a mortgage on the farm belonging to a friend of mine. Last Feby. a year in advance of the maturity of his mortgage, he wrote the Co[.] asking if they would renew when his time was out. They replied that they had concluded to withdraw all their money from Kansas, and expected prompt payment. This doubtless is the agreed purpose of all the Eastern . . . companies with reference to populist Kansas."[59] The insurance world admitted this was so. As the *Insurance Journal* said, "Loans in Kansas are naturally being called in as they become due, and nobody cares to renew them, or to make fresh loans, or to invest money in any way in a state which is governed by the emotions rather than by fixed rules of law."[60]

It is understandable that Kansans agreed that such practices hurt them and that the situation should be corrected. Early in 1895 a Populist legislator proposed that out-of-state life insurance companies invest fifty percent of their Kansas reserves in local mortgages or bonds and deposit them with the state treasurer for taxation. Although his bill received the blessings of the Farmers' Alliance, Knights of Labor, and Reform Press Association, the powerful insurance lobby, alarmed at the measure's "radical and confiscatory" nature, killed it. Lobbyists worked largely through their friend on the House Insurance Committee, Chairman Samuel Gardenshire of Shawnee County, who later served the industry as one of its New York City attorneys. A similar investment proposal in 1897 met a like fate.[61]

As in Kansas, Texas sought to force life firms to invest locally. A leading proponent was reform governor Charles A. Culberson, member of the popular and powerful James Stephen Hogg wing of Democracy. In his annual message to the legislature in January 1897 Culberson discussed the extent of the financial drain Texans faced:

> Life insurance companies, principally chartered by and domiciled in . . . New York, have for years done a large business in this State. The excess of premiums over losses paid these companies by the people of Texas for the year 1895 was $2,471,192. The premiums which our people paid three New York companies for the past ten years amounted to $13,644,124.85, and the policies which they paid aggregated only $4,947,569.51. The excess in premiums, the sum taken out of the State in that time was $13,696,555.34, less inappreciable commissions paid the agents, and is greater than the total taxable values for 1896 of either of the great counties of Bell or Collin.[62]

Following the governor's message, Senator O. P. Bowser of Dallas County, a Culberson man, introduced an investment bill that required legal reserves on Texas policies to be invested in state securities subject to state and local taxation. Although the Bowser bill received a favorable vote from the Senate Insurance Committee, adjournment of the legislature killed it.[63]

While no compulsory investment proposal passed during the pre-1905 period, on the eve of the Armstrong Investigation strong sentiment for such a plan still existed. The *Houston Daily Post* in an editorial, "Make the Life Companies Invest," repeated earlier charges of a Texas dollar drain eastward and called for passage of a Bowser-like bill. The 1905 legislature did enact an investment incentive tax. This levied a two and one-quarter percent charge on gross premium receipts but provided for a reduction of one-quarter percent and one-half percent if companies invested as much as one-quarter and one-half of their entire assets in Texas real estate or securities.[64]

The life insurance companies opposed all investment proposals, just as they had state taxation. Firms argued that to protect policyholders they needed to place premiums in the safest and most profitable securities. Since the best opportunities supposedly existed in eastern money markets, it seemed to them inadvisable to seek out Kansas and Texas investments. Most companies went on to warn legislators and others that if they were required to invest in unprofitable local securities they would be forced to leave. If this happened, states could expect an even greater loss. Firms threatened to call in all loans and mortgages and foretold the dismissal of their army of agents. These company representatives made their living from the industry's state business and spent their income locally. States additionally would stand to lose thousands of dollars that firms paid physicians for medical examinations.[65] While the life companies' arguments undoubtedly influenced some residents of Kansas and Texas, the majority of the citizenry of both states very likely sympathized with advocates of investment laws. Particularly during a time of depression such proposals easily found supporters. The public had already become alarmed at the decline of farm mortgage money. A portion of Governor Culberson's message suggested that compulsory investment was needed not only for the capital such investments would provide but also for the taxes that would accrue. Clearly an investment law meant money, funds that these two financially troubled states desperately needed.

A more subtle reason for investment law agitation is what some observers have called the "colonial complex." The idea, as discussed by Walter Prescott Webb and others, refers simply to the West's view of its financial relationship with the East. According to Webb, the states of the South and the trans-Mississippi West shared much in common economically with colonies of European nations. In both cases outsiders came in and exploited the area's wealth without showing any real concern for its economic well-being and future growth.[66] Understandably, the indigenous population resented outside "exploiters." As one Texan remarked in a speech supporting the Bowser bill, "I am fed up with these big eastern life-insurance companies coming in here and taking our money back with them. . . ." And he added, "Texas is not a colony of the State of New York!"[67]

More so than Kansas residents, Texans had a strong sense of state loyalty and pride. Although the etiology of such an attitude is difficult to pinpoint, it probably had its roots in the Texas national experience. As an independent republic for a decade, Texans commonly considered themselves citizens first of the Lone Star State and second of the United States. The "colonial complex" theme combined with this strong feeling of local nationalism to produce support for the life insurance investment movement. This feature of Texas thought may explain why the state ultimately passed an investment bill and Kansas did not.

V

IN ADDITION to taxation and investment, other issues caused consumers to favor industry regulation. These included high operating expenses, company financial procedures, and claims settlement practices.

From the 1890s on, policyholders protested against the excessive operating costs of the life insurance enterprise. Some especially objected to the munificent salaries paid most company executives, an issue that became especially sensitive during the depression. In 1897, for example, Governor Culberson called salaries paid top life insurance officials "scandalous" and declared that the nation's poor were paying for much "undeserved wealth." Later he expressed a fear that extravagant salaries were a contributing factor to the growing gap between the nation's rich and poor, which Culberson believed would ultimately result in some catastrophic event, perhaps revolution. The Kansas Insurance Department received numerous letters from policyholders asking what could be done to lower officials' salaries. One Kansan imagined that New York Life paid its president a million dollars annually; another thought his salary approached $500,000. While such statements about New York Life salaries were grossly distorted, the public obviously believed that salaries were exorbitant. Actually, most high-ranking officials received a yearly compensation that ranged from $10,000 to $125,000.[68]

A similar complaint lodged by consumers pertained to the high commissions paid life agents. "It seems to me that it would not be a very bad plan to require companies to give a more intelligible statement of commissions paid to agents, instead of merely the gross sum," commented one New York resident. "Who, knowing the fact, would take out life insurance in a company that was paying commissions as high as 90% of the first year's premiums, with 7½% or greater [for] annual renewals, as is done in many cases by some of the largest and most extravagant companies?" He added, "What would the public say if other institutions were run upon rates of such excessive extravagance?"[69] In the same vein, a Missouri woman became angry upon learning that a sizable portion of her premium payments went directly to the life agent. "I can't understand this practice. What has my local agent done to deserve all my money? Can't something be done to end these huge commissions?"[70]

There were those, too, who became alarmed about the actual financial operations of the large life insurance companies. Although possibly concerned about excessive salaries and commissions, their attention focused on internal money practices. Typical were the remarks St. Louis publisher William Marion Reedy made in his journal, the *Mirror:* "It is natural to expect that when our present peculiar prosperity 'blows up,' as it must, some of the securities in which the money of insurance companies are invested will be found worthless. It is time that [the] State Insurance Department should begin to look into the abuses or the possibility of abuses of insurance company funds, which are usually funds in trust. The insurance companies are becoming too speculatively gay and they should be curbed before they do irreparable harm to their policy holders."[71]

Disputes over policies caused a severe rift between insured and insurers. While charges of contract abuse were long-standing, they became more numerous and perhaps more bitter during hard times. Although by the nineties many companies had instituted some reforms in the policies themselves, they had not ended all shortcomings. Certain firms, particularly marketers of industrial insurance, seemingly condoned cheating and deception of policyholders by agents and managers. One New Yorker described the activities of the Metropolitan Life Insurance Company in that city during the mid-1890s. "You can find hundreds of victims in New-York City alone who were defrauded and cheated out of their money by the Metropolitan Life Insurance Co. . . . There is a poor woman in 10 Forsyth St. who had her policy taken away from her on a flimsy excuse and in a few weeks was given a policy for half the amount, the poor woman did not discover the fraud untill [sic] it was too late."[72] The pitiful condition of some abused consumers was almost unbelievable. In March 1898 a Kansas City, Kansas, lawyer wrote to that state's superintendent of insurance:

> We desire to call your attention and notice to the just and meritorious claim of a very poor, illiterate old colored woman of the age of sixty years, by name Anna Williams of this City. She is the beneficiary of her only son Eugene Moore, who died in the early part of July 1896; the insured Eugene Moore secured a policy from the Metropolitan . . . about July 1894 for the sum of $500.00 for the benefit of his aged mother. . . . All premiums were kept fully paid up on said policy, until a short period prior to May 23rd, 1896, at which time and date he was reexamined by the Company's Physician, and then and there paid all arrears claimed by said Company, to-wit $3.14 for which sum we now have Company's revival application receipt; signed by their agent and dated May 23rd, 1896; at which time and date said Agent took said policy to have same stamped renewed, or to issue a new policy to insured; which so taken away has never been returned, or any other policy in lieu thereof has never been delivered to them, though frequent demands upon said company and their agents for said policy had been made, but of no avail.

The attorney went on to add:

> We further find from Company's premium receipt book left with insured, that since the payment of all arears [sic] and receipt for renewal, and taking away of policy above mentioned, that since

said date the Company's agent had called at insured's residence and received five weekly premium payments of 27 cents each, since the payment of the $3.14 which last payment was made only two or three weeks prior to insured's death. A number of neighbors and friends of Mrs. Anna Williams have written the Company, but they *refuse* and ignore to answer any and all correspondence except denying liability. Why their agent should call and collect five additional premiums and keep them is a mistery [*sic*], it certainly is a disgrace and an insult to the laws enacted to protect our people. Another thing since the death of her son, she has lost her only daughter who leaves two small children to be cared for by their grand mother . . . in her old age, and is compelled to do so by means of the wash-tub, besides the additional burden of her only son's and daughter's last sickness and funeral expenses are cast upon this poor old gray headed woman, which they seek to cheat and rob in order to enrich themselves.[73]

Another common abuse was reluctance or complete unwillingness to pay death claims in full. Companies frequently offered beneficiaries only a portion of the amount on the policy, forcing them to accept reduced payments or take legal action. Since this usually involved long delays and court costs, beneficiaries often accepted the companies' terms of settlement. Such a procedure angered those from all walks of life. "I think times are getting better," a Mankato, Kansas, policyholder wrote his state insurance department, "but we all remember a few years back when money was scarce and a school teacher here died and left three children without a living parent. New York Life contested her policy on some technical grounds. Her children finally had to settle for $100 on a $1000 policy." And this writer noted, "The *whole* town was mad. . . . We complained to the company and later to your department, but got no assistance. We in Mankato think it is high time that these arrogant companies obey our laws."[74]

From the nineties on complaints mounted concerning the cost of life insurance protection. The depression prompted a number of companies to raise rates. For instance, early in 1897 the Big Three increased charges from $27 to $35 for each $1000 of coverage for ten-year policies, from $35 to $46 for fifteen-year ones, and from $40 to $53 for twenty-year contracts. Consumer reaction to such rate hikes was typified by these words from the mayor of the Missouri Ozark community of Ellington: "Not only do those damn life outfits make it difficult to collect on but now they go and jack up their charges. I have a big family, I work part time in the saw-mills and in town I must have protection on my life, but I don't know if I can afford it for very long." He added a warning: "I find that hard times caused people to be concerned about the cost of everything, and I know that it will only be a matter of time before the people will band together and take their fists and go after those evil insurance men if they don't mend their ways fast."[75]

Understandably, the insurance enterprise harshly denounced those who questioned their internal procedures. They claimed they knew what was best for the policyholder and branded as "radicals" or "troublemakers" anyone who sought to investigate or force a change in their established business practices. As for state regulation, the *Spectator* captured the industry's historic views on the subject in 1904: "Efforts should . . . be made to inculcate more just and reasonable ideas as to the beneficent position occupied by insurance in the business and social systems of this country; and to demonstrate, as forcefully as possible, the desirability of allowing insurance interests the greatest freedom of action consistent with a wise, though mild, supervision. The latter should contemplate the protection of the public from fraudulent concerns, but should permit legitimate companies to operate untrammeled by useless restrictions; and no greater fees or taxes should be collected from insurance interests than are necessary to maintain supervisory departments."[76]

VI

EVEN THOUGH state legislatures in the pre-1905 period failed to enact reform measures designed to control most nonmarketing abuses, support grew steadily for greater consumer protection. In the mid-1890s the first rumblings could be heard for publicly sponsored life insurance. In Wisconsin, Missouri, and Kansas some concerned individuals—policyholders and even state officials—believed that a practical solution to the host of life insurance abuses lay in government insurance. They envied the performance of similar programs, widely publicized in western Europe and New Zealand. While these advocates failed to achieve that goal, they nevertheless left a plan that later reformers used with some success. Coinciding with the movement for publicly sponsored life insurance was the promotion of fraternal insurance. Just as fire insurance crusaders backed fire mutual companies in their quest to control the "fire-trust," fraternal life insurance was emerging as one method of providing consumers with adequate coverage (at least for burial) at a fair price. Since most fraternals operated on a purely mutual plan and employed few salaried officers, policyholders participated in the company's operation and enjoyed the benefits of low overhead costs. Furthermore, a new breed of state insurance commissioners appeared around the turn of the century, who, primarily by using the existing powers of their office, defended the consumer from numerous abuses, particularly injustices stemming from contested claims.

An assessment of life insurance regulation on the eve of the New York Armstrong Investigation reveals that while progress occurred, primarily in the area of marketing practices, consumers were left unsatisfied. Granted, the new "professionals"—various industry executives and NALU and NCIC members—contributed to reform; they fought hard to establish an orderly business yet failed to tackle the tough problems associated with high operating costs and other internal industry practices. The fuel for major change was now present; only the spark of the sensational New York probe was needed to ignite a series of nationwide life insurance reforms. The intense consumerism that became so much a part of progressivism was about to erupt.

2

Consumer Triumph:
The 1905–1907 Armstrong Investigation

PUBLIC DISSATISFACTION with the life insurance business had mushroomed by 1905. Although industry personnel generally accepted the concept of self-regulation and thus backed state drives to end such marketing abuses as rebating and twisting, they continued to resist more fundamental reforms. Consumers justifiably complained about the enterprise—from companies' frequent failure to honor initial sales claims to their unwillingness to make popular investments. Sensing this vast reservoir of discontent, certain writers—"muckrakers" as they were commonly called—quickly discovered that exposé articles on life insurance evils were as well received as earlier ones on railroads and oil companies had been. Resentful of the treatment they had received and increasingly anxious about the safety of "sacred" funds, policyholders found it easy to relate to the problems and solutions portrayed in crusading stories of industry wrongs. Unquestionably, such writers acted as catalysts to precipitate the sensational explosion of life insurance reform that commenced with the New York State Armstrong Investigation during the summer of 1905.

The exposés most responsible for bringing about the Armstrong probe appeared in two popular journals, *Everybody's Magazine* and the *Era Magazine,* and in Joseph Pulitzer's crusading daily, the *New York World.* While other magazines and newspapers also described life insurance shortcomings, these publications caused the greatest sensations.[1]

The accounts in *Everybody's,* which appeared first, enjoyed a nationwide audience. Interest became so intense that the magazine sold out its insurance exposé issues, a phenomenon that surprised both Thomas W. Lawson, author of the series, and the journal's editors. The success of *Everybody's* prompted others to reveal life insurance wrongs in the hope of instigating reform and perhaps boosting circulation. One month after *Everybody's* first mention of business shortcomings John W. Ryckman began publishing in the *Era Magazine* what can be described as the first full-scale assault on the insurance industry. Ryckman immodestly claimed that his magazine "inaugurated this great insurance reform campaign." The *World* articles, although reaching a more localized audience than *Everybody's* and *Era,* appeared daily and thus applied the pressure needed to trigger a major investigation in New York, home of the nation's life giants.[2]

In July 1904 *Everybody's* embarked on a series of articles written by Thomas W. Lawson and entitled "Frenzied Finance." Lawson had already achieved considerable fame and material success as a Boston stockbroker and market speculator. In the late 1890s he promoted the Amalgamated Copper Company, the name under which Standard Oil officials reorganized the great Anaconda copper mines and associated properties. In this stock promotion venture he acted as chief broker and realized a handsome profit for his labors. However, he soon became disenchanted with the whole speculative mania that was sweeping American business. In 1902 the editors of *Everybody's,* learning of Lawson's change of mind, induced him to write the "inside" story of Amalgamated.[3]

While the "Frenzied Finance" articles focused primarily on Standard Oil and its copper dealings, Lawson wove into his story a detailed description of the shortcomings of life insurance firms. Beginning with the October 1904 issue of *Everybody's* and in subsequent installments he trained his guns on the life industry's Big Three—Equitable, New York Life, and Mutual. Lawson damned the companies for unjust marketing methods, condemned their high rate of lapsing, and exposed various investment syndicates that had garnered huge profits for leading life insurance officials. He charged, too, that the officers of the Big Three held absolute control over the funds paid in by policyholders, who had no voice in the affairs of these huge enterprises. Lawson concluded that the Big Three were as much "a participant in the frenzied speculation of the period as were the plunging Wall Street stock gamblers." In a note to his December article, he proclaimed that his intention was to set a "blaze that will make the life insurance policyholders' world so light that every scoundrel with a mask, dark-lantern, and suspicious-looking bag will stand out so clear that he cannot escape the consequences of his past deeds, nor commit further ones." Within a year Lawson would take great satisfaction in knowing that he had achieved his goal.[4]

The reaction to Lawson's blistering attack was massive and

varied. The insurance industry castigated him. The *American Underwriter* called the articles "yellow journalism" and said that Lawson's purpose was "to raise h--l and sell papers." The respected insurance trade journal the *Spectator* rushed to the companies' defense by insisting that "there is no business that takes the public into fuller confidence than does that of life insurance. Their annual reports made to the various insurance departments are open books. . . . Any attempt to connect the life insurance companies with Wall Street speculations or with the financing of any of the so-called 'trusts' is absurd and ridiculous." The enterprise widely reported that Lawson, whom they now frequently branded as a "financial black-mailer," sought revenge because the Big Three would not insure him—a charge that was unfounded.[5]

Nearly everyone else unsparingly praised Lawson's muckracking articles. One Wisconsin writer declared that "Lawson's last installment of Frenzied Finance is long and illuminating and leaves no doubt that he is doing a stupendous work in behalf of the American people. . . . [He has] convinced the people of the truth of the charges that [the life insurance companies] have been systematically robbing and supporting their robberies by perjury." The same paper later concluded that "Lawson had done more for the people of the country than any other distinctively business man in the past fifty years."[6]

Using the pseudonym Henry Shedd Beardsley, editor-publisher John W. Ryckman penned an extremely popular series on life insurance, which his *Era Magazine* ran from November 1904 to October 1905. In "The Despotism of Combined Millions," Ryckman, like Lawson, carefully exposed the reckless and unscrupulous practices of the Big Three. He hit hard at the fact that consumers suffered needlessly from industry mismanagement and wrongdoing. For instance, in 1880 the Big Three returned to policyholders twenty-four and one-half cents on their premium dollar, while in 1903 they received only seven and one-quarter cents of each dollar paid. Yet income was more than seven times greater in 1903 than it had been in 1880. Ryckman emphasized that premiums had made the industry perfect El Dorados for the favored; that millions of dollars went to support a plethora of "trusts," ranging from coal to street railways; and that other funds vanished in foolish speculative ventures.[7]

To worsen matters, the Big Three held the average policyholder in utter contempt. Ryckman revealed that agents were encouraged to misrepresent dividend returns and other policy features. Consumers were commonly threatened with expensive litigation if they refused to accept a settlement offer. Moreover, the giants spent lavishly on legislative lobbying to protect their interests. Just as Henry Demarest Lloyd once noted that Standard Oil did everything to the Pennsylvania legislature except refine it, Ryckman told readers in June 1905 that insurance men, *"not only own trust companies and banks and railroads and telegraph lines, but they control legislatures."* After thousands of words of exposé narrative, this muckraker reflected: "The investigation into the affairs and conduct of the life insurance combine leads one into such a tangled jungle of financial intrigue, gross delusion and deception, broken faith and political corruption, that I find my greatest difficulty lies in isolating certain and distinct parts of this whole ugly mess."[8]

According to Ryckman, dishonest conditions in the life insurance enterprise had reached dangerous proportions; yet, reflecting the optimism of the progressive spirit, he held out hope for a better day. Ryckman thought reform was possible if Americans heeded his warnings and acted swiftly to right wrongs. Specifically, he called for the following: "[Companies] should be put upon the same basis for the investment of their funds as the savings banks; there should be a law prohibiting a life insurance company from operating a 'trust' company, so as to make it impossible to invest in rotten 'syndicate' schemes, or lend money in sums of millions to office boys, or take over worthless securities bought by high financiers for nothing, and sold to policyholders at high prices; the delusive tontine dividend game should be prohibited; [and] there should be an annual accounting to every policyholder, so as to reduce year by year the outlay for his policy." Finally, Ryckman suggested that "the expenses of conducting the business of the policyholders should be restricted by law."[9]

As could be expected, the *Era*'s exposé series met with nearly universal public approbation. Thousands of policyholders wrote Ryckman to applaud his good work. A Scottsville, New York, consumer penned a common response: "I am very much interested in your insurance articles in *The Era* and think the good you are doing will never be fully realized by the insuring public." A resident of Dallas, Texas, complimented both Ryckman and Lawson. "I have been deeply interested in your timely articles on the rascality, duplicity and general cussedness of the high rollers, who manage the affairs of the 'Big Three.' I think you and Lawson are doing the country a great service." However, the Texan added, "Your exposé of the rottenness of the three giant life companies is, however, far more important by far than Mr. Lawson's story of the Amalgamated." And he urged Ryckman, "Don't let up; publicity is

THE EQUITABLE CONTROVERSY
Policyholder— " I wonder if they'll give me the core "
Jamieson, in Pittsburg *Dispatch*

The widely publicized clash between rival managerial factions within the august Equitable Life Assurance Society in
the spring of 1905 helped to trigger the nation's greatest
consumer probe of the life insurance industry, the New
York Armstrong investigation. (Courtesy of American
History Research Center, Akron, Ohio.)

the thing: keep hammering away at them. I doubt exceedingly if
either of the 'Big Three' could stand a thorough examination. I
believe they are rotten to the core."[10]

As with Thomas Lawson's exposés, the Big Three blasted
Ryckman and all who joined him. For example, an agency director
for the New York Life said flatly, "He is simply endeavoring to
create a sensation, thus enhancing the value, if possible, of his

writings.'' Similarly, the insurance trade press, especially those controlled by the life giants, denounced the series. The *Spectator* branded Ryckman and policyholders clamoring for reform as "dangerous individuals" who seemed to "enjoy slinging mud at a time-tested and time-honored American business.''[11]

Lawson and Ryckman struck such a rich and popular vein that Pulitzer's *New York World* began exposé installments on the Equitable Life Assurance Society of the United States. While Lawson's and Ryckman's articles strengthened suspicion in the public mind regarding the life insurance business, the *World* convinced consumers that reform was needed immediately.

The paper's first revelation came on January 31, 1905, when it covered in detail the lavish "French Ball" given by James Hazen Hyde, the twenty-eight-year-old bachelor son of Equitable's founder. At a cost approaching $100,000, young Hyde had the grand ballroom of Sherry's in New York City converted into a theater and the room below into a "Versailles Garden," complete with grass, flowering arbors, and bubbling fountains.[12]

The *World*'s editors, encouraged by the popularity of their French Ball coverage and expecting both to increase circulation and to serve the public, reported on February 15 that they had detected strife within the management group of the august Equitable. The paper described the company's internal conflicts as a fight between two factions, one led by Equitable's president James W. Alexander and second vice-president Gage E. Tarbell and the other by young Hyde, the firm's first vice-president. The Alexander-Tarbell forces hoped to oust Hyde and to mutualize the company. They and their followers believed Hyde to be totally irresponsible and feared having a "playboy" elevated to the presidency. Under terms of his father's will, Hyde was scheduled to inherit 502 shares of Equitable stock upon reaching his thirtieth birthday, which would thus give him absolute control. On the other hand, the Hyde faction insisted that its opponents sought mutualization so that they could control a $400 million corporation rather than because of any altruism.[13]

Shortly after the *World*'s initial article on the dissension sweeping Equitable, the paper printed a document in which President Alexander and other Equitable officials threatened to quit unless Hyde resigned as first vice-president. Equitable's problems now became nationwide front-page news.[14]

In response to all this unfavorable publicity, the firm made a half-hearted attempt to muffle its internal squabbles. Nevertheless, the *World* continued to ferret out company shortcomings. The paper began to charge that Equitable's reckless management had speculated widely and wildly with policyholders' money. On April 2, 1905, the Pulitzer organ published a full-page editorial on "Equitable Corruption," asserting that the New York State Insurance Department, through its negligence, shared responsibility with Alexander and Hyde for this deplorable situation. "A searching legislative investigation is now imperative," demanded the *World*. "It should extend to the other great life-insurance companies incorporated under the laws of New York. . . . Mr. Hyde has become merely the embodiment of one scandal in a circle of scandals. He is hardly more than an illuminating incident."[15]

I

JUST AFTER the *World*'s demand for an investigation, both Equitable and the New York Insurance Department launched systematic inquiries into alleged charges of mismanagement and misconduct. Equitable directors appointed a special blue-ribbon committee headed by fellow member Henry Clay Frick, the steel magnate and former partner of Andrew Carnegie, to examine the company's affairs. On May 31, 1905, the panel submitted its report. It charged that exorbitant salaries were being paid to officers and favored employees, that excessive commissions were being given to field agents, that inadequate accounting procedures for disbursements existed, and that company funds were being used to support prices of Wall Street securities in which Equitable officers were intimately interested. The Frick committee recommended a complete reorganization and the removal of Alexander and Hyde. When the board of directors refused, Frick and the directors on his committee who backed the report resigned and leaked its contents to an eagerly waiting press. The resulting publicity helped Hyde decide to leave the firm, and by the end of June 1905 he had sold his stock for a comparatively modest $2,500,000 to street railway promoter and financier Thomas Fortune Ryan. To restore Equitable's sagging reputation, Ryan placed his newly acquired stock in the hands of three trustees of impeccable respectability: former president Grover Cleveland, New York Supreme Court justice Morgan J. O'Brien, and inventor-businessman George Westinghouse. Paul Morton, Theodore Roosevelt's former secretary of the navy, became company president.[16]

A few weeks after the public learned of the Frick findings, the New York State Insurance Department released its study. This investigation had been directed by aged Insurance Superintendent

THE INSURANCE DIVIDENDS
" Why not change ends? "
Evans, in the Cleveland *Leader*

Consumer outrage toward Equitable ("Inequitable") is illustrated in this 1905 cartoon published in the conservative Republican *Cleveland* (Ohio) *Leader*. Support for life insurance reform crossed ideological lines. (Courtesy of American History Research Center, Akron, Ohio.)

Francis Hendricks of Syracuse, longtime friend of the industry and former Republican boss of Onondaga County. He had reluctantly conducted the probe, which confirmed the earlier Frick committee conclusions as to gross financial malpractice. The Hendricks investigation, for example, documented the leasing on a long-term basis of a company-owned building by Equitable personnel to a safe-deposit business in which they held a substantial interest. The lease provided for only a token rent to Equitable and absorption of all maintenance costs by it, thereby enabling the safe-deposit firm to declare huge dividends to its stockholders, who, of course, happened to be company officials. Hendricks also revealed that Equitable officers had contributed handsomely to political figures, including Chauncey Depew, Republican U.S. senator from New York, and David B. Hill, former governor and leader of New York's Democratic party.[17]

Superintendent Hendricks made two principal recommendations. First, he proposed mutualization because he believed that existing evils within the Equitable company could best be eliminated by such a change. "A cancer cannot be cured by treating the symptoms," he declared. "Complete mutualization . . . is, in my opinion, the only sure measure of relief." Second, Hendricks suggested that the next legislature provide for better control over life insurance investments, recommending specifically that investments in subsidiary corporations be prohibited. As such he abandoned the long-established philosophy of "negativism," namely, that the insurance department and the legislature need concern themselves only with matters of solvency and marketing practices.[18]

By now policyholders expressed alarm at disclosures of corruption in the Equitable ranks. Demand grew nationally for a full-scale investigation of the life insurance enterprise, and in New York attention was focused on deficiencies in the state insurance department. "We must have a searching examination of the life business to bring about the necessary reforms," wrote one Brooklyn tradesman and Equitable policyholder. "Why did not the Insurance Department years ago discover all this funny business? What was it for? Why not investigate that body as well?"[19]

Perhaps the best single expression of consumer reaction appeared in a June 25 editorial in the *New York World:*

> For years radical speakers and radical newspapers have been indiscriminately assailing Wall Street and organized capital. They have been denouncing the relations between government and predatory wealth. They have been attacking the conscience and the moral integrity of the great captains of finance and appealing to the people to throw off their "shackles."
>
> Everyone knew that there was a measure of truth in these charges, but the indictment failed to make an indelible impression upon the minds of the great mass of people.
>
> When one set of financiers stole a railroad from another set of financiers the average man might regard the transaction as immoral, but it was not close enough to his personal in-

terests to awaken his resentment. When a trust increased the cost of a necessary [*sic*] of life it was an impersonal sort of transaction which aroused wrath, but bred a corresponding sense of helplessness. After all, the consumer was not quite sure that the trust was wholly responsible. Besides, he liked to sell his own labor or products at the highest price and was willing to concede something of the same right to others.

But Equitable corruption has made its appeal to a wholly different sentiment. The man in the street suddenly comes to see how "high finance" has been fattening off his scanty savings—off the savings he laid by for the support of his widow and children in case they were left alone.

He sees how government has been debauched to protect year after year these highly respectable criminals. He sees how they have been able to purchase immunity from prosecution or publicity.[20]

With agitation high for an investigation, New York governor Frank Wayland Higgins came under suspicion for his reluctance to have the legislature interfere. The governor argued, with much cogency, that the superintendent of insurance already possessed the necessary powers and machinery to make any examination. But the current of discontent proved too strong. Higgins finally yielded to public pressure and asked the legislature, then in session, to create an investigating committee. On July 20, 1905, the Assembly and the Senate passed a concurrent resolution authorizing creation of a special unit to examine life companies operating in New York.[21] Its precise duties were declared to be:

To investigate and examine into the business and affairs of life insurance companies doing business in the State of New York with reference to the investments of said companies, the relation of the officers thereof to such companies, to subsidiary corporations, the government and control of said companies, the contractual relations of said companies to their policyholders, the cost of life insurance, the expenses of said companies and any other phase of the life insurance business deemed by the Committee to be proper, for the purpose of drafting and reporting to the next session of the Legislature such a revision of the laws regulating and relating to life insurance in this state as said Committee may deem proper.[22]

Shortly thereafter the legislature named Senator William W. Armstrong of Rochester as chairman of the eight-member committee. Armstrong's selection was a boon to the embattled consumer, for he enjoyed a reputation as a thorough, conscientious, and public-minded legislator. His work had already gained him the title of "watchdog of the Senate." The appointment of the brilliant and resourceful Charles Evans Hughes as general counsel further strengthened the committee. Hughes had just recently achieved fame and public admiration by investigating the high cost of gas in New York City. As the *Outlook* observed, "Mr. Hughes, in conducting the gas investigation in New York, displayed qualities of courage and efficiency invaluable in carrying out a public inquiry."[23]

Scholars—particularly those commissioned to pen company histories—have discussed the well-remembered Armstrong Investigation in detail. Yet the analysis has been largely from the corporate perspective. The scenario runs as follows: yes, the life insurance enterprise committed wrongs before 1905. However, subsequent self-regulation and legislative restrictions, most of all in New York, created a new era that brought happiness to policyholders and regulated companies alike. This interpretation unfortunately understates the public pressure and support for reform. The Armstrong episode can best be regarded as a consumer's probe of a great American business—the quintessence of public outrage during the progressive era.

The Armstrong Committee, officially organized on August 1, 1905, began its hearings in the jammed tension-charged aldermanic chamber of New York's city hall on September 6. At the outset Senator Armstrong underscored the body's intentions: "Our object will not be to punish anybody for wrongdoing in the past." Rather, he said, it will be "to get at all of the salient features of the modern insurance business, so as to suggest to the next legislature an adequate law that will . . . protect the policyholders in all life insurance companies."[24]

It became immediately apparent that the choice of Charles Evans Hughes as counsel was superb. "His straightforward, steady, frank gaze and strength of his face," wrote one admirer, "make any thought of double dealing or cowardice impossible." Thorough and precise, he interrogated scores of witnesses about wasteful, hazardous, and dishonest practices. As the editor of *McClure's* noted, "Before he began to ask questions, [Hughes] knew what there was to know and from this vantage point began his search for information. Every question answered necessarily opened fresh avenues of inquiry. He has not only known what to ask, he has had the wisdom to stop his examination when necessary to digest his new information, to correlate it and so to come at his witnesses from entirely new and unexpected quarters.'' By calling prominent witnesses over the course of the three-month investigation, Hughes kept the public intensely interested.[25]

Charles Evans Hughes was perhaps at his best in interrogating high-ranking life insurance executives about their respective powers, as his quizzing of New York Life president John A. McCall reveals:

> HUGHES: As president of the New York Life Insurance Company have you had occasion from time to time, to direct the drawing of checks on executive orders?
> McCALL: Yes, I have.
> HUGHES: Without approval or reference to any committee of the company?
> McCALL: Absolutely.
> HUGHES: Has that been a frequent occurrence?
> McCALL: Daily.
> HUGHES: For large amounts?
> McCALL: For large amounts.
> HUGHES: Amounts in excess of $25,000?
> McCALL: Yes.
> HUGHES: Has that been so for a period of years?
> McCALL: Almost from the beginning.
> HUGHES: In what way are such checks audited?
> McCALL: On my certificate they are sent to the comptroller's department, where a warrant is drawn, and checks issued on that warrant.
> HUGHES: In what way is the propriety of the payment determined by other officers of the company?
> McCALL: I am the sole judge of that.[26]

Reactions of the witnesses varied. Some cooperated and even seemed apologetic, some appeared nervous and confused, while still others were openly hostile. Portly Richard A. McCurdy, president of Mutual Life, proved antagonistic and declined to answer questions at one of his early appearances. He later commented, ''I think the whole course of this investigation, as it is called, is entirely outside of what was in contemplation of the Legislature when the Committee was constituted.''[27]

As Hughes exposed industry shortcomings, some prospective witnesses decided that it would be in their best interest to become unavailable. Andrew Hamilton, who directed a nationwide network of lobbies for New York Life, fled to Paris and refused to return until after the investigation. Mutual Life lobbyist and supply superintendent Andrew C. Fields claimed that health prevented his appearance. Thomas Jordan, Equitable's comptroller, mysteriously disappeared, while President Frederick Burnham of the Mutual Reserve Life

This portrait of Charles Evans Hughes was taken in 1905 when he served as general counsel for the New York Armstrong Committee, which led the country's greatest probe of the life insurance industry. (Courtesy of American History Research Center, Akron, Ohio.)

Association had testimony introduced stating that he was not in condition to appear or to have his deposition taken. Quipped the national opinion weekly, the *Independent:* "Indisposition on the part of insurance officials seems to be rapidly approaching the epidemic stage."[28]

Notwithstanding the uncooperative witnesses, the committee arrived at a number of highly significant conclusions. Its official report, released on Washington's birthday in 1906, sustained the conclusions reached earlier by Frick and Hendricks; and it supported the findings made by Lawson, Ryckman, and the *World.*

Specifically, the Armstrong Committee discovered that trustees lacked any effective check upon management. Often one or two officials in each of the Big Three companies possessed sufficient shares or proxies to wield czarlike power. These individuals could and did disperse huge sums of company funds without proper accounting or auditing. The report noted that salaries of presidents and first vice-presidents of the three largest firms were enormous and that pay increases often came without the knowledge or consent of the trustees. Similarly, high-paying nepotism was rampant. The committee revealed that major life insurance enterprises kept unnecessarily large balances at low interest rates in banks and other financial institutions in which firms themselves or individual officers held interests. It also demonstrated that the cost of getting new business was excessive, that rebating was common, and that companies sold mostly tontine and semitontine policies that paid dividends far short of estimates given consumers at the time of purchase. The Armstrong Committee charged industrial companies like Prudential and Metropolitan with encouraging policy lapsing and condoning twisting.[29]

One disclosure had special meaning to both reformers and consumers. The committee detailed the industry's massive lobbying activities, which had not only thwarted earlier attempts at meaningful reform but also had consumed vast amounts of money. The industry annually poured tens of thousands of dollars into Albany to prevent passage of "unfriendly" bills. A portion of this money went to maintain the so-called "House of Mirth," a rooming house jointly operated by the firms for the "entertainment and pleasure of our dedicated public servants." Andrew Hamilton, who operated from there, received at least $475,000 from New York Life for the period 1900 to 1905 to "act for the company in matters relating to taxation and legislation." Equitable's Thomas Jordan spent company funds for the defeat of unwanted legislative suggestions and on a host of noninsurance bills that he considered "detrimental" to America's well-being—for example, proposals regulating child labor, tenements, banks, and real-estate firms. Furthermore, these lobbyists occasionally drafted "reform" legislation themselves—"strike bills"—which they introduced and then spent company funds to defeat. The net result was that the simplest measure affecting life insurance needed industry approval before it stood a good chance of becoming law.

The life insurance enterprise did not limit its influence buying to New York. The Big Three, particularly, had become deeply involved in such activities throughout the country. The Mutual, Equitable, and New York Life companies operated a coordinated program of lobbying, with each firm having responsibility for keeping track of all legislation in assigned sections of the nation. Some companies reportedly purchased newspaper space to influence public opinion "against vicious legislation and in favor of lower taxation for life insurance," and they contributed heavily to candidates willing to support their views. The industry usually shared such expenses. Responding to these revelations, one insurance commissioner aptly stated a major cause for the paucity of significant change. "No wonder reform drives frequently ran into stone walls. Even *vast numbers of disgruntled policyholders* [emphasis added] have little chance when the legislative process is controlled by the great insurance interests."[30]

The Armstrong Committee also examined a number of the smaller life insurance companies and found most with similar shortcomings—high sales costs, excessive incomes for top officials, extensive use of tontine policies, and poor auditing and bookkeeping methods. The committee further castigated the insurance department for failure to detect "marking up" of real-estate holdings by these lesser firms so they might report an annual surplus to the superintendent and for its feeble efforts to compel these companies to carry the reserve funds required by state statute.[31]

The committee's report urged New York lawmakers to intervene. It asked for an immediate enlargement of the powers of the insurance department so there would be no question of its right to supervise the entire administrative management of the industry. The committee proposed modernizing statutes that would require firms to maintain easily detectable financial enterprises and suggested development of standard policy forms. But committee members did not confine themselves merely to superficial corrections. Consumer justice emerged as a primary objective. The official report sought limitations on company size by restriction of new business, curtailment of the amount of commissions and compensation paid to agents, checks on corporate salaries, and elimination of industry contributions to political campaigns. It further recommended prohibition of tontine insurance, limits on surpluses, annual payments of dividends, and surrender values on all contracts in force for three years. Similarly, the committee called for ending control of subsidiary financial institutions by life insurance firms and restrictions on deposits and loans to banks and trust companies. The findings also included recommendations for strengthening of existing antirebate statutes, stringent regulation of lobbying, and prohibition of insurance trustees from having business affiliations that might in any way cause conflicts of interest.

Finally, the authors of the report suggested effective participation by policyholders in administrative functions, as they advocated the voiding of standing proxies and the calling of new elections in all the major life insurance mutuals. Committee members were impressed by the operations of the largest life insurance company in the British Empire, the Australian Mutual Provident, a firm that possessed a remarkable record for good management and low-cost protection. This company was a "pure" mutual with direct policyholder election of officers. Moreover, consumer involvement made sense to legislators infected with the desire to "democratize" American life. In New York, as elsewhere, demands were being made for the direct election of senators and especially for the initiative and referendum.[32]

By early spring the Armstrong Committee's recommendations, mostly in the form of bills drafted by staff members, quickly passed the legislature and received Governor Higgins's signature. The public was elated. Thus ended the nation's first full-scale probe of a group of major corporations and the single most important investigation in the annals of American life insurance.[33]

III

THE ARMSTRONG INVESTIGATION sent shock waves ranging far outside New York. Nationally policyholders expressed their anger and concern; extensive evidence of these consumer attitudes can be found in letters and the press. One Wisconsinite commented, "I am greatly troubled by the recent events in New York. My wife and I have decided to cancell [*sic*] our New York Life policy. . . . Why throw our money away?" A Missouri banker suggested that "with all of this wholesale looting by the big New York companies . . . public [state] insurance should be seriously considered." In a letter to his state's superintendent of insurance a Kansan declared, "I am astonished at the disclosures of crookedness in the management of the three principal life insurance cos. of New York. . . . It makes me sick to know that I am paying for all of this foolishness." A Texas minister exclaimed, "Never, never had anything hit me as has this investigation. What troubled times!"[34]

Press reaction to the New York disclosures reflected a similar mood, buttressing the wave of adverse comments that the Frick and Hendricks reports had inspired. "The people are in open revolt because of the extravagance of the big life insurance companies," declared William Allen White of Kansas in his *Emporia Gazette.* "The shock with which most people have read the confessions of life insurance officials has unquestionably been a moral stimulus," observed the *Outlook.* "It has been a dash of cold water upon the face after a time of moral drowsiness. It has set the public conscience stirring. If the Committee chosen by the Legislature . . . to investigate the conduct of life insurance companies had done nothing else than administer this shock, it would have already justified its existence." One Missouri editor believed that the revelations had "reached the point that [they have] become a national scandal and a national concern. The acts that have been committed in the three companies of New York are crimes against society. It is worse than a robbery of the living, for it is the despoiling of the dead and taking bread out of the mouths of widows and orphans."[35]

Disclosures of the Armstrong Committee excited insurance agents and executives alike, but for reasons quite different from those motivating consumers and the press. As daily reports appeared, worried individuals began to cancel policies, and agents found it increasingly difficult to find new customers. In fact, the volume of life insurance in force when the Armstrong hearings began would not be equaled again until 1910. In addition to their anxieties about the decline of business in force, life insurance men feared policyholders would begin to patronize fraternals for their needs or, worse yet, agitate for publicly sponsored insurance.[36]

The trade press, which had initially ignored or tried to minimize the Armstrong hearings, now did its best to reassure agents, especially, that all was well. One publisher went so far as to request that the Kansas superintendent of insurance help in calming consumer uneasiness on the grounds that, "I believe that those whose duty it is to conserve the best interests of life insurance should, at this time, use every effort within their power to counteract the false impressions that are gaining foothold with policy-holders."[37]

The industry had ample reason for alarm. The Armstrong hearings triggered a chain reaction of reform throughout the continent. During the height of the New York investigation, the Missouri superintendent of insurance, Willard Duncan Vandiver, temporarily suspended New York Life's license to operate in the state because of disclosures that its officers had made sizable political contributions to the Republican party's campaign coffers during the elections of 1896,

HAZING TO WHICH THE PUBLIC DOES NOT OBJECT
Thorndike, in Philadelphia *Press*

Revelations forced from New York Life president John A.
McCall by the brilliant and resourceful Armstrong Com-
mittee general counsel, Charles Evans Hughes, thrilled the
American consumer. (Courtesy of American History
Research Center, Akron, Ohio.)

1900, and 1904. Legislatures in New Jersey and Wisconsin responded to policyholders' demands for a still more thorough probing by establishing investigating committees. Indiana's reform governor J. Frank Handly, through special powers granted him by the legislature, appointed a commission to examine the life insurance companies operating in the Hoosier State as well as the local insurance department, which had fallen under public suspicion because of its laxity in enforcing regulations. The Dominion of Canada conducted its own probe of life insurance.[38]

One indication of intense interest in life insurance matters occurred with the convening of a special Chicago convention in February 1906 to discuss common problems of regulation raised by the Armstrong disclosures. This meeting came in direct response to a call made by Thomas E. Drake, superintendent of insurance for the District of Columbia, at the suggestion of two astute politicians, President Theodore Roosevelt and Governor John A. Johnson of Minnesota. More than a hundred delegates—including governors, attorneys general, and state insurance commissioners—attended this conclave. Although reflecting consumer concerns, members' motivations varied. Some placed the public interest foremost, while others seemed more anxious to convert fear and anger into personal political support. Said one journalist, "There are those here in Chicago who are the type to jump out in front of a parade that is about ready to march."[39]

In a three-day session the Windy City convention passed the expected resolutions. It strongly denounced tontine insurance and recommended that legislation be passed to outlaw that evil. The group requested conservative rather than speculative investments and argued for "pure" mutuals. Of lesser import to the consumer, such "bureaucratizing" reforms as streamlining local insurance departments and developing standard policy forms became additional recommendations. The gathering quickly appointed a Committee of Fifteen, with Minnesota's active reform commissioner Thomas D. O'Brien as chairman, to consider and suggest model legislation to implement its suggestions.[40]

While the Chicago convention constituted a major response to the Armstrong hearings, the most important single reform drive coming in the aftermath of the New York disclosures arose in Wisconsin. As the Armstrong hearings drew to a close, Wisconsin's progressive Republican governor Robert M. La Follette, who had previously expressed no interest in insurance reform but sensed a popular issue, declared that his state should conduct an Armstronglike investigation. At a special session of the legislature held in late 1905 to consider a variety of matters, La Follette presented his case: "With the exception of the corporations which control the transportation facilities of the commonwealth there is no class of corporations more in need of careful and economical administration than those which make a business of life insurance. . . . Wisconsin [should] take such action as shall make impossible a repetition in this state of what has occurred in New York, and, at the same time, satisfy the people as to the condition of Wisconsin companies."[41]

Lawmakers warmly received La Follette's message and, spurred by an aroused public, appointed a Joint Legislative Investigating Committee to examine in detail the insurance companies' political contributions, lobbying activities, types of investment, internal management procedures, and marketing methods. The joint committee, organized in January 1906, had progressive senator James A. Frear as its chairman and another progressive, Assemblyman Herman L. Ekern, as its secretary. (Ekern subsequently gained national acclaim for his reform activities as insurance commissioner.) The committee employed the services of one of America's outstanding life insurance experts, Miles M. Dawson, who had just advised Hughes.[42]

The joint committee singled out for close examination three insurance companies that the Armstrong group had not dissected. Two were domestic, the giant Northwestern Mutual Life of Milwaukee and the small Wisconsin Life Insurance Company, which was headquartered in Madison. The third was the Cincinnati-based Union Central Life Insurance Company, which had a large number of Wisconsin policyholders and conducted an extensive farm loan business in the state.[43]

During the course of sixty public sessions between April and September 1906, the committee carefully examined the records of the three firms. Although its investigation disclosed no abuses of the magnitude found in the operation of the Big Three, numerous problems were identified, mainly in the area of internal management.

Testimony before the committee concerning Northwestern Mutual Life began on April 12, 1906, and revealed that a self-perpetuating oligarchy dominated the organization. More than half the proxy ballots cast in the company's 1904 election had been voted by nonpolicyholders whom Northwestern Mutual president Henry L. Palmer controlled. The hearings also showed that the firm was guilty of nepotism and of granting excessively high salaries to ranking officials. The investigating body disclosed that twisting and even rebating still existed, and it charged that the firm wasted funds battling passage of the Orton tax bill. It also discovered that some policyholders had been discriminated against in favor of others, and that the company had profited from an excessive number of lapsed policies and surrenders during the previous decade.

Union Central Life fared much better than Northwestern Mutual. The committee warmly commended the firm for having efficient and conservative investment practices but criticized President John M. Pattison and his family for their tight control over the company's affairs and their excessive salaries, which in some instances exceeded $50,000 annually. The committee furthermore took a dim view of Union Central's practice during the depression of the nineties of refusing to honor a number of policies on trivial technical grounds and of its long-standing interest rate structure, which discriminated against Wisconsin farm mortgagors.

The last of the three firms examined, the Wisconsin Life Insurance Company, was found to be poorly managed. Reorganized four times since its founding in 1895, it continued to suffer from insufficient operating capital and disastrous investment practices. The committee concluded that Wisconsin Life was insolvent and that a fifth reorganization was urgently needed. The company also came under attack for charging unnecessarily high premium rates, for selling speculative tontine policies, and for harsh forfeiture practices and related policy contract abuses.[44]

Five months after the close of the last public session the Wisconsin Joint Legislative Investigating Committee, like its prototype in New York, published its findings and recommendations. In transmitting the committee's suggestions to the legislature in January 1907, Governor James O. Davidson, La Follette's militant progressive successor, said, "Protect the rights and property of the people, erect such legal safe-guards that insurance shall be such in fact, that trust funds shall be honestly applied, that there shall be a limit to the expenditure of the insurance money and that just punishment be meted out to all violators of the law." The governor warned, "Legislation failing in these respects falls short of the public will."[45]

During their spring 1907 session lawmakers took up the committee's recommendations, which consisted of twenty-four bills, and similarly considered sixteen model bills prepared and submitted by the Committee of Fifteen appointed at the Chicago convention. After considerable debate and revision the progressive-dominated body approved the joint committee's principal recommendations and a substantial proportion of the model bills. A true reform flavor characterized the measures; they called for the direct election by policyholders of directors in domestic life companies, required reports on all political contributions and statements of monies used to influence legislation, and limited the salaries paid officials and general agents to

$25,000 annually. Other bills prohibited discrimination against any individual or class of policyholders, forbade misrepresentation while soliciting new business, ordered companies to suspend business when liabilities exceeded assets, and forced the annual distribution of surpluses accumulated by mutual firms. The laws even limited the amount of expenses that could be incurred and required the reporting of them. The newly passed bills also set "loading" for expenses at one-third of the net single premium, specified payment of yearly dividends on all future policy contracts, abolished all proxies, and outlawed rebating.[46]

Wisconsin consumers applauded the reforms. "As an owner of a NML policy, I am pleased to read that this company has now been brought into line," wrote a Prairie du Chien policyholder. Similarly, the public-spirited editor of the *North Crandon Forest Leaves* commented, "I know the policyholders in the three companies investigated who live in Forest County enthusiastically endorse the reform statutes which will hopefully be signed shortly by the Governor."[47]

Life insurance firms understandably exerted pressure on the Wisconsin legislature against enactment of the committee's proposals. Industry spokesmen branded them as "in some respects vicious, in others, indefensible and unnecessary," and warned that they would "prove harmful and expensive to policyholders and to companies." When the major bills passed both houses, Northwestern Mutual and Wisconsin Life urged Governor Davidson to veto the measures, especially those that restricted premiums and operating expenses. The companies warned that if these became law most of the non-Wisconsin firms would flee the state. Moreover, with passage of these bills, other states would surely enact retaliatory legislation, making operations there difficult for Wisconsin-based companies. Out-of-state firms likewise appealed to Davidson, charging that the bills were detrimental to all parties. The governor, without comment, signed them on July 16, 1907, and they entered the insurance code the next year.[48]

While only New York and Wisconsin of this study conducted their own life insurance probes, varying degrees of reform activity occurred in the other states. Missouri, Kansas, and Texas collectively had only a handful of small and generally benevolent locally based life insurance companies, so movements to hold Armstronglike investigations there understandably failed to materialize. Instead, general disgust with the industry, commonplace by the fall of 1905 and exacer-

ON MR. HUGHES' CIRCULAR TRACK
Webster in the Chicago *Tribune*

Prominent politicians and business leaders (e.g., Chauncey Mitchell Depew, Edward H. Harriman, James Hazen Hyde, and Benjamin Odell) sought to protect their public reputations, even at the expense of associates, during the famed 1905 Armstrong investigation. (Courtesy of American History Research Center, Akron, Ohio.)

bated by the Wisconsin disclosures and a new surge of muckraking literature, boiled over in Texas, and to a lesser degree in Kansas and Missouri, in the form of investment bills.[49]

The suggestion to require out-of-state companies to invest a portion of their premium payments in the state where they had been collected was not new. Texas seriously considered such a proposal as early as 1897. By 1907 journalistic exposés and legislative investigations so angered residents of the Lone Star State that the legislature passed the Robertson Investment Act. Robert Lyman Cox, who fought the measure on behalf of the Association of Life Insurance Presidents, said, "The passage of [the Armstrong] laws . . . stirred the country from one end to the other. People everywhere had gained a distorted view of the business. Therefore, in 1907, there came a veritable flood of legislation intended to be corrective and helpful. . . . It was out of this turmoil and misunderstanding that the Robertson Law came."[50]

During the two years immediately preceding the enactment of the Robertson bill, Texans increasingly spoke out in favor of a life insurance investment law. During the 1905 gubernatorial contest one candidate discovered that his plan to compel firms to invest seventy-five percent of their Texas policy reserves locally was amazingly popular. In 1906 Thomas B. Love, a Dallas lawyer who would later head the state Insurance Department, made numerous pleas for passage of an investment bill. Love argued that, above all, such a measure would keep capital at home. It would also help curb life insurance abuse—particularly internal management shortcomings, which he believed were caused principally by excessive surplus accumulations. Finally, he viewed a Texas investment statute as a superb complement to New York's Armstrong laws.[51]

Shortly after the January 11, 1907, opening of the thirtieth Texas legislature, James Harvey Robertson of Austin (the Travis County representative who had been a judge and was a law partner of former governor James Stephen Hogg) introduced a bill that required all life insurance companies to invest seventy-five percent of their Texas reserves in the state's public or corporate securities. The proposal stipulated that such paper was to be deposited in Texas and would be subject to state and local ad valorem taxation. "The purpose I had," Robertson later explained, "was to stop the long continued practice of taking from Texas money belonging to Texas people, and hoarding it in New York to be there used by the officials of the great insurance companies, as was developed under the investigation by the Armstrong Committee. . . ."[52]

Illustrating the cross-class interpretation of progressive support, the Robertson bill received backing from a variety of groups, including consumers' leagues, trade unions, farmers' organizations, and individuals of all political stripes. Their reasoning ranged from desire to ensure public control over the life insurance industry, especially in directing the total amount of the companies' uncommitted capital reserves, to increasing the amount of available investment funds. Virtually all supporters of the Robertson proposal agreed with one Texas politician when he said, "There is a general belief in this State that for many years the life insurance companies have not paid a just and fair rate of taxation and the legislature responding to this sentiment endeavor[s] to fix a fair basis."[53]

The small but vigorous lobby of Texas-chartered insurance companies pressed hard for passage of the investment bill, but hardly for altruistic reasons. Lone Star firms thought it would give them an edge over those headquartered elsewhere. Several months before the convening of the thirtieth state legislature, officials of the Fort Worth Life Insurance Company launched a concerted program among Texas-based insurance organizations to pressure lawmakers for an investment act. Soon after the legislature opened, the *Dallas Morning News* observed that the fight over the investment bill was "being closely drawn between the Texas home companies . . . [on the one side] and the New York companies on the other." Without question, the American life insurance industry was far from monolithic.[54]

While Texas firms organized for the bill, eastern companies actively opposed it. The leading opponent of the Robertson bill was lawyer and former New York assemblyman Robert Lyman Cox, whom the Association of Life Insurance Presidents employed to speak on behalf of out-of-state interests. Cox forcefully charged that the deposit feature would subject firms to heavy state and local taxes and would thereby work a hardship on both the companies and their policyholders. He emphasized the need to allow firms flexibility in their investments: "the best returns may or may not be in Texas." Cox warned lawmakers and all Texans that if the measure passed, foreign concerns would leave the state. Cox's arguments, however, went unheeded. The Robertson bill easily passed the legislature; the governor immediately signed it, and the act took effect on July 1, 1907.[55]

Investment proposals similar to the Robertson Act appeared in the legislative hoppers of Missouri and Kansas during the 1907 sessions and at various times until World War I. Lobbying by the life insurance enterprise was one factor in explaining the repeated defeat of such bills in the two states. But perhaps of much greater importance in explaining failure of investment measures was the apparent split among reformers over whether these changes were needed at all.

"There is the feeling among many in Topeka and Jefferson City who are interested in correcting life insurance evils," observed a writer for the *Kansas City Star,* "that an investment act would solve nothing especially in light of the Armstrong statutes which are curbing excessive expenses and foolhardy investment." Furthermore, companies voluntarily liberalized overall investment policies in Missouri and Kansas and in other western and southern states; money perhaps was "loosened" by the Robertson Act.[56]

In addition to wrestling with the question of investment Missouri, Kansas, and Texas lawmakers helped lead the enactment of "supplemental" life insurance reforms following the New York disclosures. These came in response to public clamor for meaningful change and to new model bills proposed by both the National Convention of Insurance Commissioners and the Committee of Fifteen. But advanced consumer advocates must have been disappointed. The thrust of these statutes was frequently not radical; instead, once again "modernization" emerged as the common theme. This corrective legislation covered such diverse matters as a rigid antirebate law in Missouri, a legal definition of "life insurance agent" in Kansas, and a Texas act that reorganized the insurance department and granted the commissioner increased powers. All became part of the states' respective insurance codes in 1907.[57]

In addition, in Kansas the Armstrong disclosures sparked a drive to clean up the insurance lobby. Emporia's William Allen White did much to publicize this movement. A nationally recognized journalist and author, he enjoyed the uncanny ability of being able to take the pulse beat of Kansans and to convert his findings into newspaper stories of great popular appeal. White unceasingly hammered away at the "insurance grafters." In *Gazette* editorials he repeatedly called on those who favored reform to fight for the direct primary and the initiative and referendum as ways to weaken the insurance lobby. White and his supporters saw this interest group as a major roadblock to economic justice for all Kansans. After several legislative sessions and much political bickering the state finally brought the lobby under control.[58]

IV

BY THE END of 1907 most of the key life insurance reform measures of the progressive period had been passed. Policyholders had been vindicated in their complaints; shortcomings in areas such as contract abuse, operating expenses, and internal operating practices had been corrected. The Armstrong laws brought much of the industry under strict supervision, and Wisconsin's new statutes further tightened public control. The nation was affected by Wisconsin's curb on the enterprise when it brought two domestically based companies under close regulation. Missouri, Kansas, and Texas, while passing several Armstronglike laws, likewise benefited from the New York and the Wisconsin reforms, since companies based there wrote the lion's share of life policies in these states. And in Texas the Robertson Act resolved a long-standing local complaint about the inadequacies of industry investment policies.

The statutes enacted by the various governments nicely illustrate the two principal categories of progressive reform. On one level, measures instigated by "professional" types, and even supported by the companies themselves, brought mere superficial change. Policyholders, for example, profited from standard forms and new methods of auditing, but these were hardly earth-shaking improvements. However, true consumer-oriented statutes accompanied modernizing ones. For instance, when New York curbed corporate expenses and guaranteed surrender values, the public received monumental advantages.

Adjustment to reform from the viewpoint of the life insurance enterprise and the public characterized the years between the Armstrong episode and the coming of the Great War. However, to imply that improvements suddenly ended in 1907 would be wrong. During this period additional changes occurred, including the most radical of all, state life insurance.

3

Time of Adjustment: 1907–1915

ADJUSTMENT to life insurance reforms marked the period from 1907 to 1915 in the form of attempts to modify, supplement, and even repeal recently enacted measures. Quite logically, such activities initially centered on New York's Armstrong laws. Moves by consumers to implement or enforce provisions of the new statutes collided with industry efforts to change the provisions of the new code that they felt were most obnoxious.

One section of the 1906 Armstrong laws required mutual firms to elect totally new boards of trustees. Simultaneously, a consumers' movement arose, which was designed to insure selection of reform-minded directors. The first rumblings about uniting policyholders were heard in early 1906 when Thomas W. Lawson of "Frenzied Finance" fame organized a rally of policyholders in Madison Square Garden "to make the insurance companies in fact as well as in name mutual concerns." Shortly thereafter the International Policy-Holders' Committee (IPC) appeared.[1]

A quintessential consumer group headquartered in New York City, the IPC drew members from all walks of life and all sections of the United States and even from Great Britain and Canada. Missouri's superintendent of insurance W. D. Vandiver characterized IPC's membership this way: "It is composed largely of those politically conscious policyholders who for years have sought insurance justice." Vandiver noted, "Politically the Committee wears no label. . . . Democrats, Republicans, Socialists . . . have enlisted in the cause." Leaders in the affairs of the IPC included such political progressives as Minnesota governor John J. Johnson, instigator of the February 1906 Chicago insurance conference; Indiana's governor J. Frank Hanley; and Napoleon Bonaparte Broward, the flamboyant and iconoclastic Democratic governor of Florida. Also prominent were Alton B. Parker, the 1904 Democratic presidential nominee; Richard Olney, Cleveland's attorney general and secretary of state; and Thomas B. Wanamaker, the wealthy Philadelphia merchant.

These three individuals could hardly be labeled "progressive." In fact, some IPC members, while vigorously supporting the reform goals espoused by these basically conservative men, expressed real concern that they "may merely be seeking to *control* the several life-insurance companies . . . and once in power their reform interests may become as fleeting as a summer rainbow." Indeed, the control of $1 billion was at stake.[2]

By late summer 1906 the IPC busily campaigned in behalf of slates of reform directors running for posts in the Mutual Life and New York Life companies. Spending in excess of $300,000, the IPC dispatched more than six million circulars describing its position to policyholders and other interested individuals. The IPC warned: "It is a practical certainty that, unless the policy holders wish to condone the mistakes and offenses of the two companies and desire the policies pursued by them to be perpetuated, they must insist upon being represented by entirely new boards of directors." Furthermore, according to the IPC, "What is wanted in the members of the new board is not expert life insurance talent, but homely virtues of common honesty and due regard for the requirements of the trust relation—requirements which forbid the trustee not only from stealing himself, but also from indulging in the negligence which enables others to steal."[3]

The elections, which consisted of policyholders mailing in ballots to the home offices, took place during the fall months of 1906. The final tabulations, canvassed under the supervision of the New York Insurance Department, showed a resounding victory for so-called "administration tickets" in both the New York Life and Mutual Life companies. In the former all IPC candidates lost while in the latter firm only two IPC candidates won election to the fifteen-member board.[4]

The results angered IPC members and reform types alike. St. Louis publisher William Marion Reedy expressed the feelings of most consumers about the IPC defeat, " 'Administration tickets' won. . . . The old officers and the agents throughout the country had the best kind of a machine. They had control of the voting lists and the ballot boxes. They had plenty of money. They worked as men work whose jobs are at stake. They voted dead men and men who had lost their votes by lapse of their policies." Furthermore, he argued, "Policyholders' opposition had no chance from the start. Their time and money and effort were wasted. Moreover, wherever one of the insurgents can be reached things will be made uncomfortable for him in his relations with the financial interests of his community through the influences emanating from the insurance headquarters in Gotham."

Reedy concluded, "The insurance elections have been a stupendous farce. They have only strengthened in power the old crowds of the milked companies."[5]

Although the IPC charged election fraud, the New York Insurance Department, final arbiter in the contest, was unwilling to probe into the affair. Fearing another insurance scandal and deeply involved in a political fight with the governor's office, the department simply did not want controversy. "Inaction in this matter," argued Superintendent Otto Kelsey, "hopefully will not produce popular reaction. . . . What we need in the insurance world is peace not policyholder-company war."[6]

Speaking for the industry, the trade press admitted that the administration slates enjoyed an unfair advantage over IPC candidates insofar as "agents in the field . . . [had] a personal interest in keeping those they [had] insured in sympathy with the company and [kept] up their efforts to secure their votes for the 'administration' ticket." Insurance publications, however, went on to argue that since the elections had been carried out, all parties should now abide by the policyholders' decisions. Sensing the futility of any future effort at company reform, the IPC melted away soon after the election verdicts. Members agreed that this particular Armstrong reform failed. Insurance experts concurred and added that the election machinery had proven costly and clumsy in practice.[7]

Shortly after passage of the Armstrong laws, life firms actively sought to change several sections of the newly amended insurance code. The Big Three directed most of their energies toward seeking the repeal or severe modification of sections 96 and 97. Section 96 limited the annual amount of new business for the larger companies to $150 million per year, while section 97 set a maximum rate on agents' commissions, forbade granting of prizes or rewards to agents, and disallowed the practice of giving them advances against future renewal commissions. The New York legislature had passed these sections with several goals in mind. Lawmakers feared great aggregations of funds in a few firms, they believed that limitation of new business and checks on agents and expenses would cure extravagance and lower marketing costs, and they hoped that sections 96 and 97 would cause companies to be more careful in their selection of customers and agents. Legislators wanted new policyholders who would faithfully pay their premium statements and wanted additions to agency forces to be "only those *professional* [emphasis added] life-insurance men who will strictly adhere to the ethics prescribed by the National Association of Life Underwriters."[8]

The major life concerns, led by New York Life president Darwin

P. Kingsley, called the sections "socialistic," "illogical," and even "un-American" and pleaded for their revision or outright repeal. Members of the Life Underwriters' Association of New York similarly objected to them and actively backed management's stand. Certain interest groups also favored modifying sections 96 and 97. Several New York City business organizations, including the politically powerful Chamber of Commerce, believed that provisions might cause the "loss of the financial supremacy which has so long been exercised by the Metropolis of the country."[9]

In 1908 Kingsley and fellow industry executives from New York convinced the legislature that section 97 should be modified. The state's lawmakers apparently also believed that certain revisions were appropriate. As one assemblyman, who had vigorously backed the 1906 reform measures, put it, "Really, we had no idea how the laws would work when we passed them two years ago. . . . For one thing, agents' commissions must be great enough to get the best quality of men to serve policyholders' needs." The legislature's proposal, designed primarily to permit the liberalization of agents' commissions, passed with little more than a murmur of dissent. When the bill reached the statehouse, Charles Evans Hughes, by then New York's governor, promptly vetoed it. Reflecting considerable consumer sentiment, Hughes did not concur with those who argued for insurance code revision. He justified his veto by contending that it was still too early to determine what changes, if any, might be advisable in the Armstrong reforms, especially in regard to sections 96 and 97. The limitation requirements, Hughes noted, directly affected only three companies.[10]

Undaunted by Hughes's veto message, President Kingsley continued to agitate for code revision. In early 1909 he charged that his firm had been prevented from acquiring sufficient new business to make good the losses resulting from policy cancellations. He pointed out that during the preceding year New York Life had lost 69,000 patrons and that the Armstrong laws limited the company's annual new business to about 63,000. Virtually all life firms were in sympathy with the Kingsley position, and the New York Life head received some outside support for his stance. The *Times,* for instance, said, "The argument that a good company should be restricted merely because of its size is difficult to maintain now that we are calmer."[11]

On the other hand, policyholders and organizations such as the National Convention of Insurance Commissioners and the National Municipal League saw no need for any major changes in either section 96 or 97. Although New York Life and two other companies were forced to suspend a number of their agents because they could no longer afford to keep them, the *New York Sun* commented, "The malefactors who have been discharged may not starve for lack of employment, but they will not be so well fed as they have been. No patriotic citizen can feel otherwise than gratified at the splendid triumph that has been won against the devouring demon of success." Most of the public agreed.[12]

Those advocating revision scored a minor victory when the 1909 legislature approved, with Hughes's blessings, a measure that permitted certain technical changes in the Armstrong laws and section 97. Even advanced progressives sanctioned this event. "The recent New York revisions in the insurance code of that state are wholly consistent with the original purpose of section 97," noted the former Kansas state coordinator for the IPC. "The changes made simply reward those companies that follow economical practices. In no way has [sic] the Kingsley crowd or the life insurance agents achieved their desired goals of having only 'friendly' state regulatory statutes."[13]

Proponents of sections 96 and 97 eventually won backing of the underwriters themselves. At an Albany meeting of agents in March 1915 the powerful New York group, by resolution, opposed any change in the section and voiced support for the orderly selling of insurance. At last sensing the public relations advantage of these two sections, the organization's president Lawrence Puddy said that his associates objected strongly to any change because "it would tend to put the insurance business back to the basis of extravagance which existed before the days of the Armstrong investigation." In a classic illustration of the "search for order" concept, Puddy underscored the notion that underwriters desired "harmony" and "complete stability." He believed that "chaos of the old competitive days is now hopefully over."[14]

While life insurance companies objected to additional Armstrong laws, particularly the provisions of section 100—a stock-disposal statute[15]—the feeling steadily grew that the advantages of the laws outweighed their evils. In 1915 the Life Underwriters Association noted, "All of the great companies which opposed the bills in 1906 . . . are now opposed to any change because their experience has proved that the theories on which the laws were based are sound and workable except for the limitation on new business and expense clauses."[16]

Not long after the Armstrong laws went into effect, companies began to realize that it was advantageous for them to advertise that they were supervised by the stringent New York statutes. New York–regulated firms discovered that prospective clients were more willing to buy coverage, for such persons now had confidence in the security of their investments and the certainty that their beneficiaries would receive the full value of protection. As one state official commented, "The people feel that the business of life insurance has been settled on a solid and lasting basis by the New York laws." By 1910, business in New York and the nation surpassed the pre-Armstrong highs, and management became openly optimistic about the future. Companies unaffected by the Armstrong laws found that admission to the Empire State gave them prestige. Because of the nature of the new code, a firm accredited to transact business in New York might well expect to be welcomed by any state in the union or any foreign nation.[17]

I

UNLIKE the New York story, Wisconsin's regulatory legislation produced a spectacular industry response. Shortly after Governor James O. Davidson signed the life insurance reform bills in 1907, twenty-four firms, including some of America's largest and constituting about two-thirds of those doing business locally, decided to pressure the state by withdrawing. Their principal objections centered on the strict regulation of elections, limitations on operating expenses, and the restriction of loading expenses to a stipulated portion of the premium. Similarly, firms took an extremely dim view of the provision making violations punishable by a jail sentence and a stiff fine. Departing companies believed these statutes to be legally "unclear" and feared the effects of interpretation by a "hostile" insurance commissioner. However, several major carriers—including New York Life, New England Mutual, and Prudential—decided it would be best to continue doing business in Wisconsin and announced publicly that they felt the laws were not overly drastic. The decision to remain more likely stemmed from their hopes of capturing a greater share of the local market. The 1907 withdrawal left ten out-of-state and two domestic companies to serve the life insurance needs of the Badger State.[18]

The departing firms badly misjudged the Wisconsin situation. Residents overwhelmingly viewed withdrawal as the supreme act of corporate arrogance. For instance, a Pepin County farmer in a letter to the insurance department angrily declared, "Who do those companies think they are trying to force us to change the insurance laws? Those interests had better act like other citizens have to act." He concluded, "I know now our reforms will have to remain." Some Wisconsinites felt that departure of the firms constituted "good riddance," and hoped that the dozen or so remaining would abide by the new reform laws. "If the twenty-four old line life companies do not want to serve the people," proclaimed Insurance Commissioner George E. Beedle, "then the people should serve themselves."[19]

Beedle's comment echoed earlier sentiments in Wisconsin favoring state insurance. In 1903 the legislature created a state insurance fund to insure public property against fire, wind, and flood damage. Two years later the Senate appointed a three-member committee to investigate the practicability of state life insurance. This committee included progressive Republicans James A. Frear and Julius E. Roehr and Socialist Jacob Rummel. At hearings the body seemed favorably impressed by reports on the success of government-sponsored life insurance programs in Great Britain, Germany, Norway, and New Zealand. The two Republicans, however, recommended that certain reforms of existing companies—such as moderate salaries for officials, lower commissions for agents, and liberalized policy forms—be tried prior to giving serious consideration to any plan of state life insurance. Senator Rummel disagreed. He strongly urged creation of government insurance, for he had definite reservations as to whether regulation would ever succeed.[20]

Although Commissioner Beedle did nothing more than suggest the possibility of state life insurance, his successor, Herman L. Ekern, zealously sought it. Prior to his election as insurance commissioner in 1910, Ekern had been Speaker of the Wisconsin House, member of the 1906 life insurance investigating committee, and a close ally of former governor La Follette. Ekern developed great expertise in insurance matters; he long championed life and fire mutuals and reforms designed to favor the consumer.[21]

During the 1911 legislative session the new commissioner worked closely with the chairman of the House insurance committee, Lewis L. Johnson of Door County, and D. J. Saposs, Johnson's secretary, in drawing up the life insurance plan. All agreed that regulation of the industry had not been totally satisfactory and that the vacuum created by the company exodus increased the need for other life insurance. They undoubtedly realized that withdrawal enhanced chances for enacting a program of public protection, for consumers desired low-cost coverage and sought revenge for what they viewed as the industry's contemptuous act.[22]

Proponents of government life insurance soon faced an obstacle. Wisconsin's constitution prohibited the state from assuming a debt greater than $100,000. Accordingly, Ekern suggested creation of a special fund consisting of paid-in premiums, which would resemble the one used since 1903 for insuring public property against fire loss.

Shortly thereafter Assembly Speaker Charles A. Ingram—working closely with Ekern, Johnson, and Saposs—introduced a state life insurance bill. Ingram argued that the measure recognized "the responsibility of the state to its people and the progressive idea that preventive action is often wiser than remedial legislation." The bill met with little opposition, either in committee or on the floor. The insurance lobby offered only token resistance, partly because popular feeling seemed to favor the proposal and any opposition would only further tarnish the companies' already soiled reputation. Furthermore, several of the nation's most powerful firms had departed from Wisconsin and seemingly cared little about conditions there. Since no provision had been made for active solicitation of business, carriers doubted if they would have serious competition from a public concern selling insurance over the counter. This may explain why a representative of Northwestern Mutual told the House committee that his firm did not oppose the measure because "insurance is stimulated by competition."[23]

Governor Francis E. McGovern, a La Follette progressive, signed the public life insurance bill in late 1911 and thus made Wisconsin the first state to offer its citizens government life insurance protection. The effective date of the act was set at 1913 to allow the insurance department time in which to develop its machinery. The plan offered protection to all Wisconsinites between the ages of twenty and fifty, with a maximum coverage of $3,000. It guaranteed loan surrender values on all policies in addition to annuity ones for those who desired them. Monthly and weekly premium rates were allowed, so that individuals with small incomes could take advantage of the program. One highly imaginative feature was that the fund utilized existing government machinery. Since the plan lacked paid agents, applications were received by clerks and treasurers of cities, towns, and villages and by officials of banks in which state monies were deposited. The state auditor's office became the fund's accounting department, the state treasurer served as chief fiscal officer, the state board of health was its medical board, and the attorney general acted as legal counsel.[24]

The life insurance fund sold its first policy on October 27, 1913, but few were subsequently purchased. The industry correctly anticipated the program's chief weakness: prospective customers had to take the initiative in applying for policies. Notwithstanding widespread publicity and public approbation, by the summer of 1915 the fund had sold only 328 policies, representing $227,000 of insurance in force. Assets amounted to a scant $13,074.49. Protection coverage did not reach $1 million until 1927 and never exceeded a small fraction of the total written domestically by private carriers. Still, Wisconsin residents had the opportunity to buy inexpensive and safe coverage. The fund, moreover, gave the state an invaluable yardstick against which to measure the performance of private life companies.[25]

With the election of Republican stalwart Emanuel L. Philipp to the governorship in 1914, members of this new conservative administration tried to abolish the life fund. Their position stemmed principally from their dislike of "socialistic" state insurance, which they considered "dangerous" and an "unhealthy" precedent. "The State has *no right* to engage in a private business in competition with legitimate concerns," argued one tory lieutenant. A number of business groups and associations concurred. But the majority of local lawmakers recognized the advantages of public life insurance and thwarted Philipp's attempts to scrap the program. They sought to strengthen it in 1919 by attempting to authorize state agents to solicit business actively. Governor Philipp, with industry and business community support, promptly vetoed the bill, and the life fund remained semidormant. Consumer interest in state insurance flagged. After 1915 companies that had earlier left Wisconsin returned; they realized their withdrawal tactic had not intimidated Wisconsinites. Their willingness to conform to the 1907 reforms, along with the state life program, provided residents with adequate protection.[26]

The Wisconsin venture into public life insurance prompted numerous states to consider such a plan. Legislators supporting this device usually argued that they desired to guarantee the opportunity for all to buy safe and inexpensive protection. Similarly, there existed the common notion among consumer advocates that state life insurance, while no panacea for policyholders' problems, offered buyers complete protection. "With Ekern's triumph," wrote one admirer of the Wisconsin Life Fund, "Wisconsin now has a *balanced* life insurance control program which allows all purchasers of life policies in that state, whether they be rich or poor, . . . the option of cheap and reliable insurance. . . . State life insurance complements perfectly [Wisconsin's] earlier reform statutes and can surely do the same elsewhere."[27]

While the semipublic Massachusetts Savings Bank Life Insurance System debuted in 1907, other than Wisconsin only Kansas of the states included in this study came close to enacting a bona fide government life insurance plan. In 1913 J. A. Mahurin, a Coffey County Republican, introduced a bill in the Kansas House entitled, "An act to establish an annuity and life insurance fund for the payment of annuities and life policies on the lives of citizens of . . . Kansas and to provide for the investment of the reserve fund thereof.'' The Mahurin bill resembled the Wisconsin measure; for example, state officials would serve as the fund's treasurer, auditor, and legal counsel. The main purpose of the Kansas proposal, like that of the Wisconsin plan, was "to offer sound life insurance at a reasonable cost.'' Conviction still existed in the Sunflower State that life insurance costs were sometimes too high and that private firms were not always reliable. Supporters concurred with Representative Mahurin that government life insurance would be the "final capstone to Kansas's life insurance code.'' But unlike the Wisconsin act, the Kansas program would employ agents to solicit business.[28]

The Mahurin bill sailed through the Kansas House but encountered stiff opposition in the Senate. Members divided roughly into three factions. Conservative lawmakers used arguments similar to those of their counterparts in Wisconsin. Such phrases as "this socialistic boondoggle" and "radicalism has no place in Kansas or anywhere else" sprinkled their rhetoric. These statements graphically mirrored the anger and growing concern of the life industry at the prospect of having government competition in Kansas. On the other hand, reform-oriented senators split between those who vigorously endorsed state insurance and those who saw it as unnecessary. One opposition senator asked, "In light of various reform measures enacted by New York and Wisconsin and considering our own previous statutes, why get involved in a program that few Kansans really need?" But senatorial proponents countered with arguments that "state insurance . . . [would provide] Kansans an option to old line life and fraternal coverage in the event of future life insurance shortcomings," and the proposed program would be "a safeguard and deterrent to company withdrawals or mass cancellations." Part of their arguments were the widely held notions that state life insurance offered consumers a "square deal" and in conjunction with existing statutes provided them with "total" protection opportunities. Even though their proposals were soundly defeated in the Senate, advocates of government insurance continued to introduce Mahurin-type bills in the next several sessions.[29]

II

THE REACTION of the life industry to the Texas Robertson Investment Act dramatically paralleled its response to Wisconsin's 1907 reforms. Shortly after the Robertson measure became law, twenty out-of-state firms notified their Texas employees and policyholders that they would withdraw immediately from the Lone Star State. An open letter from Mutual Benefit Life's management on June 21, 1907, to its local customers succinctly expressed industry reasoning:

> The company explains its departure on three grounds: first, that as a mutual company it did not wish to follow a policy of segregating any portion of its assets for the benefit of any particular class of policy-holder; second, that the funds deposited in the State would be subject to taxation for local purposes; and third, that the large investment would drive interest rates below the point at which the investments would be profitable.[30]

The principal explanation for the mass retirement more probably stemmed from widespread fear among eastern companies that other states, particularly the more consumer sensitive ones in the West and South, might pass similar investment acts. Only if they made a vigorous stand in Texas, the firms reasoned, could such a "blackmailing" movement be "nipped in the bud."[31]

The massive company exodus infuriated Texans. State Senator T. H. McGregor expressed popular reaction to the event when he called the companies' actions "the most insolent, arrogant, brazen, impudent and insulting act in the history of the state." Residents desiring new or additional life coverage now generally turned to existing or recently formed Texas life firms. Most of the retiring companies retained a sizable number of their policyholders and serviced their needs by either establishing new offices or expanding existing ones in border communities located in Louisiana, Arkansas, Oklahoma, and New Mexico. Nevertheless, Lone Star companies mushroomed in size and, more importantly, in political power.[32]

Within a few months after withdrawing from Texas, eastern firms attempted to have local courts declare the Robertson Act unconstitutional. To their great disappointment, the test case of *Metropolitan Life* vs. *Love* was dismissed upon reaching the Texas Supreme Court in 1908. Companies subsequently turned their attention to the legislature, where they hoped to have the investment law repealed or radically modified. Here the firms faced stiff opposition to their repeal attempts, for the original backers of the Robertson law convincingly argued that their measure had been a success. In 1910, for instance, James Harvey Robertson wrote that, during the three years of the act's operation, firms had "invested about three times as much money in land mortgages and securities held by citizens of the State . . . as they had invested in the preceding sixty years." He added that "many strong home companies have organized which will further tend to keep Texas money in Texas." And Texas consumers pleasantly discovered that state-based life firms provided them with reasonably priced and reliable protection. Unlike the situation in Wisconsin, this fact blunted talk of public life insurance. Loyal support of home companies produced a powerful domestic life insurance lobby with the financial resources to fight out-of-state interests successfully.[33]

Only after 1912 did the eastern life insurance lobby begin to make gains in efforts to repeal the Robertson Act. In 1913 the Senate gave serious consideration to a bill introduced by F. M. Gibson of Bonham. Though he was not a tool of the "foreign" companies, the senator accepted their argument that the Robertson Law was retarding the state's economic development. A spokesman for north-Texas farmers, Gibson believed that if the 1907 act was repealed or modified, the state would receive more investments at cheaper rates of interest. His proposal called for the waiving of more than a million dollars in back taxes if the companies returned at once. Gibson's bill still retained the compulsory features of the Robertson Act. Although the legislation died in the Senate, the Bonham lawmaker did not abandon his efforts to change the law.[34]

Early in 1915 the leading eastern companies came to terms with the new governor, James E. (Pa) Ferguson. They consented to invest $35 million in Texas securities within five years and to pay their 1914 tax bills, which amounted to nearly $150,000. In return for these concessions, Ferguson agreed to ask lawmakers to meet in special session in April to consider a new Gibson bill. Only if this measure passed would firms honor their agreement. One company, Prudential, wired the governor to register its support and to offer $5 million in investment money over a five-year period.[35]

The central feature of the second Gibson proposal called for repeal of the compulsory investment concept of the Robertson Act. In its stead the bill placed a five percent gross receipts tax on out-of-state companies, which was to be reduced to the extent that they had their Texas reserves invested in state securities. The progressive reduction section lowered the tax rate to one percent if a firm had all its Texas reserves invested in domestic paper bearing an interest rate of less than six percent. A third part required payment of all delinquent taxes.[36]

Although this second Gibson bill gained influential backers—Ferguson men, particularly farmers who saw repeal as providing cheaper money—the proposal encountered stiff opposition. The Texas insurance lobby mustered its resources to defeat the measure, and other groups and individuals joined the crusade. The Houston Chamber of Commerce did its best to block it. In a resolution passed on April 24, 1915, Houston merchants proclaimed, "We believe that this movement [to repeal the Robertson Act] was instigated and is being conducted in the interest of certain foreign companies who resented the passage of the law and who have since done no business in the State except to keep previous business in force and collect premiums upon which they have paid no taxes. We believe,'' concluded the resolution, "that the Robertson law is right in principle and has proved a material aid in the upbuilding of our State." Many Texans agreed. In a sampling of public opinion the *Austin Statesman* found, "From all parts of the state the feeling is that the 1907 law has been a success. Perhaps modification might be popular if the companies had stayed in Texas. Their insolent actions have hurt them."[37]

Shortly after the *Statesman's* poll the House surprised Texans by passing the Gibson bill by a narrow margin. Yet anti-Gibson forces carried the day when the Senate defeated the proposal by a 16 to 11 vote. Although discouraged, Ferguson and other Gibson backers did not quit. The governor repeatedly blasted the Robertson Act; this fiery politician made the question of retaining the investment law a major issue in the 1916 Democratic primary campaign. Ferguson convinced the state Democratic Executive Committee in June 1916 that the issue should be placed as a referendum on the party's primary ballot. While Texas Democrats could not change the law, he believed that a victory would compel the party to accept an anti-Robertson plank. The Democratic primary election on July 22, 1916, gave supporters of the Gibson bill their second major defeat. By a comfortable margin Democrats said yes to the Robertson Act. Anti-investment forces made other attempts at overturning the law, but it remained until 1963. As late as the eve of World War II, only six eastern companies had returned to Texas.[38]

III

THE DRIVE to pass model legislative measures during the post-1907 period was less spectacular than the Texas adjustment to the Robertson Act. These model laws came almost exclusively from proposals made at the annual meetings of the National Convention of Insurance Commissioners (NCIC) and by the Committee of Fifteen, the group that grew out of the 1906 Chicago insurance conference. Both the Armstrong and Wisconsin hearings prompted NCIC delegates to discuss at length how best to regulate the industry. With the subsequent passage of the tough New York and Wisconsin insurance codes, a host of NCIC members sought laws for their respective states that would complement these newly enacted reforms. Since consumer-oriented commissioners dominated the organization, a large percentage of the model proposals contained a policyholder bias. Statistically, however, "modernization" rather than advanced brands of consumerism predominated. Statutes suggested by the NCIC ranged from standardized policy contract measures to insurance department reorganization proposals. As seen in Chapter 2, the Committee of Fifteen, often in conjunction with the NCIC, also formulated similar model codes. While only a handful of states enacted such laws during their 1907 legislative sessions, most passed some by 1920. This flurry of bills led one trade organ to exclaim, "When insurance gets a wink of sleep in any legislature in the United States, let us know!"[39]

Kansas led the national wave in enacting model reform proposals. The explanation for leadership in this area can only be supposition. It might be attributed to the receptiveness of politically progressive state administrations and legislatures to these suggestions. Possibly, since Kansas had not conducted its own insurance investigation (which would have probably produced corrective measures), a need for model statutes existed. Whatever the reasons, lawmakers passed a smorgasbord of model laws. In 1913, for example, one statute established a uniform system of determining the reserve liabilities of life insurance companies, and another required firms to give a fixed value to policies after customers paid three annual premiums.[40]

Life companies expressed mixed feelings on model legislative bills. They understandably criticized true consumer protection measures—salary limitation laws, stock-disposal statutes, and surplus distribution acts. Since modernizing measures characterized most proposals, sentiment grew that the industry could "live with most model legislation so long as state insurance goes down to defeat." Firms seemed especially pleased with efforts to make state laws uniform. Speaking before a conference on this overall subject held in Washington, D.C., in 1910, Prudential's president John F. Dryden described the chaos in regulation: "Conflict and dissimilarity of State laws include practically every important statutory requirement. . . . What is permitted to be done in one State is forbidden in another, and what is the law of one year may not be the law of the next." Dryden then suggested, "I am firmly convinced that a uniform code governing the essentials both of the public and the private law on the subject of insurance can be framed and the past experience of every life insurance company . . . makes it desirable and proper that such a code be prepared." Dryden was not alone in this thinking. Life insurance personnel as a whole, like business leaders in other fields, eagerly searched for order and stability during this period of political reform and economic change. They applauded efforts for favorable and uniform model laws.[41]

During the adjustment period the life insurance enterprise made it clear that it had not abandoned its old hostility toward taxation, regardless of whether it was on profits, premiums, or property. "Life insurance should not be made to carry unnecessary burdens," argued President E. W. Randall of the American Life Convention. "Taxes, beyond the cost of supervision, are unwarranted." And repeating arguments used in previous decades, the *Spectator* editorialized in 1908: "The beneficent work accomplished by life . . . insurance companies should entitle them to the most liberal possible consideration at the hands of legislators; for the encouragement of such insurance is one of the surest means of avoiding public expense for almshouses, jails, etc. Surely, a tax upon insurance is a tax upon thrift; and, having a tendency to make insurance unduly expensive, operates to discourage prudence and forethought on the part of the citizens of our country." To make its views known on taxation and other issues, the industry employed lobbyists, organized the Association of Life Insurance Presidents, and encouraged formation and expansion of state insurance federations. These latter groups consisted principally of agency directors and underwriters. In Missouri and Kansas, agents' federations sponsored anti–life insurance tax rallies. For example, the *Insurance Leader* reported in 1914 that Kansas agents hoped to fill Topeka's public auditorium with four or five thousand people to protest that state's insurance tax code. Although this event fell far short of expectations, the original proposal "brought a Niagara of applause" from life underwriters.[42]

State legislatures throughout the progressive era continued to either maintain or refine earlier tax statues. The public still vividly remembered tax dodging by the quasi-public corporations during the depression and sought to keep all businesses paying their fair load of the tax burden. As Charles Barnes, Kansas superintendent of insurance and active member of the National Convention of Insurance Commissioners, said in 1909, "There can be no turning back on matters of taxation. The American society will not tolerate special taxation favors for special corporations; all must pay their fair share of taxes." Municipal leagues, fair-tax associations, and various citizens' groups shared the Barnes philosophy.[43]

During the decade following the Armstrong hearings some adjustment to previous tax acts occurred. Backers of model insurance legislation, members of the NCIC, and the Committee of Fifteen, along with industry representatives, agreed that major differences between states in matters of taxation needed correction. Kansas, for instance, placed a two percent tax on home companies' premium receipts but doubled the tax rate on "foreign" ones. California, on the other hand, taxed out-of-state companies at two percent and exempted domestic firms altogether. The industry proposed in 1907 that a uniform tax of one percent on premiums be imposed by every state and territory and the District of Columbia. Reformers—primarily the consumer-oriented state insurance commissioners—thought this rate was too low, and the two groups wrangled for years over the matter. In 1915 Wisconsin modified its famed Orton Law, designed to tax Northwestern Mutual Life at what the public considered a "fair" rate. Yet the company felt the tax "excessive." Commissioner Ekern, supported by fellow progressives and backed by Governor Philipp and Republicans, agreed that Northwestern Mutual was being hurt. Ekern thus pushed through the legislature a new tax bill that called for replacement of the old three percent premium tax on domestic companies and the nominal fee from out-of-state groups with a tax solely on investments of domestic firms. This new measure saved Northwestern Mutual nearly $100,000 in annual taxes and strengthened its competitive position.[44]

IV

CONTRARY to what is often thought, activities to regulate life insurance did not dissipate with passage of the Armstrong and Wisconsin reforms and the Robertson Investment Act. While the industry scored a symbolic victory with its defeat of the International Policy-Holders Committee's bid to control Mutual Life and New York Life, consumers made significant gains by achieving additional corrective measures and, more importantly, by retaining most of the key changes enacted during the hectic legislative sessions of 1906 and 1907. This support for policyholder protection continued because public dislike and distrust of the operations of the life insurance enterprise did not evaporate with the triumphs of the immediate post-Armstrong era. The arrogant withdrawal of firms from Wisconsin and Texas in 1907 did much to prevent repeal of existing reforms and, in the case of Wisconsin, aided the movement for state life insurance—the most radical response to consumer unrest. The adjustment period further witnessed passage of various model measures. Some contained a true reform flavor and were designed by advanced progressives to fill voids left by earlier acts, while others—easily accepted by the industry—strove for the streamlining of state regulation. By the end of the progressive era life insurance correction, although not complete, had overcome most of the shortcomings that had originally prompted it.

4

Fire Insurance Regulation: The Antitrust Phase

EARLY REFORM of the fire insurance industry closely paralleled initial efforts to regulate life firms. Throughout much of the nineteenth century fire insurance consumers, like those who owned life policies, sought to curb activities of wildcatters and fly-by-nights and to guarantee company solvency. The larger and more reputable concerns commonly backed citizen demands for a safe and dependable enterprise. Similarly, fire companies, fire agents' associations, and individual fire underwriters, duplicating the actions of their life counterparts, encouraged popular drives to end rebating, twisting, and disruptive and dishonest tactics used by "lightning" agents. As such, the mind-set of the fire personnel fits the common business mold where stability and predictability are cherished.[1]

As with the life business, fire carriers resisted fundamental reforms. The first serious clash erupted in the 1870s over the question of "valued-policy" bills. Proponents argued that in case of total fire destruction the insuring company should pay the face amount of the policy, irrespective of the property's value at the time of loss. Consumers had good reason for advocating valued-policy legislation. Seeking to maximize profits and at times simply to maintain their own solvency, fire firms increasingly refused to pay the face value after a total loss, even though the insured had fully met all contractual obligations. As a result, owners frequently settled for a fraction of the policies' actual value rather than face lengthy and expensive litigation.[2]

In 1872 the Wisconsin legislature became the first lawmaking body to consider a valued-policy bill. It was introduced by the Dane County representative to rectify the shabby treatment of a constituent. The affair involved an elderly Madison widow whose home had been totally consumed by fire. Although she held a $700 policy, the insuring company refused payment, arguing that her house was not worth the policy's face amount. After prolonged dispute the widow accepted a $300 settlement. Angered by this unfairness, she complained to

71

her sympathetic legislator, who then composed the valued-policy measure.[3]

Although the proposal passed the Assembly, it died in the Senate, due to the power and skill of industry lobbyists and the fact that those sympathetic to such a reform had not yet organized. At the legislative session held in 1874 the sponsor reintroduced his bill. This time it easily passed both houses and was subsequently signed by the governor. Then at the zenith of their power in Wisconsin the Grangers proved instrumental in the battle for passage, for farmers identified with the measure's goals. According to one observer, "They had been continually forced by the selfish companies to accept reduced payments on their fire losses and naturally saw the bill as a way of ending the abuse."

Yet the new law was not solely a farmer's measure. Consumers statewide felt abused, since companies had been contesting more claims following the catastrophic Chicago fire of 1871. Perhaps some Wisconsinites perceived that serious financial problems, stemming largely from the Chicago blaze and universal hard times, plagued most firms operating locally, but "townsfolk willingly joined efforts to club companies with a valued policy law."[4]

The Badger State act was the harbinger of similar ones. In 1879 Ohio, Missouri, and Texas enacted valued-policy measures (or "Wisconsin laws" as they were sometimes called), as did New Hampshire in 1885; Arkansas, Delaware, and Nebraska in 1889; and Kansas in 1893. All were patterned after the Wisconsin statute. However, in 1889 at the insistence of the insurance companies, Missouri modified its original 1879 law to allow firms to withhold claim payments if "willful fraud or misrepresentation is shown on the part of the insured." A number of latter-day laws included this Missouri provision.[5]

As in Wisconsin, consumer discontent was the principal explanation for valued-policy acts. One trade publication in 1890 observed that this agitation came primarily from the "poorer class of policyholders"—storekeepers, homeowners, farmers. "It is well known," said the paper, "that when losses on buildings owned by such people have occurred, the fear of litigation has often induced them to accept a much less amount for their policies than the amount they had insured for." But there was not a single "consumer" position. Larger, more economically powerful policyholders often opposed such reform proposals, arguing that they tended to promote arson and hence increase rates. Still, one insurance official candidly remarked that valued-policy laws were "a reaction on the part of the public against the schemes and systems which we have ourselves made." Understandably, the rest of the industry did not publicly voice this point of view.[6]

By 1915 twenty-two states had enacted valued-policy statutes. While New York failed to pass this particular reform, its legislature at various sessions from the late eighties through the early years of the twentieth century considered such bills. The insurance lobby, led by the New York Board of Fire Underwriters and liberally supported by the large fire firms, kept New York off the roll of valued-policy states. New York insurance men effectively argued that the number of arson cases increased with these laws.[7]

While consumers generally applauded the valued-policy crusade, the industry without exception bitterly attacked it. At the fourth annual gathering of the Insurance Journalists' Association held in Baltimore in 1885, trade writers charged that valued-policy laws were "calculated to lead to an increase of incendiary fires and consequent fraudulent claims against insurance companies." Likewise, an insurance official argued that "a man may insure his house worth only $1500 for $3000, and recover the whole amount; and the defendant company is expressly forbidden to prove the actual value of the property and pay the insured all that he actually lost, but is compelled to pay just double the actual loss. This is simply an incentive to perjury and arson." And at the 1890 meeting of the National Board of Fire Underwriters that group vigorously condemned all valued-policy proposals. Its president contended that Wisconsin's law alone "had cost the policy-holders of the state $876,087 in increased premiums, and had cost the companies $1,767,506 beyond this amount." This situation was bad, he argued, not only for firms but for agents as well who were "attempting to keep jobs in an industry that is faced with higher annual losses."[8]

The fire enterprise began an attack to back up their complaints about valued-policy laws. Soon after passage of the 1874 Wisconsin act, lobbyists representing companies and agents alike attempted to repeal it and to prevent the movement's spread. Elsewhere the industry appealed to the courts for help. But in all cases judges sustained the statutes.[9]

When by 1885 it became apparent that neither lobbying nor legal action could successfully halt the momentum of valued-policy legislation, companies and agent associations sought a more drastic solution. In that year they threatened New Hampshire's citizens with en masse withdrawal if they did not repeal their newly enacted law. When the New Hampshire legislature refused, the firms "arose as one man, packed their gripsacks and departed from the state." Although hoping to make New Hampshire an example for lawmakers contemplating the valued-policy concept, this first case of statewide industry withdrawal did not produce the expected results. New Hampshire continued to support its valued-policy law. Furthermore, the steady growth of farmer and village fire insurance mutuals convinced industry officials that they were about to lose their New Hampshire market permanently. The need to change tactics became obvious, and by the early nineties most firms had returned.[10]

Fire insurance companies also threatened other states that passed valued-policy statutes. In the same year as the New Hampshire exodus, for instance, several firms, led by the Home Fire Insurance Company of New York, notified Texas policyholders that they would "not . . . take risks upon any buildings in Texas after the last day of [January] until the 'valued policy law' should be repealed." But the companies failed to carry out their threat, perhaps sensing that the legislature had no intention of repealing its law. Commenting on the Texas situation the *Spectator* lamented, "Had the insurance companies taken a firm stand when the first one was passed, and refused to do business in that state [Wisconsin], we should have heard no more of valued policy laws."[11]

While the valued-policy issue continued to be a bone of contention between consumers and the industry, a much more serious disagreement centered on the question of rates. A protracted struggle over the cost of fire protection dominated the years from the 1880s to the 1920s.

I

PRIOR to the midnineteenth century, competition largely determined fire insurance rates in the United States. Fierce rate cutting often resulted; in some instances this competitiveness produced charges so low that they proved insufficient to cover ordinary claims. Under such conditions a major conflagration usually meant bankruptcy for firms holding the greatest risks in the fire areas. Just as consumers joined company representatives who fought disruptive marketing practices, both regularly endorsed efforts to stabilize industry operations. When rates plummeted, there might be consumer joy, but most policyholders realized that the bottom line was not cost of protection but whether carriers could pay loss claims. Orderly conditions in this case would benefit consumer and company alike if they resulted in a solvent industry.

During the decade of the 1850s rate-cutting episodes prompted numerous firms to form rating organizations in several cities—

including New York, Boston, and Philadelphia—which eliminated or diminished such practices. These new bodies surveyed risks and suggested charges for various classes of property. Their success in helping to end rate chaos encouraged expansion and imitation.[12]

Shortly after the close of the Civil War seventy-five eastern and midwestern companies meeting in New York City banded together to form the National Board of Fire Underwriters "to establish and maintain, as far as practicable, a system of uniform rates." By 1869 the national board had launched a rating bureau and had divided the country into six districts for rating purposes. The organization, however, soon became moribund because some industry representatives believed that the largest eastern firms dominated it.[13]

The disastrous Chicago and Boston fires of the early 1870s, which bankrupted scores of companies, revived the national board. Its services in setting rates and reestablishing industry order were required if firms were to recoup their losses. The disasters likewise spurred formation of a number of other rate associations. Most were regional— the New England Insurance Exchange, the Underwriters Association of the Middle Department, and the Western Union. As with the National Board of Fire Underwriters, the new groups sought a system of orderly rate making. However, by the turn of the twentieth century these regional organizations, along with the national board, had moved principally from rate work to lobbying, publicity, and compilation and distribution of data on fire causes and losses. This shift in activities stemmed from the member companies' desire to allow more "professional" and "scientific" groups to solve the politically troublesome question of protection charges. Yet the older associations regularly dominated the rating bodies.[14]

Newly formed fire rating bureaus now conducted their work on a city, county, or state basis. Although they resembled earlier agencies established by the national board and regional associations, the bureaus claimed to have better expertise. They surveyed the fire insurance hazards of a locality, established a supposedly equitable set of rates, and sold these findings in the form of rate books and maps to various insurance firms operating in their respective districts. While such charges were intended to be only advisory, virtually all companies instructed their agents to use them. Nationally, these independent and allegedly scientific rating bureaus were flourishing by the late nineties. But they had flaws. "There has been some hasty and ill-considered rating," noted a member of the Fire Underwriters' Association of the Northwest. "Committees have made hurried visits to towns and have marked up rates without advising either with the Local Agents or the insured. Arbitrary figures thus made have been insisted upon and no reasons have been given for the advances, nor has the property owner been informed what was necessary to be done in order to improve his risk and thus get a reduction in his rate." Consumers agreed.[15]

Largely for self-survival, fire industry personnel in Missouri spearheaded the drive for specialized, professional rating organizations during the 1880s. The state's leadership came primarily from efforts of several prominent St. Louis fire insurance men to solve rate-making problems, for heavy losses and intermittent rate-war skirmishes had long plagued that community. By the early nineties Missouri had two bureaus, one rating property in St. Louis and St. Louis County and the other, headquartered in Kansas City, serving the remainder of the state. The St. Louis rating bureau, officially known as the St. Louis Inspection Department, came into being about 1883. It had been created by the St. Louis Board of Underwriters, an organization composed of fire companies and agents, which dated back to 1872. William J. Fetter, a Kansas City insurance broker, established Missouri's second rating organization in 1891. Called the Fetter Bureau, it maintained close ties with both the regional fire insurance organization, the Western Union (a group of approximately one hundred carriers), and the local Missouri State Board of Fire Underwriters and the Kansas City Board of Underwriters.[16]

Soon after the creation of rating bureaus, Missouri policyholders began complaining about insurance charges. They no longer perceived industry solvency as an issue, but rather saw greed as the central problem. It is impossible to assess the merits of company claims that massive rate increases were justified. However, once the Panic of 1873 had run its course, industry insolvencies diminished.

While there had been public outcries against steep rate hikes in St. Louis during the 1870s and earlier, similar actions by that community's new inspection department triggered a more vocal series of protests in the late eighties. "Excessive" and "needlessly high" rates prompted a St. Louis state senator, backed by local commercial interests, to introduce an anti–rating bureau bill in the 1887 session of the legislature. However, the leadership of shrewd and politically powerful St. Louis insurance executive and fire-lobby leader James Waterworth quickly squelched the proposal.[17]

Agitation against bureau rates in St. Louis subsided in the early nineties when several firms not affiliated with the local board forced companies using the inspection department's schedules to slash rates. According to one broker, competition materialized because of "the aggressiveness on the part of certain managers, usually of the smaller concerns who desire to build up their companies overnight.'' (This observer could have noted that it was this same type of aggressive action that historically played havoc with rate and traffic pooling agreements in a wide variety of American businesses, particularly in midwestern railroading during the seventies.) While rate competition delighted St. Louis residents, it especially pleased the biggest consumers—large-scale manufacturers and business owners—many of whom found themselves in dire financial straits due to the Panic of 1893. With intense competition, these individuals could expect rebates on their annual or semiannual premium payments in addition to generally lower charges.[18]

The Fetter Bureau caused immediate policyholder unrest in Kansas City. Within a fortnight after its establishment, the bureau rerated the city's packing-house district and subsequently raised rates by as much as fifty percent. The packers indignantly denounced the hike, charging that their fire loss record had been low. While most policyholders grudgingly paid, several of the more determined either gambled with nonbureau coverage or went uninsured. To exacerbate an already bad situation, the tight control Fetter and the industry exerted on the area prevented rebates to the largest operators, a consideration previously enjoyed. Fetter's actions prompted discussion in some quarters of "the packing men launching their own fire insurance mutual so as to establish on a lasting basis rates at a reasonable level."[19]

Hard times produced further anti-Fetter feeling in Kansas City and the area served by the bureau. In 1893 and 1894 Fetter made drastic rate hikes throughout Kansas City. In some cases charges skyrocketed as much as 100 to 300 percent. Not only were rates increased, but rebates to favored customers virtually ceased.[20]

Two conditions prompted the bureau's actions. Since the panic and the ensuing depression adversely affected most fire firms operating locally, Fetter and industry officials believed that rate increases were mandatory if several companies were to survive. A second contributing factor was the condition of the city's water supply. Kansas City residents received this service from the privately owned National Water-Works Company. When hard times struck, the firm, which was poorly managed and full of watered stock, declared bankruptcy. Since the company could not maintain pressure in its mains or extend lines into the expanding industrial, commercial, and residential sections of the city, Fetter rightfully argued that great sections of Kansas City were at the mercy of the flames because of National's poor performance. The Fetter Bureau seemingly took advantage of the situation to boost rates to a "burdensome" level.[21]

Residents on a cross-class basis lashed out at their local water firm. Many in Kansas City, including some of the most prominent financial leaders, demanded municipal ownership. But residents did not reserve their anger solely for the ill-managed National Water-Works Company. Fetter's rate increases infuriated them. For example, one drugstore owner berated the bureau without mercy. "That bastered [*sic*] Fetter is ruining me! I have to have fire insurance. . . . How can I pay this kind of rates when nobody has money?" Members of the Kansas City Board of Trade—warehouse operators, retailers, manufacturers—joined small businessmen and homeowners to express their wrath against the "trust," as Fetter's bureau was commonly called. They now talked of tough state regulation, "perhaps an anti-compact law, or German [municipal] insurance, or businessmen's or private dwelling owners' mutuals, anything to improve the all-embracing plight of property holders." The Board of Trade itself demanded a full-scale probe of the industry.[22]

William Fetter further suggested fire rate increases for more than four dozen Missouri communities during the depression. One case was in Mexico, where the Fetter Bureau during the summer of 1893 raised local rates from 20 to 100 percent. Fetter told policyholders of this bustling northeast Missouri county seat that companies needed a hike to offset financial difficulties, for they were "not making expenses at the old rates." Bureau raters seemed oblivious to the fact that Mexico had gone into considerable debt constructing a modern municipal water system so as to better meet the fire threat. The community also boasted an excellent record of fire prevention.[23]

Mexico residents naturally thought the increase grossly unfair, and they universally attacked this "high-way robbery." The local business group, a Chicago & Alton Railroad shop local, the Mexico Ministerial Alliance, and the Hardin College Board of Trustees all condemned Fetter's action and demanded a return to the old rate structure. The *Mexico Intelligencer* commented, "The companies under the old rates collect from the people of Mexico $20,000 annually and their losses are not one-fourth of that. The plea of not making expenses at the old rates is the merest rot." And the paper said, "Our people have cause to feel that they are being subjected to a grevious [*sic*] injustice in this action of the companies."[24]

Several months after the rate hike Fetter asked that Mexico's mayor seek council approval to abolish the small license fee required of all fire firms operating locally. This fee originally had been passed by the town fathers in the 1880s to control wildcatters; however, in 1893 it was increased to raise much needed revenues for the Mexico treasury. Perhaps this tax prompted rerating. Publicly, Fetter felt the tax to be an unfair "nuisance," but most of all he feared it might be raised to an "unreasonable level." To sweeten his request, Fetter offered to trade a ten percent reduction in Mexico's fire insurance rates for council action. His proposal proved extremely unpopular with the town's five council members and consumers generally. Councilman B. C. Johnson summed up Mexico's reaction: "I am opposed to making any concessions whatever to the insurance companies. They should pay [the] license [just] the same as any other business enterprise."[25]

The council unanimously rejected William Fetter's request, and the community reluctantly continued to pay the increased charges. Led by members of the council, some residents began plans for establishment of a town mutual company to force down the cost of protection. By October 1893 the new firm became a reality. There was also talk among Mexico businessmen favoring a program of government fire insurance. As one merchant put it, "In portions of Europe the government conducts the insurance and does it successfully. Why cannot the government protect our property as well as protect our lives?"[26]

Intense consumer unrest in Missouri over fire rates produced a series of insurance reform proposals by 1895. While unsuccessful attempts at enacting anti–rating bureau bills had come during the 1887 and 1889 legislative sessions, lawmakers in 1891 passed major corporation reform with an all-encompassing antitrust statute. Proponents of fire reform hoped this law could be used against the fire "trust," which was termed "the strongest and most thoroughly organized in the United States." From 1893 to 1895 Attorney General Robert F. Walker, aided by Secretary of State Alexander Lesueur, unsuccessfully sought to use the new antitrust statute against the St. Louis and Kansas City bureaus. "It has always been a grief to the attorney-general of Missouri," noted the *Insurance Journal* in 1895, "that the courts did not agree with [Walker's] belief that insurance companies were included in the anti-trust law of 1891."[27]

At the 1895 session of the General Assembly a bipartisan group of legislators, representing various small-town and rural interests, enthusiastically backed a bill drawn up by Secretary of State Lesueur, extending provisions of the 1891 antitrust law specifically to cover activities of fire rating bureaus. Through a series of intricate political maneuvers the insurance lobby, under the generalship of James Waterworth who had already rendered yeoman service to the industry, succeeded in excluding cities of over 100,000 population. Although Waterworth claimed that his settlement "was deeply resented by agents in the out-state districts," St. Louis and Kansas City policyholders were even more resentful of the exemption. Dr. Morrison Munford's *Kansas City Times,* a vocal critic of the fire insurance trust, later reported that in House debates on Lesueur's bill, "out-state" backers of antitrust legislation vehemently supported the proposal, asserting that "their people had been robbed until they had arisen in indignant protest." The Senate, however, modified the House bill to exclude the state's two largest cities. "Senators from Kansas City and St. Louis," according to the *Times*, "asked that their cities be exempted from the insurance provision . . . [because] the business public demanded it, and that rates would be demoralized and their cities destroyed by fire unless the local Board of Underwriters be permitted to continue in business." While this may have been true, Waterworth, no novice in Show Me State politics, saw the handwriting on the wall. Exclusion of Missouri's two most profitable markets would not only be a palatable compromise for the industry but would also be one way of disarming rural lawmakers' clamor for tough anti-insurance codes.[28]

Soon after the effects of the new antitrust statutes became known, the *Times* carefully described the Missouri fire insurance situation:

> In Missouri, outside of the two cities of Kansas City and St. Louis, where the Insurance trust has full sway, insurance rates were last week reduced. Thanks to the lawmakers, the insurance combine still has the cities, where the bulk of the business is done and from which the big profits are obtained, by the throat.
>
> Kansas City and St. Louis are just now feeling the full effects of trust domination. They are discovering the difference between competition and combination, and they are paying dearly for all their information on the subject.
>
> "Boss" Fetter who dictates the rates, so far as Kansas City is concerned, . . . says that the law does not make any difference and that Kansas City . . . is getting just as good rates as the rest of the State. The facts in the case do not bear this statement out. This history of the fire insurance business in Kansas City has been that rates have been constantly increased. The improvements in the fire service and the city's inspection service have been constant. The class of buildings erected is better every year; in every way the chance of loss is being decreased, and yet, at the same time, the insurance rates have been going up.[29]

Throughout 1897 the *Times* continued to blast the trust. The paper charged that Kansas City residents paid exorbitant rates and that other Missouri communities, notwithstanding the provisions of the 1895 antitrust act, were still at the mercy of "Czar Fetter."

The *Times*'s ringing indictment of industry wrongs did not go unheard. Responding to consumer pressure and his own sense of fair play, Missouri's new attorney general Edward Coke Crow declared all-out war on Fetter and the fire trust. The decision to attack the

Kansas City rather than the St. Louis bureau was based largely on the fact that "Fetter's rates are generally higher and affect more Missourians. . . ." The attorney general, buoyed by his just completed triumph over the "school-book" trust, attacked Fetter's bureau on August 7, 1897. Assisted by Insurance Superintendent Edward T. Orear, Crow started collecting evidence to use in annulling charters of firms associated with the Fetter combine. After several weeks of intensive investigative work, Crow and Orear jointly announced that "fire insurance rates throughout the state are excessive and exorbitant" and promised they would take appropriate measures against the cause of unjust rates, namely William J. Fetter and companies who used his rate books.[30]

On September 6, 1897, Attorney General Crow brought suit in the Missouri Supreme Court to force the dissolution of the Kansas City-based fire insurance trust. Crow charged that companies "wearing the Fetter collar" were violating provisions of the 1895 antitrust act and that exemption of both Kansas City and St. Louis from the law was unconstitutional.[31]

The attorney general's foray brought immediate response from the industry—first a denial that "an insurance combine" existed and then a twenty percent statewide rate cut outside Kansas City and St. Louis. Said the *Times,* "[The reduction] is simply thrown out to the people as a sop in the face of a fight. The dissolution of the trust will make the reduction perpetual, and nothing else will."[32]

While the fire insurance industry assessed and adjusted its strategy, Crow received strong bipartisan support in his drive to force rate competition. "It is to be hoped [Crow] will succeed in breaking up the combine," wrote the Republican editor of the *Gentry County Headlight.* "Insurance rates are inordinately high and must come down." The politically independent *Joplin Globe* commented, "The people of Missouri will have good reason to crow if their attorney general succeeds in breaking the insurance trust." The Democrats of Audrain County spoke out: "Attorney General Crow . . . will receive hearty support from the people of the State in their effort to break up the Insurance trust. For years the insurance combine has ridden rough shod over the property owners of Missouri. They have conducted their business on the high-handed method which implied: 'The people be damned.' " And the Democratic *Jefferson City Tribune* trumpeted, "It is not a fight against insurance companies, but a fight against as iniquitous and unlawful a combine as was ever formed to rob the people. That the people have been systematically plundered through this insurance combine there is no doubt, and it is time that something was done to check the evil."[33]

Newspapers were not alone in their praise of Crow's reform efforts. Prominent Missourians also spoke out in his behalf. For example, W. V. Watson, retiring president of the Kansas City Commercial Club, told his fellow business colleagues: "I . . . recommend that determined and diligent efforts be made to bring about a reduction of fire insurance rates. And headway made in this direction will necessarily be gained against great odds, due to the way fire insurance rates are now fixed." The growing grass roots support for reform can be seen in the statement of a Hannibal railroad employee. "The high-handed methods of the Insurance combination have forced a choice between the further protection of a trust which is despoiling the State and a protection of the people who have been dispoiled [sic]. We [members of the CB & Q trainmen's local] back our attorney general in his brave and noble attempts to have honest competition to fix the price of insurance just as it determines wages paid labor."[34]

Although Crow mustered a good deal of evidence in his attempt to prove the existence and harmful effect of the fire monopoly, the court sustained the industry's right to use Fetter's rate books and maps. It concluded in part that the 1895 antitrust act had clearly exempted the Fetter books, even outside Kansas City, from the law's jurisdiction. Deeply disappointed, Crow announced that remedial legislation was the only way to "crack the trust."[35]

Defeat in court coupled with continued consumer agitation prompted the introduction of amendatory antitrust legislation in the 1899 General Assembly. Lawmakers from small-town and rural Missouri sparked this drive, and they were joined by several legislators representing large urban interests, including the state's three largest commercial associations, the Business Men's League of St. Louis, the Kansas City Commercial Club, and the Commercial Club of St. Joseph. Their efforts succeeded. According to the industry's chief Jefferson City lobbyist, "Senators Morton, Major, McClintic, Farris, Dowell, all first-class speakers and energetic workers, all seeking political preferment, all inflamed with the current anti-monopolistic sentiment or at least voicing it, swept everything before them. After a close survey of the field, I concluded that no human power could stem the hostile tide at this Session." The amended antitrust act now prohibited "combinations to fix the price of premiums to be paid for fire insurance."[36]

Shortly after the measure's effective date of August 19, 1899, both the Fetter Bureau and the St. Louis Inspection Department formally dissolved. In their stead two new organizations emerged, the Kansas City Independent Actuarial Bureau and the Independent Rating Bureau of St. Louis. These advisory bureaus supposedly were completely severed from the control of local, state, and regional associations. Yet until creation of a system of state-made fire insurance rates more than a decade later, Missourians not favored with rebates repeatedly accused the bureaus of unfair rating practices, contending that most firms required their agents to use the new bureaus' books and maps.

The cost of protection during the early years of the twentieth century fluctuated throughout Missouri. In the fall of 1901 it rose dramatically in the tristate mining belt of the southwest. The Missouri-Kansas Zinc Miners' Association and the Commercial Club of Joplin understandably lodged a series of complaints. Both charged that a recent rate increase on area mining properties was "out of line. . . . The percentage of increase [being] ridiculously high considering that losses have been very light." Furthermore, these groups accused the Independent Actuarial Bureau with being the "Fetter combine in disguise."[37]

While losing his initial court battle with the companies, Attorney General Crow scored a partial victory for correcting fire insurance practices. In 1899 he initiated ouster proceedings against the newly formed St. Joseph Underwriters' Social Club. Fire firms and their underwriters organized this group in anticipation of the 1899 antitrust law. Crow charged it with being a "plain, palpable and bungling trust." The "club," whose membership consisted of some seventy-three companies, soon became an enormously powerful force in Missouri, for members wrote nearly three-quarters of the domestic coverage. Moreover, it was strongly suspected that the club controlled the two new independent bureaus. In July 1899 the Missouri Supreme Court issued a writ of ouster against the St. Joseph organization. The high court later modified its decision by changing it from an absolute ouster to a fine of $1000 for each guilty party and a promise to abide thereafter by the antitrust act. The companies agreed, and by early 1900 all had paid their penalties and affirmed their intention to behave.[38]

The success of the Edward Coke Crow campaign against the St. Joseph club very likely sustained statewide support for the antitrust approach to fire rate problems. Although there were those like the Joplin groups who bitterly castigated the rating work of the supposedly "independent" bureaus and the overall cost of protection, a variety of small-town commercial groups, homeowners, and politicians expressed greater faith in the state's insurance code. They agreed with an employee of the Ozark-based Bunker-Culler Lumber Company that "while the present antitrust laws in regard to the control of fire rates cannot be called perfect, I believe that this method of regulation is the only practical way to curb rates, except perhaps with state insurance or strong industry and farmers mutuals. If rate competition can be maintained, fair rates will result." And those predominantly urban businessmen, who traditionally reaped the benefits of the rebate in competitive market areas, continued to laud the antitrust approach to rate regulation. But when rebates ended or diminished in size they fumed and fussed. The theme of rate justice, not industry stability, is the overriding one in this phase of Show Me State fire insurance reform.[39]

II

KANSAS POLICYHOLDERS, like their Missouri neighbors, fought a long and hard battle with the industry over rate levels. Prior to passage of the state's famed antitrust act of 1889, fire agents' associations determined local insurance charges. For the most part, these associations set rates in an arbitrary manner. They paid little or no attention to an individual policyholder's fire loss record, the construction of the building, or its accessibility to fire protection. Consumers naturally resented this. And because of recurring company insolvencies, rates were frequently excessive, sometimes surpassing those in nearby states and territories.

In 1889 Kansas lawmakers, led by embattled farmers and small-town merchants, included fire insurance companies on their list of businesses to be regulated by the nation's first antitrust law. Specifically, the act said this about insurance: "That all arrangements, contracts, agreements, trusts or combinations . . . to control the cost of insurance . . . are hereby declared to be against public policy, unlawful, and void."[40]

Since this antitrust statute prohibited the fixing of fire rates by agents' associations, Kansans soon saw development of a new system of schedule making "designed to be in harmony with the law." Early in 1890 Harrison Clarkson, one-time state insurance superintendent, established a supposedly "scientific" fire rating bureau. Called the Clarkson Rating Bureau and based in Topeka, it rated the entire state. Like Missouri's two rating organizations, charges were to be advisory, but virtually every fire firm operating in Kansas required its agents to adhere to Clarkson's books.[41]

Consumer complaints about Clarkson's rates came swiftly. The effects of the decade of depression, which began in the late 1880s, tended to make residents even more bitter about high charges. An 1895 letter to Insurance Superintendent George T. Anthony from

William Moore, editor of the *Pittsburg Headlight,* best expressed the general feeling. "It seems there is a man named Clarkson in Topeka who with his assistant makes the rates for all the insurance companies doing business in the state [,] law or no law. He has made rates here on buildings that are out of reason and after making such rates refused to point out definately [*sic*] what is the cause of such big rates and the way to remedy the evil so that a person can have their [*sic*] insurance written at a reasonable rate." He went on to explain that "during these hard times, people here are especially angered by the Clarkson rates." And he asked, "Is there any way to reach this modern king of insurance?"[42]

The appointment by Populist governor John W. Leedy of consumer advocate Webb McNall to head the insurance department in March 1897 brought about the demise of Clarkson and his rating bureau. Early in his administration McNall polled all licensed fire insurance companies to determine if they used the Clarkson books. After establishing their widespread use, he issued an order based on the antitrust act, asserting that the rate books constituted a restraint of trade and requiring the companies to cease using them or else have their licenses revoked and suffer the penalties of the 1889 law. A not unexpected reaction followed when Clarkson sought relief through the courts. On November 8, 1897, a state tribunal denied Clarkson's application on the grounds that "doing business according to the rate sheets in question constitutes a violation of the anti-trust law." The judge further upheld McNall's right to revoke the license of any carrier that continued to use the books. As a result of McNall's victory over Clarkson, the cost of protection for the next two years decreased considerably.[43]

Just as Missouri witnessed formation of two new rating bureaus soon after that state's 1899 antitrust act outlawed its earlier ones, so too did a new rating organization rise phoenixlike in Kansas from the ashes of the destroyed Clarkson bureau. Shortly after McNall left office in the spring of 1899, Charles Eldridge, a former employee of Harrison Clarkson, started the Independent Fire Insurance Inspection Agency of Kansas. In the agency's prospectus Eldridge promised to rerate the state and to sell his findings on "an advisory basis only."[44]

Kansas policyholders of all stripes castigated the Eldridge agency just as they had earlier attacked the defunct Clarkson bureau. Individual consumers joined a variety of pressure groups—lumbermen's associations, public school boards, labor unions—to register their displeasure. Not only did Eldridge hike charges but most companies required their agents to use his rating books and maps. For instance, an Abilene mortician wrote in 1902 to McNall's successor, William V. Church, a standpat Republican friendly toward insurance interests, that "I find that the town was re-rated by [Eldridge] . . . and that rates have been raised from 50 to 100%. It is altogether too high, and I would advise that you look the matter up and ask that the town be re-rated again as it is on such basis now that no business man can afford to pay insurance." For emphasis he added, "The fact of the matter is, our people are going to make a desperate kick and will not for a moment stand for it." Unlike the more industrialized and urbanized states, Kansas had a limited number of large manufacturers and other giant policyholders. This situation produced strong bonds between consumers—for example, those in Abilene—since few were honored with rebates. All could agree that the status quo must change.[45]

By 1905 conditions had not markedly improved. But policyholders had reason to be optimistic. In 1904 Kansans voted into office their first reform-minded governor since the nineties, Edward W. Hoch, a progressive Republican. During his administration and those of fellow Republican Walter R. Stubbs and Democrat George H. Hodges, the state would undertake a variety of much needed political housecleaning—from outlawing the railroad pass system to adopting the initiative and referendum. Although Hoch gave greater attention to battling the Standard Oil trust, he did express the public's concern about fire charges. In his first message to the legislature the governor said, "Insurance rates are entirely too high in this state, relatively much higher than elsewhere. As the law now stands the people seem to have no protection against the cupidity of insurance companies. There is practically no competition in the business, and no present pretense of any. The laws on the subject are evaded and practically annulled." But Hoch's enthusiasm for insurance reform cooled for reasons that are unclear. Because of an absence of either a consumer-oriented insurance superintendent or attorney general, positive action against the Eldridge Inspection Bureau did not begin until a few years later.[46]

In 1907 Fred S. Jackson, the new attorney general and a spokesman for the state's rising progressive movement, sought to aid Sunflower State fire insurance customers. Jackson brought suit in district court to restrain seventy-nine fire companies alleged to be using Eldridge rate books in a noncompetitive fashion. However, the court did not find any antitrust violations and decided in favor of Eldridge and the carriers. "The defendant companies do not now, and did not at the time alleged in plaintiff's petition, by any combination endeavor to regulate or control the cost of fire insurance," argued the judge, "and the rates for such insurance are not now and were not then controlled by the Eldridge advisory rate book." Jackson appealed this decision to the Supreme Court but lost on a technicality.[47]

Kansans thus came to a critical realization: the fire industry could *not* be effectively regulated by antitrust legislation. The distasteful practices of the Eldridge rating bureau continued unchecked until 1909 when the movement for state-made rates surfaced.

III

FIRE INSURANCE REFORM in Texas closely resembled events in Missouri and Kansas. Texans likewise fought for rate justice; by the latter part of the century foremost consumer concerns clearly were not the industry's financial health and stability.

Beginning in the late 1880s and coinciding with the rise of area railroad pools and the "bagging (for cotton) trust," a statewide underwriters' association, commonly called the Texas Insurance Club, took control of rate fixing. The club set charges that residents viewed as largely excessive and unfair, and it wielded such tight control over the domestic fire insurance scene that rate cutting and rebating virtually ceased. Texas policyholders—residential, commercial, and industrial—with few exceptions complained about this situation, accusing the club of consisting of firms that are "bloated monopolists fattening by extortion."[48]

Consumers first saw positive action taken against the "insurance trust" in 1891. With backing from the newly elected and modestly reform-oriented James Stephen Hogg administration, Texans not only received their first railroad commission but the attorney general's office took up the standard of fire insurance reform. Using the state's immensely popular 1889 antitrust act as the basis to file suit, Attorney General Charles A. Culberson went into a local court to dissolve the fifty-seven-member Texas Insurance Club. Culberson charged in *State* vs. *Queen Insurance Co., et al.* "that Club members had illegally combined to regulate agents' commissions and insurance rates." The court, basing its decision on common law, enjoined the club from further rate fixing but held that the antitrust statute did not apply to insurance companies. After a series of additional legal battles, the Texas Supreme Court ruled in December 1893 that "insurance companies are not subject to the anti-trust law or the principles of the common law applicable to combinations in restraint of trade."[49]

The high court's adverse ruling prompted lawmakers to pass an amended antitrust law in 1895. The revised statute specifically included fire insurance companies along with corporations previously subjected to antitrust control. The principal factions of the state's dominant Democratic party supported its passage—businessmen, bankers, and old-guard professional politicians; members of the Farmers' Alliance; and merchants, farmers, ranchers, and younger professional politicians who were loyal to the Hogg organization. No prominent noninsurance pressure group objected to the measure.[50]

Shortly after passage of the revised antitrust act, the Texas Insurance Club, desiring to escape its provisions, decided to turn over its rate-making duties to a recently formed rating bureau. This agency, the Jalonick Rating Bureau of Dallas, provided services similar to those of the Fetter and Clarkson organizations.[51]

Soon after its creation the bureau's founder and director, George W. Jalonick, and his staff rerated most Texas communities. While sometimes lowering coverage costs, the bureau more often raised them. Because they came during hard times, these rate hikes infuriated Texans. As one Waco lumber dealer put it, "What a burden this fire trust! Now we have Jalonick and his bunch to contend with. My rates . . . were raised nearly 2 fold after his raters made their visit. . . . One thing is certain, raising fire rate during a depression will be like getting blood out of a turnip—in his case a mad turnip." In addition, rebates ended, thus angering large insurers who expected "special considerations."[52]

Public dissatisfaction with the Jalonick Rating Bureau prompted still another antitrust code amendment. Most Texas consumers continued to believe that reasonable rates could be achieved through forced competition. The Davidson Anti-Trust Act of 1899—"extremely lengthy and verbose"—tightened the legal definition of a "fire-insurance monopoly," providing, according to one lawmaker, "the ultimate fire insurance anti-trust law that could be passed." A key feature copied from a recently enacted Arkansas statute required each company doing business in Texas to sign annually an affidavit declaring that it did not belong to any rating organization.[53]

The 1899 antitrust measure produced the common pattern of one rating bureau dissolving to be replaced by a "solely advisory one." The new Texas organization was the Texas and Arkansas Inspection Bureau, designed to meet the legal requirement of each state's new antitrust code. Then in May 1900, four months after the revised antitrust statute took effect, the Texas Fire Prevention Association emerged to supplement the rating efforts of the bistate inspection bureau.[54]

Once more Texas antitrust legislation failed to produce lower charges. As the June 3, 1900, *Galveston Daily News* reported, "Insurance companies are still doing business in Texas and instances of their cutting the rates for business are unknown. The framers of the law were positive the insurance monopoly . . . would be completely destroyed, and in consequence thereof the rates would be slashed by reason of competition and the people be benefited thereby. All of which has failed to materialize."[55]

Texans continued to object vociferously to high insurance costs. Palestine policyholders offer one example. Angered by a rate increase after a Texas Fire Prevention Association inspection, they held a public protest rally in September 1901. Townspeople named a blue-ribbon committee of businessmen to negotiate with the prevention association and the companies for a rate reduction. If a decrease could not be achieved, the committee threatened to file a formal complaint with the attorney general; if that failed, launching a local mutual and boycotting all old-line fire firms were planned. The Palestine protest worked, for by January 1, 1902, rates in this east-Texas community dropped significantly.[56]

In 1903 Texas legislators once again revamped their antitrust statutes. Since the United States Supreme Court had declared Illinois's antitrust act unconstitutional (a law partially patterned after the original 1889 Texas measure), a revision was deemed in order. Written by Attorney General Charles K. Bell, an ardent proponent of business regulation through forced competition, the new act proved "short, orderly [and] well-expressed," with stiff penalties for those guilty of any "restraint of trade."[57]

Shortly after passage of the 1903 antitrust law Attorney General Bell, responding to recurring complaints about excessive rates and rate fixing, filed suit against fifty-nine companies, charging they had "fixed uniform rates in Texas." After a series of court fights the cases were subsequently dismissed on technical grounds. Texans had come to expect help only from attorneys general on fire insurance matters, for industry interests had apparently captured the state insurance department.[58]

Until after advent of the successful movement for state-made rates in 1909, additional complaints continued to be heard about unlawful combinations; strong antitrust sentiment remained in the Lone Star State. The persistence of this support can be attributed to the widely held notion that if such legislation were vigorously enforced and violators were tried before consumer-sensitive courts, competition and hence equitable rates would result. One astute observer noted that the average policyholder would not be the only one to benefit from competition. As in Missouri, certain individuals held a vested interest in achieving meaningful competition through antitrust legislation. "If competition exists, our largest merchants fervently believe that the fire companies, when faced with cut-throat competition, will be forced to grant them low-cost coverage in return for their business. . . ."[59]

IV

AT TIMES policyholders in New York and Wisconsin joined their brethren elsewhere in protesting fire insurance charges and practices. In these states, however, the pattern of reform during the antitrust years differed noticeably from that in Missouri, Kansas, and Texas.

For most of the nineteenth century fire industry practices variously affected New York consumers. Although several local tariff associations had been established following the Civil War, the extremely large number of firms operating in the state caused repeated organizational instability. Tariff associations, particularly in the greater New York City area, were constantly in a state of flux— organizing, disbanding, and reorganizing. The industry seemed helpless in its attempts to maintain rate order. The *New York Times* emphasized the extent of competition when it observed that "companies . . . under the pressure of an extreme necessity for business have been in the habit of taking risks, both 'moral' and material, on almost any building that would stand up long enough to be insured, and trusting to luck that it would not burn down until their policies had expired." As a result, competition forced rates downward, giving New Yorkers generally lower costs than virtually anybody else. The state's largest commercial and industrial policyholders, located mainly in the New York City metropolitan area, seemed to be the principal beneficiaries. According to the *Sun,* they were "paying dirt-cheap premiums or receiving munificent cash rebates from those companies desperate for their business."[60]

The vigorous competitiveness among firms in New York City produced an unusually high number of insolvencies. Undoubtedly some patrons smiled at the benefits of rate competition, but uncertainties of protection prompted others to work actively with company leaders who desired to eliminate bankruptcies and to organize business on an even keel. With stricter licensing requirements and tighter deposit laws, this problem was well in hand by 1890.[61]

The immediate effects of the Panic of 1893 led policyholders, mostly outside metropolitan New York, to protest strongly against rating practices. Their reaction seemingly stemmed from two related events. Consumers who had insured with small farmer and town mutuals discovered that hard times were wrecking scores of these companies—an understandable occurrence since the state's mutuals had a history of being exceedingly vulnerable to economic downswings. Unprotected, many former mutual policyholders sought coverage from old-line stock firms. Unfortunately, they turned to the industry at an inopportune time. By the fall of 1893 the New York

State Association of Local Boards of Underwriters, under whose auspices rates outside the city were usually fixed, forced up charges throughout much of the state to offset losses caused by depression and the cost of preferential treatment to large customers. For instance, rate increases for rural Madison County alone averaged nearly 140 percent.[62]

Angry policyholders, mostly upstaters, communicated their displeasure to the legislature. In a resolution they charged in part: "Whereas, the rates so fixed and established are unjust, exorbitant and oppressive to the people and operate to foster and promote monopoly and to yield revenue and profits in such quantities as to render the existence of such corporate monsters dangerous to the Commonwealth." The rate protesters achieved no corrective measures. According to one lawmaker this was due "in large measure to our inability to formulate a specific rate-reform program."[63]

Beginning in 1894 the cost of protection jumped sharply in the city of New York, although not to the extent that it had upstate. Factors responsible include New York City's heavy fire losses, due in part to its financial inability to provide adequate fire protection, the imperative need to save companies from bankruptcies, and the successful establishment out of economic necessity of a basic rate structure by heretofore rival firms and agents' associations.[64]

Before consumer unrest could trigger a reform drive, New York City's premium charges started a decline toward predepression levels. Better times and a resurgence of competition explain these reductions. By the spring of 1898 a full-scale rate war had broken out in the city. Rate cutting ended, however, when the city's leading fire rating organization, the New York Fire Insurance Exchange, successfully arranged a new tariff with the city's principal companies and agents' groups. This agreement pushed up rates for all classes of property.[65]

This time the higher cost of fire protection in New York City caused the customary consumer discontent. Several large department store owners, for example, argued that their rates were grossly unfair. They were supported by prominent insurance brokers who claimed that department stores "have been discriminated against unjustly, and that they were chosen as to the sources from which to make up losses sustained in other localities." Quite likely these brokers publicly backed the storeowners' cause to court their business or simply out of fear that these politically active merchants might use their influence to agitate for stringent rate reform controls.[66]

Rates continued to climb during the first decade of the twentieth century, both in the New York City area and upstate. With the steady rise in the cost of coverage for virtually every risk, sometimes as much as 200 percent, New Yorkers began to endorse antitrust proposals to combat combinations that many blamed for excessive charges. However, the possibilities of a tidy bureaucratic solution to rate injustices did not appeal to consumers. The penchant for antitrust legislation probably stemmed from a deep-seated distrust of regulatory commissions. "I do not cherish government by commission," wrote one Utica merchant to the Insurance Department in 1905. "The Board of Railroad Commissioners for more than twenty years has been an outstanding example of the ineffectiveness of such bodies to curb practices that they were empowered to correct." Indeed, the story of New York's attempts to regulate quasi-public corporations prior to the emergence of Charles Evans Hughes and progressivism in 1906 is a sordid one, full of corruption and boss rule.[67]

While antitrust bills appeared in legislative hoppers in the nineties, the first serious drive occurred in 1906. In April Assemblyman Alfred E. Smith of New York City, representing his district's homeowner and commercial interests, succeeded in getting an antitrust measure reported out of the House Insurance Committee. The Smith proposal made it a misdemeanor, punishable by a fine of $250 to $1000, for fire firms or their agents to "enter or maintain pools, trusts, conspiracies, or agreements to control rates of insurance." Insurgent Republican senator Edgar T. Brackett of Saratoga Springs introduced a similar proposal in the upper chamber. Both measures differed little in their scope from those passed earlier by midwestern and southern lawmakers. Brackett's bill was buried in committee. The Smith proposal, on the other hand, sailed through the House by an 85 to 15 final vote but never came up for Senate consideration. Politics made strange but explainable bedfellows when the fire lobby, to stymie Smith's bill, joined forces with certain reform-minded individuals desiring greater punishments for antitrust violators. The latter group, composed of some of New York's largest fire insurance policyholders—including many "mercantile, lumber and heavy manufacturing concerns" and the Merchants Association of New York City—would not accept "a diluted measure when it was thought possible to nail the fire men to the wall." These advocates of stiff antitrust statutes—like their colleagues in Missouri and Texas—undoubtedly longed for the days when vigorous competition gave them exceedingly low-cost coverage. Although defeated, Smith and others of a similar stripe continued to seek antitrust relief.[68]

By 1910 New York policyholders were facing a trust similar to the ones confronting residents of other states much earlier. In a letter from Monroe County district attorney Howard Widener to Insurance Superintendent William Hotchkiss the public's concern about the fire rate situation was duly summarized. "I thoroughly believe that some legislation is needed to reach this monopoly, as the insurance combination as it exists in this State and the United States is one of the greatest evils of the day. As from my investigation they have complete control of the business and the fixing of rates, and the business people of the cities are wholly at their mercy without redress." The initial rate reform efforts of New Yorkers—antitrust legislation—paralleled the first far-reaching insurance corrections that Missouri, Kansas, and Texas consumers supported. Yet the Empire State would lag behind in development of more sophisticated rate control statutes.[69]

V

WISCONSIN'S EFFORTS to control fire protection costs, while resembling reforms elsewhere, included notable differences. Consumers faced the recurring problem of an industry whose charges were frequently excessive. High rates stemmed from a combination of company insolvencies, the need for firms to bolster earnings during the lean years of the nineties, and rate fixing. As with other policyholders, Wisconsinites toyed with the antitrust approach to rate reform. But consumer-owned mutuals and talk of government insurance replaced antitrust agitation as the central thrust in the state's drive for equitable charges.

In the mid-1880s the leading fire insurance firms that operated in Wisconsin achieved for the first time a relatively high degree of rate order. This came with the establishment of the Wisconsin Fire Rating Bureau, or Northwestern Inspection Bureau as it was sometimes called. This rating organization supplied books and maps to virtually every Wisconsin community except for the three largest cities— Milwaukee, Superior, and Madison—where local boards did the rating work. In the late eighties Wisconsin residents became mildly concerned about this method of rate fixing. The 1887 General Assembly failed to act on a bill, backed principally by warehouse owners, that would have prevented local boards from setting charges. Strong policyholder support for such a proposal did not materialize, due in large part to the enactment of a town mutual measure that captured the public's attention.[70]

From the late eighties through the first decade of the twentieth century some Wisconsinites expressed interest in antitrust legislation. As a consequence, lawmakers repeatedly considered anticombination bills. Such measures were apparently supported by various types of policyholders—including those engaged in farming, business, and manufacturing—who perceived those proposals as "a means of protecting the public from the grips of an abusive trust." No organized consumer lobby appeared, although higher rates coming after the Panic of 1893 generally stimulated antitrust thinking. For example, a sharp rise in coverage costs coinciding with the panic deeply disturbed Superior's residents. One local newspaper described the situation: "A year ago last August [1893] a raise of 20 per cent went into effect and on December 26 [1894] a new rate book had gotten [sic] out which raised or lowered rates, mostly the former, . . . in some cases the new differential amounting to as much as 160 per cent increase over the prices in vogue a year and one half ago." The paper then pointed out that consumers, large and small, were "kicking about the stiff raise of rates which had gone into effect" and concluded that the "arrogant fire trust must be destroyed with meaningful anti-trust laws" or perhaps "boycotted and a local town mutual company launched in its stead."[71]

Those who believed that an antitrust measure could solve the problem of high rates succeeded in 1897 in passing a moderate antimonopoly law, which forbade combinations to fix rates, except locally. Since the established method of rate fixing for Wisconsin's three largest cities was at the community level, this law had little repressive effect. The 1897 statute testified to the insurance lobby's abilities at "watering down potentially dangerous anti-combination measures," at least as they related "to the source of our most profitable business."[72]

Interest continued in antitrust legislation. From 1899 to 1909 there were repeated efforts to eliminate the local exemption from the 1897 law. No legislative action occurred, mostly because consumers discovered other ways of dealing with excessive and arbitrary fire insurance charges. The popular alternatives were government and mutual insurance. No other state in this study, or for that matter in the country, carried out these programs to the same extent as Wisconsin.[73]

The first drive to establish some form of publicly sponsored insurance came in 1872. The ruinous Chicago fire of October 1871, which bankrupted scores of stock companies, convinced many Wisconsinites that insurance firms operated for profit were woefully inadequate. Therefore, a "cheap and safe plan" of fire insurance appeared for the 1872 legislature to consider. It would have created special county fire funds, administered by the local board of supervisors, to pay loss claims. A county's tax collection machinery would acquire money for the fund by assessing premiums on those desiring such protection. Although failing to pass in 1872, the bill was eventually enacted for Grant County.[74]

For the next thirty years Wisconsin experienced repeated proposals for state fire insurance. In the Granger legislature of 1874 lawmakers debated the merits of public insurance but rejected it for fear that if major losses plagued the state, the burden of repayment would fall directly on the taxpayers. Although the 1881 House session called for rural townships to set up a fire insurance scheme by using their tax assessment powers, this bill never arrived in the Senate. Milwaukee reformers—socialists and urban populists—subsequently introduced measures that would have placed the state directly into the business of insuring privately owned property. The insurance companies quickly pounced on each proposal and killed it, for they argued (as did those who would a decade later oppose state life insurance bills) that such measures "are clearly socialistic and inconsistent with our system of business" and would "ultimately be harmful to society." These lobbyists effectively underscored the widely held view that government insurance would be a financially risky proposition for the taxpayer.[75]

The event that spawned state fire insurance occurred in 1898 when flames engulfed the Wisconsin Industrial School for Boys at Waukesha. Destruction of this uninsured structure immediately prompted officials to insure other public properties, including the capitol. But more importantly, the Waukesha fire made cogent the argument advanced by some in the mutual and antitrust movements that Wisconsin should become a self-insurer, thus saving large premium payments, much of which went to out-of-state firms. With the rise to power after 1900 of Robert M. La Follette and the consumer-oriented progressives, prospects improved for public fire insurance, at least for state property. Although the proposal that would allow Wisconsin to enter the insurance field as a self-insurer by creating a special fire fund failed to pass in 1901, it became law two years later. Commenting on this unique American fire insurance reform, the *Milwaukee Sentinel* said, "It is expected that under the new law the State's interests will not only be better safeguarded than at present, but that twice the value of risks can be carried for about the present expense."[76]

The great jubilance shown by those who backed Wisconsin's new role as self-insurer soon turned to concern. Nine months after the state launched its fire insurance experiment, the capitol burned, leaving the fund with a sizable deficit. Nevertheless, for the most part Wisconsinites saw no reason to abandon the public fire insurance experiment and continued to support it. There were those, too, who encouraged expanding Wisconsin's role as a fire insurer even to the extent of insuring private property.[77]

Coinciding with the proposals for government insurance came a keen interest in mutual fire insurance. Patterned after German and Scandinavian models, mutuals were designed to provide inexpensive protection by permitting residents to share all losses cooperatively. Since mutuals usually had only one salaried official, a secretary, operating costs were further minimized.

In rural Wisconsin during the seventies farmers experienced difficulty in obtaining safe, inexpensive fire coverage. The depression of the mid-1870s magnified capital scarcity. Private joint stock companies, therefore, were reluctant to expand operations outside the state's major urban centers. When they did, rates were usually inordinately high. The Chicago and Boston conflagrations of 1871 and 1872 made it apparent to many that private firms were exceedingly vulnerable to catastrophic losses. Also, the difficulty farmers and others faced in collecting claims created further consumer resentment against the private carriers. Typical arguments in support of mutuals appeared in Granger bulletins. One urged, "Patrons, you cannot afford to pay these high premiums to joint stock companies. Insure yourselves and keep some money at home." Another said, "This immense sum [arguing that commercial carriers wasted seven-tenths of premium payments] is now an annual gift from the hard working people to a set of sharpers who ridicule us for our stupidity while reveling in luxury on our hard earnings." These factors led to enactment during the late seventies of liberal and revised amendments to Wisconsin's original 1859 mutual insurance statute.[78]

The 1878 law is of particular significance. It authorized incorporation of a host of specialized mutual companies, including ones for druggists, lumber retailers, millers, jewelers, liquor dealers, and hardware merchants. The act also called for mutuals to protect county asylums, schools, and poorhouse property.[79]

Eleven years later lawmakers extended the concept by authorizing creation of church mutuals, first for the Methodist Episcopal Church and later for other denominations. The rise in protection costs during the nineties, coupled with the inability of numerous congregations to pay insurance bills, resulted in steady growth of church mutuals throughout the decade. In 1895 the legislature permitted them to insure religious property outside Wisconsin and to protect against casualties other than fire and lightning. And in 1903 legislators,

pressured by various religious bodies, drastically expanded the scope
of church mutuals by authorizing them to cover members' property.
Thus they became general fire carriers.[80]

A major Wisconsin mutual statute was passed in 1887. This was a
general incorporation law that allowed creation of local fire insurance
companies on a mutual basis solely for cities and incorporated
villages. Urbanites who desired low-cost coverage and believed this
approach was the only logical way of solving the fire rate problem
pressed hard for this measure. The *Waukesha Freeman* ably summarized the arguments of those who sought town mutual protection:

> Enough is paid to [old-line stock] fire insurance companies by the
> village of Waukesha . . . every year to cover the average annual
> losses of the village by fire, four or five times over, whereas it
> ought not to pay out more than twice as much as it receives, at
> the most, in order to cover all margins of expenses and
> risks, . . . Waukesha would be richer by eight or ten thousand
> dollars every year than at present, from the mere savings in
> money actually paid out by houseowners.
>
> With such a saving of outgoes, the village could afford to be
> more liberal to its fire department than the insurance companies
> now are, and the result would probably be less destruction from
> fire. The township associations have caused savings of hundreds
> of thousands of dollars to the people of the rural districts of the
> state during the comparatively few years of their operation, and
> will save millions in the future. The law under which those
> associations have been organized and conducted should now be
> extended to more thickly populated localities, and the saving
> made more important still than at present.[81]

After the town mutual bill became law, several hundred
Waukesha residents launched the Waukesha City Mutual Fire Insurance Company. During the depression of the 1890s the local press
continually argued that "this company ought to be loyally sustained,"
for dependable, inexpensive fire protection was now available to all
community residents. Local consumers apparently followed this advice, for the firm prospered.[82]

Scores of other Wisconsin municipalities established town
mutuals to provide relief from high rates. A number of communities
dotting the Wisconsin River valley, for example, formed mutuals
shortly after the 1893 panic drastically boosted protection costs. By
1900 such companies were flourishing in Merrill, Wausau, Grand
Rapids (later named Wisconsin Rapids), and Portage.[83]

A variety of factors explain the Wisconsin passion for fire insurance mutuals. The success of similar concerns in Germany and

Scandinavia was well known to that large segment of the population immigrating from those lands. Moreover, the fine record of early mutual operations in providing equitable rates and dependable coverage proved the old adage that "nothing succeeds like success." Furthermore, mutuals allowed Wisconsinites the opportunity to obtain virtually instant relief; consumers simply did not have to wait for politicians to enact programs that always ran the risk of failing to meet their needs and expectations. The plan also represented indisputable principles for residents inculcated with the time-honored notions of pragmatism, hard work, and the cooperative spirit.

VI

BY THE END of the first decade of the twentieth century the initial wave of fire insurance reform had run its course. A distinct pattern developed: policy contract abuse produced valued-policy legislation; high and arbitrary rates led to a series of antitrust proposals. The chief variations for rate reform came in New York, where fierce competition delayed antitrust agitation, and in Wisconsin, where government-sponsored insurance and mutuals in particular served as satisfying substitutes to dependence upon antitrust legislation.

One of the most interesting and significant aspects of the early years of fire insurance reform is the persistence of antitrust sentiment well into the twentieth century. Antitrust solutions are usually associated with the 1890s, with reformers during the early 1900s and after supposedly concentrating on controlling business monopolies by independent regulatory commissions. Why did antitrust sentiment against the insurance industry continue? The answer is not simply the notion of the widespread belief in the virtues of competition and the free marketplace. The foremost reason is that consumers regularly viewed this form of corporate regulation as an effective means of guaranteeing equitable rate structures. While there had been early concerns about disruptive marketing practices and a lack of overall financial stability within the enterprise, that rapport between policyholders and companies quickly dissolved as protection costs soared with the appearance of the fire "trust," best represented by the newly created rating bureaus. Once again justice, not a search for order, is the key to understanding public pressure for change.

Related explanations cast light on the evolution of antitrust agitation, particularly in Missouri, Kansas, and Texas. Unlike New York and Wisconsin, these states were deeply involved in the populist revolt. Since the People's party program of business regulation emphasized antitrust legislation, it is understandable that these states repeatedly proposed this approach to problems they felt stemmed directly from unwarranted combinations. There were also reformers who continued to view antitrust laws as the panacea for all regulatory problems. One Kansas lawmaker remarked in 1907, "I believe antitrust laws can be made to solve most of our problems with big business. . . . Government ownership may be fine, perhaps for Railroads and Telegraph companies, but the basic principles we set forth in 1889 [Kansas antitrust act] are sound and should be widely used." Similarly, antitrust advocates skillfully argued that weaknesses in this approach to the fire rate problem frequently lay, not in the laws themselves, but rather in their enforcement. If a state had sincere, aggressive reformers in the offices of insurance commissioner and attorney general they reasoned, then "the fire-insurance trust can be forever smashed." Persistence of antitrust sentiment can also in part be attributed to certain individuals and groups who had vested interests in maintaining this form of regulation. When competition existed, fire firms commonly gave their largest customers special considerations to keep their business, either in the form of lower rates or rebates. Thus as favored patrons these often politically potent individuals—usually large merchants and industrialists—naturally wanted to retain such advantageous statutes.[84]

In Missouri, Kansas, and Texas, where antitrust legislation proved generally unsatisfactory, a corrective movement began by 1910. The drive for state-made rates would become the second major wave of fire insurance reform during the progressive era. As with the antitrust approach, this was another pragmatic attempt to establish forever protection at a fair cost.

5

State-made Fire Rates

Enthusiasm for antitrust legislation to combat rate abuses dramatically flagged after the turn of the century. Those advocating rate justice seemed to sense the futility of achieving meaningful competition. Hope, however, replaced despair with the emergence of a new control tactic—state-made fire insurance rates. Proponents foreshadowed the "New Nationalism" philosophy advocated by Theodore Roosevelt and his Progressive party in 1912 when they sought to recognize the realities of the corporate world. Like New Nationalists who wanted to permit big business but sought to counterbalance it with big government and big labor, these insurance reformers effectively argued that the fire "trust" had become an established fact of life. In their minds, regulation of combination in the public interest, rather than its destruction through forced competition, was the logical response to recurring rating problems. Yet objectives remained the same; while order and efficiency seemed desirable, the watchwords continued to be consumer interest.

In 1909 Americans witnessed the harbinger of this new fire insurance reform crusade, which was destined to sweep the country much as the valued-policy and antitrust campaigns had done in earlier decades. In that year Kansas and Texas lawmakers dramatically broke with their antitrust tradition by enacting the nation's first state rate measures, just as both had led with anticompact statutes. By 1915 Missouri, Louisiana, Washington, Kentucky, and nearly a dozen other states had become directly involved in the rating process. This movement repeats the theme of deep-seated consumer dissatisfaction with industry rate fixing and related practices, and it furthermore reveals another dimension to the complex nature of business regulation during the progressive era.[1]

I

THE FIRST widely publicized suggestion for state control of fire insurance charges came from Kansas. In the spring of 1892 the state's superintendent of insurance William H. McBride proposed that his office be permitted to have a say in fixing rates. Why Superintendent McBride made this proposal is not exactly clear. His career contained little to indicate that this obscure country lawyer sympathized with consumers. He served a single term in the Kansas House during the mideighties and held membership on the state penitentiary commission prior to assuming the superintendency. McBride's friend and fellow Republican, the archconservative governor Lyman U. Humphrey—a man generally disliked by Kansas reformers, particularly by the state's emerging populists—appointed McBride to the insurance post in July 1891.[2]

The superintendent's thoughts on the general subject of business regulation, however, hint at the origins of this all-important regulatory concept. Alarmed at the potentially "radical" and "confiscatory" nature of the Kansas antitrust act of 1889, McBride thought this approach to control would severely injure the state's economic well-being. It would certainly limit opportunities for profits, and capital would be withdrawn. The superintendent fervently sought continuation of the now badly deflated boom that had characterized Gilded Age Kansas. He strongly believed that regulatory statutes administered by commission could be made compatible with overall business interests. And, too, the ideals of order and efficiency may help to explain McBride's brainstorm.[3]

The fire enterprise did not approve of the innovation. At that time a leading insurance trade journal expressed the companies' overwhelmingly negative response: "Just now this seems quite laughable, but there are various signs in various quarters that this tendency of hostile legislation toward compulsory rates . . . is a serious menace." And the publication correctly prophesied that "the companies will find a few years hence that this form of attack will have many supporters."[4]

To the great satisfaction of fire firms, Kansas lawmakers for the time being failed to consider McBride's proposal seriously. Instead, they continued to endorse antitrust solutions to the fire rate problem. One opposition spokesman reflected a fairly common point of view in the states that tenaciously backed anticompact legislation. "Frankly, I am leery of any change in direction of state-set rates. . . . People want a system of free enterprise and competition." He concluded by emphasizing that "private property is near and dear to all" and not one "to be tampered with by state laws." Such a position is understandable when one considers that many Americans from the time of the McGuffey readers and earlier had been committed to a traditional value system with its emphasis on free enterprise, laissez-faire, and private property.[5]

Despite the initial coolness of Kansas, the movement to pass a state-made rate measure came into its own in 1909. Shortly before the convening of the regular biennial session of the legislature, Superintendent of Insurance Charles W. Barnes drew up a rate control proposal. A member of the progressive wing of the Kansas Republican party, Barnes consistently championed business reform. As a newspaper editor in Osage City he had endorsed tighter public control of a host of quasi-public corporations, ranging from railroads to express companies. And as deputy insurance superintendent from 1903 until his election to the superintendency three years later, he repeatedly sought to curb insurance abuses. However, Charles H. Luling, his more cautious superior, restrained his reform impulses.[6]

The Barnes rate control measure was straightforward. It required fire insurance firms to file with the superintendent "general basis schedules showing the rates on all classes of risks insurable by such . . . rates or the value of the insurance issued to the assured." The proposal empowered the insurance department head "to pass upon the rates when filed, and if he shall determine that any rate is either excessive or inadequate, he is authorized to direct the company or companies filing such rate to file a lower or higher rate, which shall be commensurate with the . . . risk." However, the proposal granted companies the right to appeal to the courts whenever they felt any reduction order was unjust. The bill, moreover, contained all-important antirebate and antidiscrimination provisions.[7]

The exact origins of Barnes's proposal are obscure. It is known that the antitrust approach to rate regulation dissatisfied the superintendent, and he willingly abandoned the philosophy of limited government to which Kansans had clung steadfastly in the past. "We have wasted too much time with anti-trust law," he said. "Reasonable rates cannot be guaranteed with this kind of legislation." And Barnes argued, "If the State Board of Railroad Commissioners can fix freight and passenger rates, I see no reason why this department should not be authorized to fix insurance rates."[8]

A Barnes colleague and a fellow champion of consumers' rights, Attorney General Fred S. Jackson, similarly directed the state's attention to the problem of rate regulation. In his annual report to the legislature in 1909 Jackson, embroiled in a bitter two-year dispute with fire companies over alleged violations of the state's antitrust laws, concluded that the time had come for Kansans to rethink their rate control approach. He informed lawmakers "that some kind of combine, by fire companies, looking to the establishment of rates, is essential for the best interests of policyholders. . . ."[9]

The legislature accepted the thinking of Barnes and Jackson. The proposal's favorable reception stemmed partially from the men's lobbying skills and from Barnes's indefatigable labors for its passage. The legislators' common belief that fire costs continued to be uniformly high and inequitable, especially for small policyholders, aided Barnes's bill tremendously. From a sense of desperation and as a practical necessity, lawmakers seemed willing to accept the concept of state rates. As the representative from Crawford County remarked, "Kansas faces a *crisis at this time* with the insurance industry on the rate question. . . . While I think the anti-trust law is basically sound, I can see that it has not worked to the advantage of the average policyholder." He concluded, "The Superintendent's bill may hold the key to successful regulation of fire rates. . . . Beside[s] state fire insurance what other alternatives do we have?" This reference to government insurance suggests one factor that very likely guaranteed success for the Barnes proposal. When compared to a program of public insurance patterned, for example, after Wisconsin's fire insurance fund, a system of state rates seemed less radical and more palatable to laissez-faire–minded Kansans. Furthermore, as Superintendent Barnes noted, his measure (as well as other pre-World War I state-made rate acts) still allowed companies to realize reasonable profits.[10]

The Barnes Law took effect on June 1, 1909. Industry representatives immediately castigated it. For instance, the *Weekly Underwriter* let go a powerful blast: "It should be submitted to only under protest! The right of the State to dictate terms of sales once admitted, the regulation of all the other details of a company's business logically follows, even to fixing the compensations of its clerks and limiting the amount of its gas bills." The paper went on to speculate that "were it possible for such a law to stand in Kansas it would speedily be adopted in other States and throughout the country, and fire insurance would struggle amid conditions nearly if not quite intolerable." The *Western Insurance Review* echoed the *Weekly Underwriter*'s views. Following a line of argument reminiscent of those who had opposed state-made rates in the 1890s, it warned, "No time should be lost in an endeavor to have the law repealed upon the ground that it fixes the price of a commodity dealt in by private corporations, a thing which is contrary to the genius and traditions of our Government."[11]

For the most part, policyholders disagreed markedly with the opinions of the fire companies. Within a month after the law went into effect, residents inundated the insurance department with letters and telegrams expressing the desire that their rates be made more just. Favorable sentiments came mostly from smaller consumers who held coverage on family-sized businesses or homes.[12]

Because the largest policyholders had previously been granted rebates and cheap protection under anti-rate combination statutes, they tended generally to criticize the new act. The *Topeka Journal* observed what would become a typical consumer response to various state-made rate measures: "The new insurance law has been batted about over the state by policyholders like a baseball on a townlot. This was especially true as regards the big policyholders who had enjoyed rebates in the past under the provisions of the old law. These rebates have been cut off and the big and little fellows treated alike under the new law." Yet in Kansas (unlike either Texas or Missouri, the two other states that blazed the rate control trail) fewer big, powerful policyholders received rebates. Kansas was predominantly made up of farms and small towns. Since the state was without major industrial centers (in 1909 Kansas City, the largest community, claimed less than 80,000 residents) the number of large manufacturing and mercantile interests was limited.[13]

Shortly after the rate measure became law, Superintendent Barnes received several formal complaints about charges, mostly from small businesses. A group of Abilene merchants asked that their cost of coverage be reduced. After investigating, Barnes ordered a substantial rate reduction. The continuing influx of rate complaints, particularly from small-town businessmen, prompted him to dictate a flat twelve percent reduction on all business property by September 1, 1909. After making this announcement, Barnes told the press that this "will mean a saving of $488,583.72 to the business interests of the State annually." He added parenthetically, "I believe that our history does not show where a single legislative . . . [act] has brought similar benefits to the people of the state within so short a period. This law is the most enlightened legislation ever enacted by any state, and the judgment of the members of the legislature will be fully confirmed before another session is held."[14]

The reduction order was immediately opposed by the insurance companies. At a hurriedly called meeting held in Chicago to discuss the Kansas situation, the firms decided to appoint a seven-member committee to explore court action. Even before the committee could report, Barnes cautioned a Frontenac, New York, gathering of industry officials to obey his reduction order and not to take legal action against the law.[15]

Barnes's warning went unheeded. The committee suggested that the industry challenge the constitutionality of the act. "It is the purpose to carry the case to the Supreme Court of the United States for final adjudication upon the rights of a state to pass laws so drastic and so pointedly constituting an interference with private business as the rate regulation statute of Kansas." Subsequently, in a test case the German Alliance Insurance Company brought suit in federal court to enjoin Barnes from enforcing the statute. The plaintiff argued that only businesses "impressed with the public interest," such as railroads and telegraph companies, could have their rates regulated by state governments. And, according to the plaintiff, fire insurance was "not impressed with the public interest to such an extent as to make this [rate regulation] possible."[16]

While the test case moved slowly through the courts to a final United States Supreme Court decision, Charles Barnes continued to pressure the industry to charge fair rates. In late 1909 he discovered that companies were dodging his September reduction order. Only rates in effect as of September 1 had been lowered, while new policies were being written at prereduction levels. The superintendent immediately notified firms that if they failed to comply in good faith he would either take court action or revoke their Kansas licenses. By mid-January 1910 Barnes happily announced that the industry accepted his advice.[17]

A month later Superintendent Barnes submitted a glowing report on the operation of the law to the state's progressive governor Walter Stubbs. Barnes claimed the new act had already saved Kansans nearly a half-million dollars. "The average rate for [187] towns under the old law was $2.25 [per $100 of insurance]. The rate in force under the new law for the same towns is $1.93, an average reduction in the cost of insurance in these 187 towns of 14 per cent." And Barnes told Stubbs, "We have disposed of hundreds of cases to the entire satisfaction of the policyholders." Official insurance department records confirm this statement.[18]

Also in February 1910 Barnes ordered a rate reduction ranging from twelve and one-half to seventeen percent on dwellings, private barns, boarding houses, and apartment buildings in urban areas. These new schedules were to become effective on March 10. Residential policyholders wished to share in the benefits of rate reduction previously limited only to business property, and Barnes agreed that they deserved such consideration. Once more companies protested. Several threatened to withdraw, but most expected court invalidation of the rate act.[19]

Individual agents, especially those who represented more than a single firm, regularly supported Barnes's reduction orders. Underwriters who had earlier disagreed with the marvelous predictions envisioned by Barnes commonly saw positive benefits in the statutory regulations, particularly the antidiscrimination feature that curbed rebating, which was a longtime annoyance. During the legislature's deliberations on the Barnes proposal, agents and their associations had expressed interest only in antidiscrimination and had agreed with the industry's dire prediction that "from the regulation and reduction of rates to regulation of [agents'] commissions is an easy and inevitable step." But in time Kansas agents began to notice improved consumer attitudes toward fire insurance. As one underwriter noted, "Policyholders here in Dodge City are more friendly. . . . I find it much easier to sell fire policies and to get renewals. Nobody seems to be talking much about starting mutuals any more . . . business prospects appear bright."[20]

After Charles Barnes completed the traditional one term in office, he encouraged his deputy and close friend Ike S. Lewis to seek the Republican nomination for the post. Like Barnes, an ardent progressive, Lewis easily won the superintendency in the 1910 general election.[21] Much to Barnes's satisfaction, his successor actively continued support of the rating act and other general policies. As one of his first official acts Lewis ended the practice of charging tenant farmers higher premiums than those collected from owner-operators. Within a few weeks the leading fire insurance firms accepted the Lewis order.[22]

Up until the time he left office in 1915, Ike Lewis continued to strengthen the original rate law. Its major weakness, he believed, stemmed from the superintendent's inability to determine precisely whether a rate had been fairly set. Because of a woefully inadequate staff, the only way the superintendent could investigate charges was by the unsatisfactory method of correspondence.[23] Therefore, in 1913 Lewis proposed creation of a salaried three-member advisory commission to check rates. In his message to the lawmakers he said, "There are hundreds of cases of unreasonable rates that need correction and we have no way to make these corrections at this time. Many of the new rates are too high and many are too low. We have no way to find out. What we want is a commission of experienced men and a contractor and builder who will follow up the inspectors of the insurance companies and see that the rates they use are correct."[24]

An economy-minded legislature failed to approve Lewis's request, but it did give the insurance department a special assistant to check rates and a modest increase of $1000 in its annual budget.

Although disappointed, Lewis continued vainly to seek approval for an advisory commission.[25]

While the legislature failed to satisfy Ike Lewis fully, the judiciary badly disappointed the companies. In June 1911 a federal circuit court in the case of *German Alliance Insurance Company* vs. *Lewis, Superintendent of Insurance of the State of Kansas* upheld the 1909 fire rate statute. The tribunal did not see that the law conflicted with either the Kansas or the federal constitution, and it held that legislators had the right to delegate the power to adjust rates to the superintendent of insurance. At the insistence of the industry the plaintiff appealed the verdict. Then on April 20, 1914, the United States Supreme Court, in an epoch-making decision, sustained the Kansas law. "The decision is without doubt the most important single factor which has entered and influenced fire insurance in twenty years," observed Wisconsin insurance commissioner Michael J. Cleary. "It changes the whole status of the business. . . . It has elevated this to a place of importance alongside the railroad and other great quasi-public enterprises."[26]

II

WHILE Kansas legislators debated a state-made rate bill, Texas lawmakers enacted a similar measure. In many ways the Texas fire rate movement duplicated the Kansas experience. The idea of state participation in the rate-fixing process predated the 1909 legislative session. As in Kansas much local dissatisfaction existed with the antitrust approach. Texans commonly argued that meaningful competition did not exist and that companies required agents to apply exorbitant charges that were unfairly set by the "advisory only" rating agencies. Certain small policyholders claimed the industry favored large urban customers with lower costs or rebates. But while Kansas lacked large cities, Texas did not; members of the Local Agents' Association of Texas, an urban-based organization, from an early date strongly objected to this favoritism. Preferential rate treatment frequently involved underwriters in unpleasant experiences with powerful clients.[27]

Shortly after 1900, agents joined unpampered policyholders to suggest publicly that the state consider a rate control law. Even the infant Texas fire insurance industry boomed their cause. The president of Austin's tiny Southern National Insurance Company, J. G. Hornberger complained bitterly that larger and more powerful out-of-state firms often sought to freeze out the smaller Texas concerns through wholesale rate cutting on the most profitable accounts. He said tartly,

"The Texas companies are the especial objects of their efforts at benevolent assimilation." Thus representatives of locally based firms blessed state-set rates primarily for the same selfish reasons that prompted the Texas life insurance industry to push for the Robertson Investment Act.[28]

Although the first seriously considered proposal for a Texas rate control act came in 1904, the persistence of antitrust sentiment, together with pressure from those benefiting from the status quo, prevented adoption of an alternative approach. Writing in 1906, one informed observer explained: "Although it may seem terribly illogical not to have some sort of State controlled [fire] rates when one considers the high costs of protection and the treatment many receive, policyholders nevertheless seem to have an unabated faith in the merits of competition." Responding directly to the question of why this Texas penchant for antitrust legislation existed, this commentator said, "The largest policyholders naturally expect rate drawbacks . . . [and] the small ones have grown up on the notion that the proper function of government is to act only as a referee and not as an active participant in business affairs."[29]

Just as Superintendent Charles Barnes proved to be the guiding force behind passage of the Kansas statute, so did Insurance Commissioner Thomas B. Love deserve much credit for the 1909 Texas rate act. Like Barnes, Love was a longtime champion of consumer interests. Popular disenchantment with fire rating practices helped reinforce and shape Love's opinion, as did an exchange of ideas with fellow reform commissioners, including Barnes, Frank Blake of Missouri, and Reau Folk of Tennessee. Love fervently believed the antitrust approach was a failure. Even if competition could be successfully maintained, he felt owners of small properties would not receive the preferential treatment accorded their more wealthy neighbors.[30]

Therefore, Commissioner Love drew up a proposal for a state rating board. Love's agency would contain three members—the insurance commissioner and two other qualified persons appointed by the governor. All companies would submit their schedules to the board, which in turn would have the authority to raise or lower rates as circumstances determined. Rebates and other variances from the stated charges would be prohibited.[31]

Thomas Love won the crucial support of the House and Senate insurance committees. Legislators generally agreed that rate reform was overdue. A representative echoed the common cry: "Fire insurance companies are overcharging the public. . . . Rates must be brought into line immediately!" The clamor for state-made rates then became chiefly a desire for lower protection costs. Yet the antidiscrimination dimension of the Love proposal excited some. "Discrimination is rife all over the State," one farmer-lawmaker emphasized. "Some cotton is written at 2% and that other cotton on the same platform is written for 3%. . . . Big cotton growers so often pay less."[32]

The legislature adopted the bill's central features by a wide margin in April 1909. The law exempted local mutual or profit-sharing companies because they were small and already offered consumers reasonable rates. On April 19, 1909, the state's Democratic progressive governor Thomas M. Campbell signed the measure; but it did not go into effect until January 1, 1910, seven months after Kansas formally launched its rate control program.[33]

Opposition to the act was generated swiftly from two unrelated but understandable sources. Member companies of the fire insurance lobby objected; they did not relish that "rates—the vital life blood of fire insurance—are to be fixed by law." Some predicted dire consequences for any firm operating in such an environment, suggesting that many faced financial ruin. Insurers who previously benefited from the antitrust law, particularly large urban wholesale and jobbing concerns, likewise battled the proposal. "The purpose of the bill," they contended, "is to do away with competition in fire insurance rates in the State, and to legalize the most gigantic trust that has ever got a footing on Texas soil."[34]

Operation of the rate law, as administered by an unsympathetic insurance commissioner, jolted its backers. Soon after the act took effect, scores of companies filed rates with the state board, mostly "enormous increases." The new insurance commissioner, William E. Hawkins (who assumed office on Love's departure in February 1910), along with one other board member, approved these hikes. Hawkins believed that rigid enforcement of the generally higher rates would result in the "obnoxious" act's repeal, for he had long sympathized with the antitrust approach to rate regulation. Close personal ties with several big consumers, however, very likely explain his position. In fact, politically important commercial interests probably saw to it that Hawkins succeeded Love.[35]

William Hawkins received the policyholder protest he expected. Complaints from all sections of the state flooded the board's Austin office. Perhaps the most notable protest came from El Paso where local businessmen called a mass meeting in early June to discuss the rate increase. According to one of the meeting's organizers, "The town is in a ugly mood. . . . We expected a rate *reduction* not increase. El Paso has a first class fire department, good buildings, adequate water supply and even a city fire marshall and reward for

anyone convicted of arson.'' At the meeting El Paso residents, both
the powerful and the weak, agreed to send a delegation to Austin to
ask that the board suspend the increase pending a thorough review.
Soon their representatives met with the rate body. Although two
board members agreed to a suspension, Hawkins refused. The commissioner subsequently issued a statement warning that he would
revoke the license of any firm that violated the board's El Paso rates.[36]

Hawkins's uncompromising stand on the El Paso controversy,
together with his negative attitude toward the rating board, prompted
Governor Campbell to ask for his resignation. Hawkins declined,
whereupon the governor called a special legislative session for the announced purpose of reconsidering the act. Since Hawkins held only a
recess appointment, convening the legislature meant the end of his
tenure in office unless he was reappointed. He was not, and his successor, Frederick C. von Rosenberg, proved friendlier to the philosophy of state rates.[37]

The special session of the Texas legislature convened in late
August 1910 and studied the previous year's statute. Both houses
agreed that the original law, although a valid reform concept, was
deficient. The initiative in rate fixing, they believed, should be re-
moved from the companies and placed directly in the hands of a state
insurance board. Lawmakers, however, disagreed on the extent to
which rates should be binding. The Senate bill, which fixed a maximum rate, permitted firms to cut rates at will. The House, on the
other hand, insisted that a mandatory rate be set on all risks, holding
that "the Senate provision would bring back the former discrimination in rates in favor of the larger property owners."[38]

The legislature did manage a compromise bill, which Governor
Campbell signed on October 6. The amended version created a State
Insurance Board, the new designation for the former Fire Insurance
Rating Board. Unlike the old body the second had power to take the
initiative in setting fire rates; it retained a staff of experts for technical
assistance. Although the measure allowed companies to write policies
below maximum rates, the board could prevent any specific reduction.
As the 1909 statute did, the modified one prohibited all rebating and
discrimination.[39]

This revised rating law worked. While some of the largest property owners correctly contended that its antidiscrimination feature
raised their rates, the average price of protection fell noticeably statewide. In 1909 a consumer paid $1.48 to buy $100 of fire-insurance
coverage, four years later the cost dropped to $1.15, and this rate con-
tinued through World War I.[40]

The downswing in fire costs generally disturbed company officialdom. Although fire firms did not react as dramatically as their life counterparts had when the Robertson Investment Act was passed in 1907, several threatened to leave and others warned Texas to "watch its step" in rate matters. The *Western Insurance Review,* for example, responded to the whole notion of state fire insurance regulation by saying, "It would be a splendid card for the state of Texas, for its reputation abroad, and for the growth and expansion of its trade and commerce at home, to have both the rate making law and the antitrust law . . . wiped off its statute books."[41]

Notwithstanding insurance industry rebukes, Lone Star lawmakers in 1913 made the 1910 law even more stringent. The new measure contained two key revisions; one tightening the antidiscriminatory features of the original act, the other financing the rate program. The State Insurance Board, henceforth to be called the Texas State Insurance Commission, not only continued to set maximum rates for all classes of property but forbade companies to write at rates lower than the maximum fixed by the commission. One exception, however, allowed firms to charge a cheaper rate on all risks of the same type in the same community. The legislature added a tax of one and one-quarter percent on all gross premiums to cover the expenses of the new insurance commission.[42]

Proponents of equitable rates continued to be enthusiastic over the revised act's operation. They had no desire to return to the era of antitrust control. As Thomas Love later observed, "If justice and equity are to prevail in fire insurance rating . . . the Texas system of state regulation of . . . rates and the strict prohibition of all discrimination and rebates [or] the writing of all fire insurance . . . by the state itself" are the only two methods of realistic fire insurance reform.[43]

III

MISSOURI followed Kansas and Texas and abandoned the antitrust approach in favor of state rates. But the Missouri story proved much more complicated. Contrary to the situation in Kansas and Texas, local Missouri fire agents played the principal role in passing the 1911 Oliver Rating Act, the state's initial venture into fire rate control. In 1909 the president of the Missouri Association of Local Fire Insurance Agents, Samuel D. Capen of St. Louis, sparked agitation to free local underwriters from both rating bureaus and antitrust statutes in establishing rates. Why such a movement surfaced at this particular moment is not totally clear. Probably restlessness among fire agents over several long-standing consumer complaints prompted Capen to formulate a fresh approach to rate fixing.[44]

Samuel Capen argued that rating bureaus produced inflexible charges, a distinct disadvantage to policyholders. In an article for the *Western Insurance Review* he spelled out his position: "Frequently an agent for the advantage of his customer, could point out to him how he could reduce his rate by slight and inexpensive changes in his building, such, for instance, as the installation of metal clad shutters, the fire proofing of portions of the building. . . ." Capen added, "The company he represents now insists that the rate made by the experts [the advisory only rating bureaus] shall be collected, no matter how easily the risk might be improved."[45]

Local fire insurance agents whom Capen represented felt furthermore that rates adjusted to individual risks would be more popular and would provide the companies with favorable publicity. It was hoped that business and commissions would increase, even though rates would not differ from agent to agent. Local underwriters thought they were best qualified to determine charges in specific situations. If they themselves did not fix rates, they could at least set guidelines for a rating bureau.[46]

Missouri agents voiced an additional complaint. Like generations of underwriters nationwide, they despised rebates. To fight competition, most had been forced into such a practice to keep their best clients. Firms might back an agent in rebate situations by taking the loss themselves, but more often rebates meant cuts in an underwriter's own commissions. Furthermore, agents often viewed abolition of rebates as fundamental to improving agent-policyholder relations: "Our profession will be aided greatly if we insure the 'greasy silver dollar of a poor man' buying as much insurance on the same class of property as the 'crisp new gold certificate of the rich fellow.'"[47]

Notwithstanding quickly mustered industry objections and complaints from several large St. Louis and Kansas City commercial interests, members of the Missouri Association of Local Fire Insurance Agents soon found sympathetic legislators to consider a proposal designed to meet their needs. Like their counterparts in Kansas and Texas, a majority of Missouri lawmakers expressed real concern about rate costs and discrimination. They seemed willing and ready, as one newspaperman reported, "to cut the umbilical cord that has so long connected the state and the unworkable and often meaningless antitrust laws."[48]

The agents' bill, which breezed through both houses in May, authorized fire insurance agents to form associations and to adopt rates that in their judgment were "just and reasonable." The measure empowered the superintendent of insurance, "upon written complaint that any rate was unfair to make an investigation and order the rate reduced, if in the opinion of the Superintendent, it was excessive."[49]

Governor Herbert S. Hadley jarred agents and lawmakers alike when he vetoed the bill as soon as it reached his desk. According to Capen, the veto came about "because of the fact that our Bill did not definitely give the State proper supervision [over rates]." Moreover, Hadley believed that the legislators had acted in haste. He suggested that "the agents' association itself could be potentially as dangerous to policyholders as the fire-insurance trust" and added that "the present anti-trust approach is not all that bad." Such a statement coincided with the governor's views on business regulation. As attorney general during the previous Joseph W. Folk administration, Hadley had achieved considerable success and national recognition by using Missouri's antitrust code against the "oil trust"—Standard Oil and two satellite firms, Waters-Pierce and Republic.[50]

Undaunted by the governor's veto, Samuel Capen and his association planned to reintroduce the measure at the next General Assembly. During the intervening period agents waged an active campaign, reiterating earlier reasons why their proposal should become public policy. They emphasized (somewhat contrary to fact) the "completely satisfactory" operations of the Kansas and Texas rate statutes. For instance, in various public addresses delivered during 1910 Capen alluded to "nearly universal satisfaction" with the recently enacted reforms in those states. "What can be done successfully in Kansas and Texas," he argued "can surely be done in Missouri."[51]

Shortly after the Forty-sixth General Assembly convened in January 1911, Senator Arthur L. Oliver of Cape Girardeau County introduced a fire rating bill similar to the earlier one. As he had in 1909, Charles F. Bates, a lawyer retained by the Missouri Association of Local Fire Insurance Agents, drafted the proposal. Under provisions of the Oliver bill every company would be required to file general rate schedules within thirty days after the act went into effect and to file specific ones for each kind of risk in every community within ninety days. After the rates for the entire state had been filed and approved by the superintendent of insurance, they would become mandatory. Competition would then cease, since all firms would be using the same schedules. And it would be unlawful for any agent or company to deviate from established charges.[52]

Samuel Capen and fellow association members actively lobbied for the Oliver bill, as they had done two years earlier. Their cause received a powerful boost when Superintendent of Insurance Frank Blake, a progressive Republican whom Governor Hadley had appointed in 1909, announced his support. Blake liked the proposal, but he had one reservation. "There is always the possibility of having a man in the Insurance Commissioner's office who will favor the companies," he said, "but it seems to me it is better to leave the fixing of rates to a public officer, responsible to the people through the Governor, than to leave it to the companies without regulation, as at present." The superintendent called attention to the Kansas and Texas rate measures. He seemed particularly impressed with the effects of the Kansas act, which had reportedly saved consumers an estimated $600,000. Accordingly, he reasoned that there would be similar reductions in Missouri's fire insurance charges. Blake supported the anti-rebating section, saying that "this bill will prevent rebating and will prevent some individuals who have much business along insurance lines from receiving a low rate at the expense of small insurers, who must pay a higher one."[53]

Now somewhat better organized, most firms urged their agents to defeat the Oliver bill. The industry's arguments repeated earlier statements against various state-made rate proposals; top officials continued to have qualms about any government power over rate fixing and saw such suggestions "as the beginning of state socialism in America." Their protests failed to influence the "mutinous" agents, particularly those who wrote insurance for multiple companies. Contrary to the stated position of the industry at large, several locally based fire firms expressed a more optimistic point of view. "A careful reading of the bill will indicate that it is not so bad as some have supposed it would be. In other words, it does not aim to wrench from the companies the prerogative of rate making, but is simply a measure to get around the objections to the anti-compact law."[54]

The companies failed to lobby extensively against the Oliver bill in Jefferson City, perhaps anticipating disappointment because of the powerful organization of rebelling agents and the bill's apparent appeal to Missouri lawmakers. Lamented one industry spokesman, "What's the use of trying to fight this bill? We don't have a chance. . . . The legislators showed two years ago that they must have this law." Company representatives expected or at least hoped for court invalidation of all Oliverlike measures. "I am not panicked at the thought of hostile rate regulation in Missouri," said an officer of the Liberty Fire Insurance Company. "I am certain that if and when we are defeated, the courts will take our position on this matter." Yet certain eastern fire insurance men held conferences with several of their largest Missouri clients. In these behind-the-scenes sessions both parties agreed that they had much to lose with a state rate law—smaller long-term profits for the industry and the end to the pampered status for the big policyholder. The companies privately encouraged them to "exert all possible pressure" to stop the Oliver bill.[55]

As expected, the Oliver measure easily passed the Senate on February 16, 1911, and passed the House two weeks later. Because of minor differences in the House version, the bill was returned to the Senate for final consideration on March 7; the favorable vote was unanimous. High margins of support came from the desire of lawmakers for rate justice (certainly a popular political position) and from the belief that the ideal of competition envisioned by authors of earlier antitrust statutes was a failure. "A more workable approach to fire rates has been deemed in order by the General Assembly," explained one veteran statehouse commentator. Seemingly satisfied with changes in the initial proposal, Governor Hadley signed the Oliver bill on March 18, 1911.[56]

Implementation began badly. Since the Oliver Act called for rates to be filed with the insurance department within thirty days and for more complete rating information within ninety days, the industry hurriedly employed the Missouri Actuarial Bureau to rerate the state. However, it proved impossible for the bureau to establish specific rates for the entire state within the period specified by law. Although displeased by this turn of events, Blake understandably extended the filing deadline.[57]

As soon as the Missouri Actuarial Bureau started the rerating process, it asked the insurance department for permission to publish these new specific rates as advisory ones. The bureau believed that while schedules at this point would serve merely as guidelines, agents should be permitted to write policies at the suggested rate where bureau work had been completed. While not opposing the bureau's request, the fire agents' association wanted the charges for each rerated community to become legal immediately, contending that to wait until all the state had been rerated would violate the letter of the law. But the association's stand should be viewed in light of the new rates. Since bureau schedules were substantially higher than the old ones, agents were losing commissions.[58]

Several weeks after the bureau's request to publish rates, Superintendent Blake obtained its agreement that none of the new charges would go into force until all rerating was complete. But the bureau broke its promise. Within six weeks it had published revised rating books, and fire agents in some communities began using them immediately. In October as these books appeared, Blake asked Attorney General Elliott W. Major for a ruling on the Oliver Act. Six weeks later the attorney general held that the law would not go into effect until the entire state had been rerated and the results properly filed with the insurance department.[59]

While Blake awaited Major's opinion, a majority of companies that operated locally formed what was commonly called the "Missouri Pool," at the insistence of the Missouri Fire Insurance Agents. Differing little from such groups in other industries, it was held together by nothing more than a "gentleman's agreement" and the desire to exert control over a business—in this case to place the Missouri Actuarial Bureau's rate schedules into operation. This arrangement, however, did not receive full industry approval. Several leading insurance firms serving Missouri refused to support what Blake called the "conspiracy." These companies, perhaps fearing punitive measures on the part of the insurance department or hoping to capitalize on the situation by increasing their own volume of business, refused to substitute the new rating books for those of the old system.[60]

In areas of Missouri rerated by the bureau, certain policyholders did benefit from this conflict within industry ranks. Rates charged by firms refusing to use the rating books were as much as fifty percent cheaper than bureau ones. And in a few localities such reductions triggered rate skirmishes on certain risks. These incidents, however, were exceptions to the trend toward higher coverage costs.[61]

Although Superintendent Frank Blake warned the pool repeatedly that "it was committing a crime against the people of Missouri," he did not immediately issue a restraining order. Office correspondence reveals that while the bureau's violation of the rate agreement infuriated him, the internal industry conflict, with its lowering of charges in various sections of the state, had been a pleasant turn of events. The bureau's high rates nevertheless greatly concerned the superintendent. By the second week of November Blake decided that he must act, even though he would be shortly surrendering his office to a Democratic successor.[62]

Why Blake delayed so long in taking official action is not certain, although he probably wanted to wait until the bureau had finished its rerating job. As of the first of October 1912—almost nineteen months after Governor Hadley had signed the Oliver bill—only 200 of Missouri's 700 communities had been rerated. Blake at last concluded that the bureau was deliberately taking an inordinate amount of time in the hope that his successor would adopt a more favorable position. He also charged that the techniques used by the Missouri Actuarial Bureau seemed as "unscientific" as those used by the state's earliest rating bureaus. To use Blake's words, "Under the present methods, all rates charged property owners are founded upon guess and conjectures. The experts who construct the schedules and who apply them to the risks of the state, pay no attention whatsoever to statistics or experiences of the companies."[63]

On November 12, 1912, Frank Blake ordered all fire coverage to be written under the pre-Oliver method of rate competition. If agents continued to use the new rating books, he would revoke their licenses. The superintendent still accepted the philosophy of the Oliver Act; the old method was unscientific, and Missouri deserved to be rerated by experts who would take all aspects of fire insurance costs into consideration. Only in this way could equitable rates be determined. Yet agents continued to use the bureau's rate schedules, arguing that Blake openly violated the Oliver Act.[64]

Considerable consumer opposition to the Oliver measure emerged during the latter months of 1912. Citizens of rerated communities commonly had paid little attention to the law. But as policies expired, they experienced the results of bureau rate making. Early in March 1913 Missouri's new attorney general John Tull Barker reported to the press that his office had received over five hundred complaints concerning excessive bureau rates. The correspondence revealed that charges had increased 50 to 300 percent over previous levels. The attorney general pointed out that in his hometown of La Plata "fire insurance rates have been advanced under these new schedules about 200 per cent."[65]

The sharply increased rates shocked and angered the state's businessmen. The plight of one St. Louis shoe manufacturer typified their concern with the operation of the Oliver Act. In 1913 this individual was forced to pay $10,000 more for the same amount of protection than he had the previous year. And some of the largest consumers in the urban areas of St. Louis, Kansas City, and St. Joseph were still unhappy about the loss of rebates and the end of other "special considerations."[66]

Early in March 1913 concerned members of the business community, headed by J. D. Cathey of the Regal Buggy Company of St. Louis, gathered in the Gateway City to form the Associated Merchants and Manufacturers of Missouri. The organization had a single purpose, the repeal of the Oliver Act. Reacting to "unjustified rate hikes," businessmen throughout the state quickly subscribed the money necessary to defray the group's immediate expenses. They zealously embarked on an extensive letter-writing campaign to local merchants, business groups, and public officials. The businessmen's crusade against the 1911 act had officially begun.[67]

On January 17, 1913, even before opposition to the Oliver Act became formally organized, Representative E. G. Orr of rural Liv-

ingston County, angered by high rates, called for the repeal of the
Oliver Act and a return to the antitrust code. But his plan contained
one provision designed to put teeth into the antitrust laws. "It shall be
prima facie evidence that [a] company is a pool, trust . . . if it be
shown that such company, or any agent . . . in writing insurance has
used any insurance rate . . . kept or furnished by any person, association . . . bureau employed by, representing or acting on behalf of
any other insurance company or association. . . ."[68]

From his writings on the subject, this Chillicothe lawyer and Jef-
fersonian Democrat appears to have had a long-standing faith in the
merits of forced business competition. While applauding the General
Assembly's 1909 and 1911 determination to obtain fire insurance rate
justice, Orr saw lax state enforcement as the principal fault of the antitrust approach and only lukewarmly supported a regulatory solution.
His bill made rapid progress through the lower chamber and easily
passed on February 5 by a vote of 123 to 3. Once again, as with the ill-
fated Oliver Act, most Missouri lawmakers felt they were supporting
equitable fire rates.[69]

The Orr proposal fared less well in the Senate. Although the
Senate Insurance Committee received the bill on February 11, it did
not report it back to the body until the third week in March. During
hearings the seven-member committee split into three factions. One
was led by the committee's chairman, Robert McClintic, who saw no
need for change. Rather, he favored minor revisions in the Oliver Act.
This group seemingly spoke for the agents' interest. The second faction, headed by attorney Michael Casey of Kansas City, likewise
favored the continuance of the Oliver Act but for different reasons.
The Casey advocates believed that since meaningful competition never
existed under the antitrust measures and chaotic conditions often
resulted, the answer to Missouri's high fire rates could be found in the
state rate approach. They attributed high rates, not to the Oliver law,
but solely to "the failure of the late insurance commissioner Blake to
enforce [it]." These senators might best be labeled efficiency types,
since they sought fire rate order based on rational, even scientific,
methods. The third group, sparked by St. Joseph realtor Thomas
Lysaght, agreed with the Casey people that rates were excessive but
favored the antitrust concept. Lysaght's own motives are open to
question. Closely identified with large St. Joseph property owners,
Lysaght and his friends might enjoy handsome rebates with a return to
the antitrust days of rate regulation. Nevertheless, some antitrust
backers, both on the insurance committee and in the Senate, consistently held that forced competition was the only workable solution
to problems posed by economic combination.[70]

While the Orr bill was in the upper chamber, lobbyists on both sides exerted great pressure on the senators. As expected, the Associated Merchants and Manufacturers of Missouri led the fight for the bill's passage, while the insurance agents and a majority of the companies, sensing advantages of the Oliver Act and fearing a tough antitrust statute, opposed it.[71]

The factionalism within the insurance committee resulted in Chairman McClintic returning the Orr bill on March 18 without recommendations. Three days later the Senate passed the measure by a count of 18 to 12. The opposition votes did not represent a significant proinsurance sentiment but merely reflected the split in the committee's ranks over how best to curb high rates and arbitrary practices. On March 29 Governor Elliott Major signed the Orr bill. In his initial message to the lawmakers the governor said it would be wise to repeal the Oliver Act and "to re-establish the principle of competition by the strict enforcement of laws against combinations and agreements in the fixing of fire insurance rates in the state." The Orr Act was to become effective on June 23, 1913.[72]

The industry reacted almost immediately. Representatives of the Western Union, a group of nearly one hundred leading carriers, met in Philadelphia on April 10 and unanimously agreed to discontinue writing insurance in Missouri at the end of the month. The firms reached their decision "because of the enactment by the Missouri Legislature of a drastic anti-compact law, intended to force lower fire insurance rates by forbidding any agreement or co-operation as to rates."[73]

News of the Philadelphia meeting promptly reached Jefferson City, but state officials did not panic. Charles Revelle, the new Missouri insurance superintendent and a staunch "New Freedom" Democrat, seemed optimistic. "I can hardly believe that the large companies expect really to withdraw from this State. I am sure some of the companies will not withdraw, and I also am sure some will leave." And he added, "I am not apprehensive that the situation will become acute. It would be only a short time until some of the companies not affiliated with the central organizations would be able to take care of the business. The formation of . . . co-operative companies in the meantime could take care of most of the losses." Revelle went on to assure policyholders that cooperative or mutual firms could operate at a much lower rate and could therefore share savings with consumers. Attorney General Barker agreed with Revelle that Missourians might meet their insurance needs if Western Union members carried through their withdrawal threat. "There is enough capital and enough State pride among Missouri capitalists to see that the State does not suffer from the drastic threats of the big fire companies."[74]

In answer to the companies' charge that the Orr Act was a "drastic anti-compact law," the superintendent retorted, "If the companies do business on a competitive basis and do not form combinations to fix rates, they need have no fear of the Missouri insurance laws. But if agencies are established for the purpose of increasing rates or preparing agreements with the approval of the different concerns, they will face prosecution under the anti-trust provisions of the statute." The governor and the attorney general echoed Revelle's sentiments.[75]

Two weeks after the Philadelphia assemblage sixty-two companies of the Western Insurance Bureau, at their annual convention in Pittsburgh, likewise decided to withdraw from Missouri on April 30 because of "antagonistic legislation." At the bureau's meeting former Missouri governor Herbert Hadley appeared before the delegates as special representative of the Kansas City Board of Underwriters. He urged the companies to send envoys to Jefferson City to confer with Major, Barker, Revelle, and other state leaders before deciding to leave. His suggestion fell on deaf ears.[76]

Missouri's first official reaction to the threatened withdrawal came on April 26, when the attorney general filed *quo warranto* proceedings in the state supreme court against firms holding membership in the Western Union. Barker asked the high court to fine the companies for voting to suspend their Missouri operations and to restrain them from attempting to quit business on April 30. His *quo warranto* petition alleged that "the fire companies which met at Philadelphia unlawfully, illegally and willfully, misused and abused their said franchises, rights and privileges as foreign fire insurance companies authorized to do business under the laws of the State of Missouri." Hearing of the Pittsburgh meeting, Barker filed identical charges against members of the Western Insurance Bureau, prohibiting them also from withdrawing and from canceling policies already in force. On April 28 the Missouri tribunal ordered the firms not to withdraw or to void policies.[77]

In spite of *quo warranto* writs and supreme court action, companies of the Western Union and the Western Insurance Bureau made good their planned withdrawal. One hundred eighty-two firms, writing over ninety percent of the state's fire coverage, left by the first of May. Missourians saw this as gross industry arrogance. Elias S. Garver, owner of the *Worth County Times,* expressed the rural viewpoint when he editorialized, "The time has not come whe[n] arrogant corporations may write the laws of the state for the furtherance of their own interests and then threaten the commercial welfare of the people when they enter protest against greed." William Marion Reedy, editor of the *St. Louis Mirror,* aptly captured the state's urban reaction: "The insurance companies are exercising upon the people of this State as wanton a tyranny as any community has ever suffered. They are trying to dragoon the State into wiping out laws they don't like."[78]

The decision to withdraw alarmed businessmen. Almost immediately, numerous out-of-state banking institutions prepared for the mass insurance company exodus by announcing that they would no longer accept Missouri mortgages or make loans on property until the controversy had been settled. The paralyzing effect on local commerce was evident in Metropolitan Life's withdrawal of a $1,200,000 loan for construction of a ten-story St. Louis office building.[79]

The Associated Merchants and Manufacturers of Missouri, which had led the fight for repeal of the Oliver Act, now found itself confronted with the possibility of drastically reduced fire insurance protection and a tightening of credit. Meeting in St. Louis during the third week of April, the organization agreed to push for a statewide referendum on the Orr Act. These business leaders concluded that this tactic would be the quickest way to entice the companies back. By obtaining 27,500 signatures on initiative petitions in the state's eleven congressional districts, the Orr Act would be suspended until the November 1914 general elections. At that time voters could decide the measure's fate.[80]

Other Show Me State business groups backed the Associated Merchants and Manufacturers' proposal, and by the end of April a campaign to acquire the needed signatures for the initiative petition was well under way. Similarly, a number of businessmen sought more direct and immediate action; they asked the governor to call a special session of the General Assembly to deal with the crisis. But Governor Major showed no inclinations to bend to such pressure, saying that "no matter how many business men appeal to me for an extra session, I will not call it." Major's negativism is explained by his belief that insurance people, rather than "concerned" public groups, were behind demands for an extra legislative session.[81]

The proposed statewide referendum and the request for a special legislative session were not the only plans formulated to meet the companies' withdrawal threats. The League of Missouri Municipalities, meeting in Sedalia for its annual convention in late April, created a study committee to investigate the feasibility of state government entering the fire insurance field. The league felt that public insurance could provide needed protection, which the "arrogant companies" had threatened not to do, and would furnish this coverage at reduced rates.[82]

The league's surprisingly radical proposal found support. An editorial appearing in the *Kansas City Star* on April 27, 1913, and

widely reprinted in small-town weeklies, expressed the popular sentiment favoring state fire insurance: "There is no reason why the state
itself should not undertake the business of insurance. Governments
are doing this in several countries abroad." Furthermore, the *Star*
added, "People have been hearing about state's rights for a hundred
years. The public has been feeling more and more that the business of
fire insurance in this country has been badly conducted. The people
are in a temper to try to conduct it them[selves.]" William Marion
Reedy, like many journalists, endorsed the plan. "The solution of the
present and all future difficulties with the insurance grabbers," he
said, "lies in state insurance. . . . State insurance is only the mutual
idea upon a large scale."[83]

While the Missouri League of Municipalities and members of the
press called for state insurance, several communities considered
organizing fire mutuals. For instance, Fayette attorney Jasper
Thompson urged formation of a mutual for residents of that central
Missouri county seat. "The people of Fayette should take a lesson
from the prudent farmers of the country who through the mutual insurance company save thousands of dollars per year," Thompson told
local fire policyholders. State officials, too, publicly endorsed mutuals. Speaking for the Major administration, Superintendent Revelle
claimed that "co-operative companies can operate much cheaper than
regular fire companies for the reason that they have no salaried officers," and predicted that if the firms remained out of the state,
mutuals would be loyally supported.[84]

In contrast to popular reaction against the carriers the state's insurance agents, who claimed to have spent nearly $200,000 through
the Missouri Actuarial Bureau in a vain attempt to rerate the state
under the Oliver Act, overwhelmingly supported withdrawal. Like the
companies, they thought it would force Missourians to "respect" the
fire industry. Yet underwriters planned to keep "their hands off the
fight between the insurance companies and the state authorities over
the . . . Orr insurance law." While waiting for the April 30 withdrawal deadline, they worked day and night issuing policies.[85]

It took fourteen weeks to resolve the Missouri insurance controversy. From May 1 until August 12 state leaders, industry representatives, and private groups conferred on an almost daily basis. The
most significant of these meetings took place during the first week of
August. On August 5, leading members of the insurance community,
concerned by the talk of state insurance and the planning of local
mutuals, met in New York City's fashionable Down Town Club and
agreed to return to Missouri on the condition that the state dismiss all
conspiracy suits. They also approved an earlier proposal made by Ma-

jor and Revelle that the governor appoint a special six-member investigating commission to study fire insurance matters. This body would make recommendations for possible legislative changes to the 1915 General Assembly. News of the New York meeting reached the Missouri capitol the next morning. At an all-day meeting attended by Governor Major, Attorney General Barker, and Superintendent Revelle, the state accepted the industry's New York City decisions.[86]

Two factors explain Missouri's willingness to drop the conspiracy suits. First, equitable rates could be permanently guaranteed by a law based on a careful study of insurance problems, one that the governor's special investigating committee could specify. And second, the prima facie section of the Orr Act was of questionable legality.[87]

Not all parties applauded the settlement. The Missouri League of Municipalities continued to express its faith in the merits of state fire insurance, and those who backed community mutual insurance still argued that this proposal made sense. Both groups lacked confidence that the settlement would permanently guarantee either fair rates or freedom from future acts of corporate abuse.[88]

Within a week Attorney General Barker dismissed all legal proceedings against the 183 companies. On August 12 most firms reentered the state, and in December Governor Elliott Major appointed the investigating team. Known officially as the Missouri Insurance Commission, it consisted of six individuals whom Representative Orr described as public spirited and, more importantly, "free from the influence of the insurance interests." After months of hearings held throughout the state, the commission's recommendations formed the basis for a new insurance act, which the General Assembly passed in the spring of 1915. Containing features common to both the 1909 Kansas and Texas rating statutes, this consumer-oriented measure included these central provisions: companies writing risks at rates lower than their competitors were required to give this advantage to all customers; rates filed with the department that were lower than former ones would become effective immediately, while higher charges had to receive affirmative approval from the insurance superintendent; and agents could use their long-favored rating bureaus but only in an advisory capacity and in conjunction with state-approved rating experts.[89]

To the delight of policyholders, the 1915 law brought a noticeable decrease in premium costs. In widespread instances they dropped twenty-five percent from pre-Oliver rates. These reductions understandably caused the drive for state insurance to collapse, although that idea still lingered in the minds of some. The *Kansas City Star* thought it a grievous error to abandon the notion of state fire insurance. "The big club [against the industry]," the paper editorialized, "is the authority for the state to provide state insurance. Missouri need not embark in the fire insurance business if it does not want to at this time. But the state should be ready if the fire companies should attempt to withdraw again, to say 'Go ahead. The state will furnish the insurance.' Then, and only then, can a permanent settlement be made." The revised insurance act also caused interest in community mutual insurance to flag, but not before several towns launched such companies. Because of bad management and inadequate capitalization, these were largely short-lived.[90]

The fire industry grudgingly accepted the 1915 rating act. For example, the St. Louis–based trade journal, the *Insurance Leader,* vigorously objected to the fact that "the power of rate-making [is] too largely in the hands of the Insurance Commissioner," yet the *Leader* held out hope for the future: "Enough is known of the . . . law to seemingly justify the opinion that it means something of a new era for fire insurance, and will set at rest the unsettled conditions." Apparently by 1915 the industry preferred rate order and harmony even if it meant major concessions to Show Me State consumers in the form of lower premiums and state-made rates.[91]

IV

ALTHOUGH New York and Wisconsin did not spark the movement for state rates, both adopted such concepts in time. Rate control by independent regulatory commission rather than by antitrust statute started to capture the fancy of local reformers after 1910. While their rate control measures exhibited features common to the Kansas, Texas, and Missouri acts, there were important variations. However, the story of reform experiences in New York and Wisconsin further illustrates the nearly universal quest among consumers for rate justice.

New Yorkers objected to the high cost of fire protection with increasing frequency after the turn of the century. Previously, industry competition, which often erupted into full-scale rate wars, kept costs at acceptable levels. Policyholders occasionally paid premium charges well below what firms could reasonably afford to carry. But as companies combined to fix rates, consumers statewide found themselves at "the mercy of a despotic monopoly." While Assemblyman Alfred E. Smith pushed for antitrust statutes to smash newly created or expanded tariff associations, a stronger movement emerged around 1910 to have the state guarantee coverage costs and to control industry practices by commission.[92]

Unlike similar crusades elsewhere, the larger urban merchants and manufacturers dominated New York's rate control drive. Such individuals, like policyholders nationally, blasted high rates and industry malpractices. The president of Rochester's Pilot Ribbon and Carbon Company voiced a common reaction. "The raising of an Insurance rate in [an] arbitrary manner should not be allowed to pass the Insurance Department without some definite action, and the making of rates is a matter which should be taken up by this department. In fact, it would seem to me that the Fire Insurance in the State as well as the Country, is one of Public Utilities, even more so than Railroads, as every person who owns a building is obliged to carry Insurance, and should be under control of the Insurance Department of this State." He suggested that the insurance department be "enlarged so as to cover everything pertaining to Fire Insurance in this State. It should have powers similar to the Public Utilities Commission in order that the public will not be boycotted and that their losses cannot be held up indefinitely."[93]

Blacklisting and unsatisfactory claim adjustments became two more reasons why such individuals demanded stiff state regulatory controls. The insurance department received repeated complaints from a variety of policyholders—including many of the state's largest—charging they no longer could obtain coverage even at exorbitant rates. If they had sustained a major loss or had property in a high-risk location (commonly the older manufacturing-warehouse districts of urban areas), their chances of being "uninsurables" were excellent. Those unable to obtain protection understandably accused the industry of blacklisting; a practice that not only existed but appears to have been widespread.[94]

New Yorkers often did not receive prompt and equitable settlements on large loss claims. This obviously affected the biggest policyholder, and he complained the loudest. Insolvency explained the unwillingness of some companies to pay claims. However, the desire to maximize profits for stockholders and the added financial burdens stemming from the Baltimore conflagration of 1904 and the San Francisco earthquake and fire of 1906 caused a number of firms either to delay paying or to scale down claims in hopes of smaller cash settlements.[95]

Superintendent of Insurance William H. Hotchkiss of Buffalo, a progressive Republican whom Governor Charles Evans Hughes appointed early in 1909, perceived the extent of consumer ill-will toward fire carriers. Shortly after assuming office, he wrote to the Monroe County district attorney concerning the imminent need for reform: "I thoroughly believe that some legislation is needed to reach this monopoly, as the insurance combination as it exists in this State and the United States is one of the greatest evils of the day, . . . they have complete control of the business and the fixing of rates, and the business people of the cities are wholly without redress."[96]

Hotchkiss launched his attack by exposing legislative corruption. Well aware of the reform effects of the Armstrong Committee's disclosures of life insurance lobbying, the superintendent decided to capitalize on recently unearthed documents disclosing the illicit activities of the Phoenix Fire Insurance Company of Brooklyn. Inquiries into the affairs of the Phoenix and other New York–based firms, which began in January 1910, climaxed with monthlong public hearings in March at the department's New York City office. During these sessions Hotchkiss found evidence of considerable legislative graft in companies' promotion and prevention of legislation during the previous decade; firms had spent about $150,000 on vote buying between 1901 to 1906. Understandably, the industry reacted negatively to the superintendent's sensitive probings. The investigation, which was accorded ample and judicious coverage in the state and national press, prompted Governor Hughes to ask the legislature on April 11 for an extensive inquiry into fire insurance practices. As Hughes said, "[These revelations] have caused every honest citizen to tingle with shame and indignation and have made irresistible the demand that every proper means should be employed to purge and to purify."[97]

The Hughes request came at a time when the state's progressive movement was in full bloom. Indeed, in 1910 a milieu conducive to consumerism helped create a special eight-member committee known as the New York Legislative Investigating (or Merritt) Committee. Chairing it was Edwin A. Merritt, Jr., an able Potsdam legislator and Hughes man, whom New Yorkers already knew as the co-sponsor of the highly acclaimed public utility regulation law of 1907. The Merritt Committee held forty-two sessions during the autumn and early winter months of 1910–1911. A multitude of industry wrongdoings were uncovered, particularly discriminatory rating practices. The committee quickly substantiated larger policyholders' long-standing contentions that firms hiked rates exorbitantly, boycotted customers, and unfairly challenged loss claims.[98]

Committee members urged more thorough state supervision of the whole process of rate fixing. Rejecting the antitrust approach in favor of regulatory controls, they deemed antitrust acts "utter failures." Even this rebuke of a concept long cherished by many reform-minded New Yorkers found a positive reception. Antitrusters like Alfred E. Smith seemed willing to consider other methods of regulation, and in time much of their earlier suspicion and hostility toward regulatory commissions melted away. Their change of heart can be attributed partly to the success of the Page-Merritt Utility Act and partly to the exigencies of reform. The Page-Merritt law, which gave New York sweeping regulatory powers over all forms of public service corporations (except telegraph and telephone companies), had wisely incorporated the successes and avoided the pitfalls of a variety of regulatory commission statutes, including the 1887 Interstate Commerce Commission Act and Robert La Follette's Wisconsin utility reforms. Agreeing with Hughes's dictum that the "public's interest must be our foremost concern," these antitrust supporters, who at times criticized the very people directing the movement for regulatory controls of fire insurance, saw the value of a flexible and multifaceted attack on all forms of "corporate arrogance."[99]

The Merritt Committee's investigation led to the enactment of the rate-making association law of 1911, despite intense industry criticism and active opposition. Unlike typical rate statutes of the period, this measure failed to give the state actual rate-fixing powers. Instead it allowed New York's four regional rating associations to combine to set charges, a feature that made the act much more palatable to companies and agents alike. Each association, however, had to submit to certain controls—to publicly disclose its membership and its overall purpose, organization, and methods of operation; to allow periodic public examinations; and to keep complete and accurate records of all proceedings. The insurance superintendent was empowered on consumer complaint to conduct rate hearings and, if needed, to order removal of any existing discrimination. The purpose then was the prevention of inequities in connection with fire premiums rather than actual rate making. As such, the measure's initial backers (the larger policyholders) scored a clear-cut victory.[100]

The new law did much to eliminate unjust discriminations. Yet on occasion, policyholders charged it was difficult to prove a rate discrimination. While some contended that the rate-making association statute "afforded complete protection to the insured," consumer dissatisfaction persisted. The chief complaint voiced was the cost of coverage. Letters and telegrams from angry policyholders periodically showered the insurance department, demanding an end to rating associations and asking that the state assume the duty of fixing or approving rates. The stock response from insurance department officials seemed to be this simple but true statement: "[We] do not have power to regulate the ratings of the organizations, if no discrimination between similar risks is uncovered." It would not be until the 1920s, and then only after bitter policyholder-industry wrangling and consumer prodding of recalcitrant lawmakers, that the insurance department would receive more complete authority to control rates and practices.[101]

While New Yorkers debated the merits of state-made rates, Wisconsinites also sought to find the best way to lower costs and eliminate rate discrimination. In 1911 state lawmakers adopted a resolution, introduced by progressive assemblyman Lewis L. Johnson, that called for the appointment of a joint Senate-House investigating committee to study the industry, with special emphasis on rates, agents' commissions, and marketing methods. Wisconsin then became one of nine states to conduct full-scale legislative probes between 1909 and 1915 into fire insurance operations.[102]

The hue and cry of consumers over rates, coupled with the crusading zeal of reform-minded commissioner Herman L. Ekern, prompted this legislative action. Policyholders agitating for change came principally from urban areas where stock rather than mutual companies wrote the greatest number of policies. Here frequent complaints charged the industry with rate excesses and discriminations, particularly on types and locations of risks insured. Contrary to conditions elsewhere, the largest policyholders tended on the whole to be participants in successful cooperative concerns—mutual groups of lumbermen, millers, and furniture dealers, to name several of the leading ones. Since these individuals enjoyed inexpensive and dependable mutual coverage, they had no need to seek stock company favoritism.[103]

Herman Ekern, whose role in the creation of the Wisconsin life insurance fund was discussed in Chapter 3, dedicated his four and one-half years as commissioner to the establishment of fair insurance practices. Ekern saw the importance of regulating both life and fire companies in the public interest. "Insurance interests every citizen. It protects his business, his future and the future of his family," he told Wisconsinites in June 1910. "It affects more property than does any other business. It represents more savings than does any other form of investment. It is the most universal safeguard of the economic independence of our people. Its efficient regulation and supervision in the interests of the policyholder and the public is . . . one of the highest duties of the state."[104]

The newly formed Wisconsin Fire Insurance Investigating Committee conducted extensive probings into the fire world beginning in January 1912. Public sessions were held in Madison, Milwaukee, Oshkosh, La Crosse, Superior, Fond du Lac, and Chicago. After a total of fourteen weeks of hearings and more than three thousand pages of testimony, the committee concluded in part that enforced competition as envisioned by the architects of earlier antitrust laws had failed the consumer. Committee members revealed that the "independent" fire rating boards that had replaced the fire "trust" had not made rates for the benefit of the insured. Rather, these boards, which consisted of individuals appointed by the state's underwriters, commonly kept premiums at high levels so as to produce handsome commissions for agents. Other fire rate practices similarly hurt policyholders. One problem causing considerable unrest was the public's inability to appeal charges set by local Wisconsin boards.[105]

The committee drafted legislation that called for a modified system of state rate control, based on the concept of fire insurance as a public utility—a philosophy in tune with the popular progressive notion of a positive service state. Specifically, the reforms allowed firms to cooperate in rate making, but from a common inspection bureau or bureaus that were subject to close scrutiny by the insurance department. The commissioner could check rates when problems of discrimination arose between classes of property or different localities within the state. A special commission composed of five experts appointed by the governor would also review questions as to whether statewide charges were excessive and discriminatory. Companies were to use rates fixed by the inspection bureaus and not by other sources. Finally, all agreements between firms were to be open to public examination.[106]

The legislative investigation committee asked additionally that Wisconsin fire insurance agents be subjected to more stringent state controls. It called for limitations on commissions paid to agents and said that individual companies could have only a single representative in a particular territory. All underwriters must be qualified for their work, and those entering must be examined by a civil service commission. Thus it was the state and not the industry that sought the "professionalization" of agents.[107]

Understandably the package of reform recommendations clashed with formidable foes when introduced into the 1913 legislative session. Stock companies, together with their agents, marshaled forces to defeat the committee's basic proposal—state control of the rating process. Industry motives in opposing this legislation, especially controls on rate fixing, followed the rationale used elsewhere. Company officials again argued that "fire insurance rates are a sacred right. . . . No commission, no commissioner, no law is going to fix rates. . . . State meddling is uncalled for." Agents, who occasionally demonstrated enthusiasm for state rates and related reforms, balked at the investigating committee's chief proposals. Joined by the

National Board of Fire Underwriters, local underwriters vociferously opposed interference with rate fixing and restrictions on their commissions. ''We believe that complete freedom from state supervision or control of rating,'' uttered a Green Bay agent, ''constitutes the most certain way to the permanent establishment of satisfactory rates and practices. Only the industry knows or can ever understand the complexities of fire insurance. Commissions charged must remain the decisions of those who are most knowledgeable.''[108]

Bickering among Wisconsin reform leaders, namely, a rift between Governor Frances E. McGovern and Commissioner Ekern, further aided the opposition's cause. Although Ekern was a political progressive, McGovern strongly disliked him. This feud, rooted in the factionalism within the Republican party during the La Follette era, blossomed into a protracted struggle during the presidential election of 1912. In January 1913 McGovern attempted to oust the commissioner on charges of ''political activity'' and ''misconduct in office.'' However, after much name-calling and political maneuvering the state supreme court ruled in June that Ekern had done nothing wrong. Remarked one source, ''It was a case where the state's chief executive took the law in his own hands in a sorry attempt to remove an official of the state whose fidelity to the public interest [has long been recognized].'' Clearly, both men expended energies that might otherwise have been more profitably directed at achieving fire reform.[109]

After 1914 the political climate in Wisconsin changed noticeably. No longer did consumer champions have the upper hand. Voters elected refrigerator car magnate and stalwart Republican Emanuel L. Philipp governor in November 1914 and again in 1916 and 1918. Ekern himself left the Wisconsin insurance scene when Philipp appointed his secretary, the conservative Michael J. Cleary, to the commissioner's post in July 1915. Even with a radical shake-up in Wisconsin's political scene, the movement toward state rates did not cease abruptly but, rather, ultimately succeeded.[110]

Those who sought state control over fire charges and industry conduct made a surprisingly strong showing in the legislature on the eve of Ekern's departure. An Ekern-authored rate control bill passed the Senate by a unanimous vote in early June 1915; but the Assembly, dominated by stalwart Republicans, subsequently killed the proposal by a five-vote margin. Opponents received help from lawmakers who themselves were in the insurance business. The lower body's reasoning for rejection mirrored earlier industry and agent objections—fears that such state controls would be too harsh on companies and underwriters alike, and an unmanageable and expensive bureaucratic octopus would be created. Some thought a majority of Wisconsinites opposed the measure, for in the previous year voters had rejected referendums that would have permitted state entry or expansion into major insurance fields.[111]

Legislative defeat in 1915 did not silence rate reformers. Two years later a compromise measure of a largely bipartisan nature met with the lawmakers' unanimous consent. "At last the legislators have shown sensitivity to many policyholders' unhappiness with the way certain facets of the fire business have been conducted in Wisconsin," wrote former commissioner Ekern to a Kansas friend. "It took years of hard work to educate those who claim to represent the people. But now they see the success of various state-made laws and realize that our state's policyholders can benefit."[112]

The 1917 act contained two principal clauses. It gave the insurance commissioner power to fix a reasonable rate after establishing the inequality of any charge. And if he found a rate to be discriminatory, he could order the newly created statewide rating bureau—one that had compulsory company membership—to correct it. The new statute worked. In the postwar period rates dropped noticeably, and the number of letters to the insurance department protesting arbitrary and unfair charges dwindled. "The regulation was not merely a paper regulation," observed one insurance specialist. "On various occasions Commissioners suspended the bureau's rulebook, denied a war-motivated plea for increase premium rates, . . . [and] ordered lower rates on Milwaukee dwellings."[113]

One revealing dimension of industry attitudes toward the state rate crusade developed soon after it began. Company representatives repeatedly argued that the wrong type of change captured the fancy of the consumer-lawmaker coalition. "If rates are to be permanently lowered," suggested an officer of the Liberty Fire Insurance Company, "then a better class of buildings must be constructed and careful scientific inspection of all insured properties has to occur."[114]

The public—policyholders, insurance commissioners, legislators, and insurance industry personnel—had for years overwhelmingly backed ways to decrease insurable losses. Safer buildings and improved fire protection capabilities became popular and possible with new technology. Telegraphic alarms; water towers; sprinklers; and such fireproof construction materials as "slow-burn" wood, steel, and terra-cotta were either introduced or more widely used during the 1870s and 1880s. Similarly, strong support materialized for tough public regulation of flammable petroleum products, nonsafety matches, and even fireworks (often a response to a publicized disaster). Thus when at the turn of the century the National Board of Fire Underwriters proposed model electrical and building codes (inspired by European experiences) and created Underwriters' Laboratories (UL), Americans approved. Most states and territories patterned laws after these proposed statutes, and consumers preferred UL-sanctioned products. Backed by the industry, governments also began creating the office of state or city fire marshall to institutionalize fire-prevention work permanently. Yet policyholders did not see fire marshalls as a panacea to unfair rates; they wanted more than the professional-scientific approach. Consumers could not accept a *Western Insurance Review* statement that "this [fire marshall law] is what the rate reformers should be considering."[115] They correctly perceived that self-interest caused companies to stress this "reform."

V

THE DRIVE for state-made rates followed a distinct pattern. It developed early and rapidly in states that relied almost exclusively on the antitrust approach to control industry charges. And it met difficulty where either vigorous rate competition or alternatives to stock companies existed, namely, thriving fire mutuals.

When states turned to publicly set rates, the specific acts varied significantly. Kansas legislators required firms to file rate schedules with the insurance superintendent, who could then adjust them. The Texas law gave the power of rate regulation to a three-member rating board rather than to the head of the insurance department. In Missouri the 1911 Oliver Act empowered companies through a fire rating association to set charges, while at the same time granting the superintendent of insurance power to lower them when, in his opinion, they were excessive. In New York and Wisconsin, two states not in the vanguard of the movement, the approaches also differed. New York's Merritt Committee statute regulated the rating process but stopped short of actual state rate making. In 1917 Wisconsin rate reformers finally called for compulsory company membership in a statewide rating bureau, which would fix charges in accordance with policies established by the insurance commissioner. These variations in state rate measures, even more so than differences in earlier antitrust laws, demonstrate that reformers during the progressive era were not committed to any one specific rate reform plan; rather, corrections were pragmatic and adaptable to local needs and conditions.

Support for state rates also varied. The smaller policyholder, who was previously discriminated against, provided key backing for the movement in Kansas and Texas, while Missouri's local fire insurance agents instigated that state's initial rate control act. Large commercial and manufacturing interests in New York agitated for public supervision of rate practices; and in Wisconsin nationally prominent insurance commissioner Herman L. Ekern teamed up with disenchanted urban consumers to spark a rate reform drive.

The role insurance commissioners played in the state rate story should not be minimized. Ekern diligently worked for reform, as did Charles W. Barnes and Ike Lewis in Kansas, Thomas B. Love in Texas, Frank Blake and Charles Revelle in Missouri, and William A. Hotchkiss in New York. In all states these insurance department heads were directly associated with politically progressive governors and active reform movements. While it is true that certain consumer advocates, including these commissioners, had by World War I sought a "bureaucratic" solution to the nagging problem of soaring and frequently unfair fire costs (that is, having a department official or board control rate practices), they were not attempting to establish order out of chaos so much as they were seeking to obtain justice for policyholders.

As with antitrust legislation, the fire insurance industry overwhelmingly opposed state control of rates. Clearly, most companies did not believe that insurance departments or fire rating boards would become mere tools of the industry. Rather, they agreed with the statement of a fellow insurance official that "no rate control is the best kind of control." Still, it was not a monolithic industry that opposed such measures. In Texas that state's locally based fire insurance industry backed state-made rates; and agents themselves, in Texas and especially Missouri, also said yes to such charges.

The movement for state rates can be termed a success. Both immediately and in the long range there was a general lowering of protection costs and an end to the most flagrant discrimination. Compared with antitrust statutes, the newer schemes for regulating high and discriminatory fire insurance charges were vastly superior. A few consumer advocates did continue to believe that rates could be reduced further if individual states would launch their own insurance programs or have extensive numbers of fire mutuals. Some even tenaciously clung to the antitrust approach of rate regulation—a split in reform ranks similar to the division within the larger progressive movement between Roosevelt New Nationalists and Wilson New Freedomites over how best to regulate the new industrial state.

6

The New-breed Insurance Commissioner

SHORTLY BEFORE the turn of the century, America produced a cadre of "new-breed" state insurance commissioners, who, unlike their predecessors, demonstrated a genuine interest in the rights of consumers. Often associated with popular reform governors, these individuals emerged as staunch and resourceful champions of the public interest. The states of this study could claim the most famous of the country's new breed of commissioner; indeed, they were the central figures of Chapter 5.

Prior to this period, most insurance commissioners concerned themselves strictly with mundane procedural matters. They did not view their office as a tool to advance reform, either through rigidly enforcing existing statutes or by suggesting new ones. It is understandable that "old-breed" commissioners should be unreceptive to change, since they frequently came from the industry and returned there (often to high-paying and prestigious positions) following their terms of office. Consequently, serious consumer problems bothered them little. The new breed, on the other hand, usually lacked this incestuous relationship; most came from outside insurance—from law, journalism, education, and agriculture—although they quickly mastered the details of a highly technical business.[1]

State insurance departments controlled by the old breed consistently accumulated poor records of consumer protection. The New York department is a splendid example. Older than any other except that of Massachusetts, it did not gain the reputation of defender of policyholders' rights until the progressive era. Historically, the office of insurance commissioner was highly political; large insurance firms played a major role in the selection process. But there was more. "An inadequate clerical staff," remarked one observer, "has hitherto encouraged superintendents to content themselves with ascertaining the solvency of companies, rather than probe into and expose errors of judgment or even intentional wrongdoing on the part of those in control of companies.''² (Through sheer determination, the new breed often overcame the same paucity of assistants.)

Fortunately for the consumer still another variety of commissioner existed. This group aggressively sought several related reform objects (albeit ones endorsed by most insurance carriers)—to end operations of fly-by-night and insolvent firms; to abolish marketing abuses such as rebating, twisting, and the like; and to streamline existing insurance statutes.

More often a contemporary of the new breed, this second type dated from the earliest days of supervision. For instance, Elizur Wright, who assumed control of the Massachusetts department during the Civil War era, fits the mold. As commissioner he fought hard to secure the reserves of life insurance companies in order to protect policyholders' claims. Then toward the end of the century two individuals appeared who were in the tradition of Elizur Wright— Daniel Webster Wilder and Dr. William A. Fricke. Both made insurance headlines for their modest quests for uplift. Wilder, the Kansas superintendent from 1887 to 1891, valiantly combated fly-by-nighters. "Only dishonest or weak companies attempt to come into our State without authority," he often told residents, "and it is against companies of this class that our people need protection." In the same vein, Fricke, the Wisconsin department head between 1895 and 1898, continually sought to end rebating and to revamp that state's insurance code. "The rebate is the number one evil for the policyholder," he repeatedly proclaimed. "It promotes lapses and encourages policy twisting." Fricke ceaselessly battled for uniformity in the Wisconsin laws and for "the need to have company examinations conducted in a systematic and logical fashion, which would mean real benefits to the insured since company structural weaknesses could be detected.''³

This brand of commissioner placed a strong emphasis on industrywide "professionalism." Superintendent Wilder, for example, prophesied in 1891 that "most of those nasty letters from policyholders will cease when the best company men with the highest ideals assume control. . . ." Insurance agents who subscribed to a "code of standards" thus were urgently desired. Wilder and those who shared this perception of reform worked closely with professional agents' organizations and similar industry groups and played a prominent role in the National Convention of Insurance Commissioners.⁴

Generally speaking, the Wilders and Frickes did not attempt major changes within the life and fire insurance industries. They might best be thought of as "modernizers"—narrow administrative reformers—while their new-breed peers could be labeled "insurgents.'' Thus the Wilders and Frickes fit nicely into the category of progressive era reformers who placed a premium on economy, efficiency, and professionalism; while the insurgents represent the advanced brand of consumer-sensitive crusaders.[5]

To understand the reasons for the appearance in the 1890s and early 1900s of insurance commissioners dedicated to public service and not to economy and efficiency alone and to recognize the role they played in insurance reform, it is fruitful to examine in detail the careers of two distinct types: Webb McNall, Kansas superintendent from 1897 to 1899, and Willard D. Vandiver, Missouri's insurance chief between 1905 and 1909. Both men superbly illustrate the diverse motives and objectives of insurgent commissioners and show how a state insurance department head might become the policyholder's best friend.

I

WEBB MCNALL (1848–1910), the first Kansas superintendent and perhaps the nation's earliest insurance department official to battle exclusively for the policyholder, arrived in the Sunflower State from Iowa in 1871. In his adopted home he worked hard for what he considered to be the best interests of his community. In the early seventies, as a farmer in Smith County, McNall led residents in a successful vigilante battle against a band of horse thieves. Shortly thereafter he volunteered his services as a township official and later as the county's deputy sheriff. Although admitted to the bar in 1879, McNall continued his farming operations near Gaylord until his death.[6]

Being a lawyer and farmer did not prevent Webb McNall from embarking on still another career. In the spring of 1880 he purchased his hometown newspaper, the *Gaylord Herald*. McNall succinctly expressed his philosophy as a journalist and later as a state politician in his maiden issue: "The paper will be devoted to the building up of Smith County, Gaylord and the north-west [section of Kansas], and on all subjects it will be found on the side of the people." This deep concern about the commonweal prompted McNall in 1884 to become his county's Republican party nominee for the Kansas House. Since the Central Branch of the Missouri Pacific Railroad victimized his community with high and discriminatory rates, McNall concluded that the time had come when "selfish railroad interests" should be made to act like responsible members of society by charging equitable rates "on all commodities to all destinations." After his election McNall succeeded in obtaining the chairmanship of the key Committee on Railroads. During the 1885–1886 legislative sessions he sought strict railroad control measures and vigorously backed passage of the Simpson maximum freight rate bill.[7]

By the end of the eighties McNall, like a great many other Kansans, concluded that the financial plight of the state could only be relieved by the free coinage of silver. At the Sixth District Republican convention held at Colby in 1890, the party selected him for Congress on a soft-money platform, but in the general election he lost to the Independent (People's) party candidate by a slim margin. The silver issue along with his proconsumer views finally caused McNall to bolt the Grand Old Party in 1896. He subsequently helped organize and later chaired the Kansas Silver Republican party, which in the 1896 election backed the victorious Populist-Democratic fusion ticket. As reward for his services, the new Populist governor John W. Leedy named McNall superintendent of insurance.[8]

In early March 1897, one month after assuming office, Webb McNall launched his first battle against the unpopular insurance industry. To demonstrate his commitment to policyholders, he refused to relicense three large eastern life insurance firms, charging they had failed to settle an eighteen-year-old death claim. The case, subject of a number of trials since it first entered state courts in 1880, involved a suit brought by Sallie E. Hillmon of Lawrence to collect $45,000 of insurance on her late husband's life. Since Hillmon had disappeared under mysterious circumstances, the companies charged fraud, arguing that he and his wife conspired to substitute a body in order to collect on three separate policies. The Kansas courts, however, showed their sympathy toward Mrs. Hillmon's claims; and juries, in four of the five trials up to the time McNall entered the controversy, voted overwhelmingly in her favor. Nevertheless, New York Life, Mutual Life of New York, and Connecticut Mutual Life continued to contest payment.[9]

Webb McNall believed his refusal to renew the licenses of the three firms would force them to pay the Hillmon claims and, more importantly, would make them (and other companies also) more cautious about challenging such obligations in the future. McNall repeatedly argued that firms commonly offered beneficiaries only a portion of death claims due, making it necessary for them to accept reduced payments or take court action. Since this involved delays in payment and legal costs, beneficiaries often accepted the companies' terms of settlement.[10]

The three firms quickly responded to McNall's attack. On March

Kansas Superintendent of Insurance Webb McNall
emerged in the late 1890s as the nation's most famous new-
breed insurance commissioner. This fiery consumer advocate terrorized the life and fire insurance enterprise.
(Courtesy of Kansas State Historical Society.)

17, 1897, their lawyers filed a formal complaint contending that the superintendent's refusal to renew their licenses constituted contempt of court, inasmuch as he was seeking to dispose of a pending case. Shortly thereafter, federal district judge Cassius G. Foster ruled that no technical contempt of court had been committed but suggested that McNall had laid himself open to the more serious charge of attempting to coerce witnesses. The case of McNall versus the three life companies was then turned over to a federal grand jury in Topeka, which soon indicted the superintendent for acting illegally. The court quickly placed an injunction on his activities. McNall ignored this ruling and turned the matter over to a sympathetic state attorney general.[11]

In his stand against New York Life, Mutual, and Connecticut Mutual, Webb McNall seemed mildly but pleasantly surprised by the widespread bipartisan support from state and local officials, the press, and the public generally. "I knew I was doing the right thing in the Hillmon case," he told the *Gaylord Herald*. "I realized that policyholders had long complained about a variety of company practices, but frankly, I apparently struck an extremely sensitive nerve." McNall added, "I am not about to quit." Letters like this one from a Great Bend resident must have reinforced McNall's reform inclinations: "Our folks here are outraged at the way those giant life insurance cos. are treating that Hillmon family. It is about time that we have some-body over there in Topeka looking after the little fellows [*sic*] interests. People here wish you all the luck possible in your very corageous [*sic*] battle."[12]

Thus encouraged by cross-class popular reaction and following his own convictions as to his public responsibility, Webb McNall next responded to numerous complaints made against the Metropolitan Life Insurance Company, which had the dubious distinction of having one of the highest policy lapse rates in the industry. Because of this, insurance departments across the country annually received thousands of complaints charging the firm with deliberately encouraging policy lapsing. McNall's mail was full of such correspondence. The event that precipitated action was the company's refusal to pay a $548.42 death claim on the life of a Wyandotte policyholder. On May 20, 1897, McNall revoked Metropolitan's license and forbade it to do business in the state. In characteristic fashion, the company refused to accept this decision. A telegram from a Metropolitan vice-president to his Kansas director of agencies declared, "Commissioner McNall's action against us is absolutely without authority of law and is void. Go on with your business the same as if he had not acted. You will be amply protected." The protection the official had in mind was an injunction, which a district court granted on June 6, 1897.[13]

This second injunction understandably infuriated McNall. The next day the superintendent called a press conference where he blasted the court:

> This is twice . . . in the last ninety days that [the court] has reversed the Supreme Court of the United States in granting a temporary injunction against the superintendent of insurance . . . in the case of *Doyle* vs. *the Continental Insurance Company* . . . the court held that an injunction would not lie against a superintendent of insurance to revoke a license at his pleasure whether he had any cause to do so or not. You might say also that I am of the opinion that the injunction is not very binding.[14]

Unfortunately for McNall, the court decided on June 30, 1897, that he lacked authority under Kansas law to revoke the Metropolitan license because the company, during the intervening period, decided to contest the claim. Metropolitan continued its Kansas operation.[15]

Webb McNall, however, did win important victories in his battle to force life insurance companies to treat their customers fairly. In December 1897 Mutual, a defendant in the Hillmon case and under constant pressure from McNall and the state attorney general, voluntarily withdrew from Kansas. A month later the Kansas Supreme Court prohibited its readmission until the company settled its differences with the department. In January 1898 New York Life, another Hillmon case defendant, came to terms with McNall.[16]

Being one of the new breed did not mean that consumer activist McNall could not function at times as a modernizer. In 1897 he won still another skirmish with the life enterprise when he forced the exodus of the Travelers Insurance Company. During the summer he had become concerned about the firm's financial health. Since the superintendent believed that the head of the insurance department was obligated to protect the policyholder in every possible way, he felt he must prevent company insolvencies, thus responding in the best "modernizing" tradition. After a careful examination of Travelers's 1896 annual report, McNall discovered that, although the company claimed assets of $17,500,000 and liabilities of $16,000,000, it had placed its own valuation on its properties and other tangible assets. A preliminary investigation of the firm's Kansas holdings led him to conclude that these were largely overvalued. The company, for instance, listed the worth of its Depot Hotel in Abilene at $30,000. When McNall received three independent appraisals of the structure, the highest listed the value at $8,000, the lowest at $4,500.

Superintendent McNall subsequently notified company president James G. Batterson that the department would have to make a careful investigation of Travelers's financial condition, which under Kansas law it could do. Batterson first replied that he did not have the authority to allow such a probe. Several weeks later on October 4, 1897, Batterson and the company's board of directors won a temporary court injunction enjoining McNall from making an investigation. The superintendent quickly asked the court for a hearing and succeeded in having the injunction overturned. Batterson then told McNall that the firm's records subsequently would be turned over to the Connecticut insurance commissioner (the home state department), so the investigation might begin. But McNall replied that the Kansas department "would proceed in its own way and manner to investigate the company's assets in the state of Kansas," for McNall realized that the Connecticut department had a poor reputation for consumer protection. Deciding that he could not tolerate any such probe, Batterson arranged for Travelers to retire from Kansas at the end of 1897.[17]

Until he left office in March 1899, Superintendent McNall continued to pressure all life insurance companies to obey Kansas laws and to respect consumer's rights. He actively prosecuted unlicensed firms and agents, acted swiftly on complaint letters, and energetically investigated all dubious activities.[18]

As earlier noted, the public not only objected to dishonest life insurance practices but it also resented high and arbitrary fire insurance rates. No Kansas superintendent prior to 1897 had meaningfully responded to a plethora of complaints about fire protection costs. While McNall's fight with the Clarkson Rating Bureau is recounted in Chapter 4, his victory over the fire "trust," based on his vigorous enforcement of the state's 1889 antitrust law, proved impressive. One Kansas-based firm, the Shawnee Fire Insurance Company of Topeka, for example, in 1897 wrote $12,048,000 in policies and collected $196,000 in premiums, while a year earlier it had written $11,950,000 in policies and collected premiums amounting to $208,000. Thus, following the demise of Clarkson's influence, the company collected approximately $12,000 less while writing $98,000 more coverage.[19]

In addition to unfair fire insurance charges, Kansas consumers bitterly opposed industry violations of the state's 1893 valued-policy law. Typical of complaints received by the department was this one from a Wichita policyholder: "I recently had a business building here completely destroyed by fire. It was insured with the Hartford . . . for $5,000, but that evil company said it was worth only half that amount. As I understand the law they have to pay the value of my policy." The complainant was correct. When a total loss occurred, the firm owed the policy's full value.[20]

As he had with the Clarkson rating bureau, Webb McNall acted upon these valued-policy complaints by first polling the companies as to their practices regarding payments on total fire losses. When the questionnaires were returned, he found "that in a larger number of instances where a policy had been written on real property and there was a total loss the full amount had not been paid, and in some cases there was a difference of hundreds of dollars between the amount the statute required to be paid and the amount actually paid."[21]

After conclusively establishing the statute's widespread abuse, the indefatigable McNall personally wrote all violators and threatened that if they did not abide by the law he would have their licenses suspended immediately. The ultimatum proved effective and the superintendent reported in his 1898 annual report that "in a great many instances—I would say, in fact, all cases that I have reached—the companies have complied with the provision of this law, on the request of this Department."[22]

Although Webb McNall's favorite method for achieving reform came through enforcement of existing state statutes, he, like other new-breed commissioners, also proposed corrective ones. Suspicious of the often narrow thrust of model legislation proposed by the National Association of Life Underwriters and the National Convention of Insurance Commissioners, McNall formulated his own measures. His pet idea became a program of state-operated fire insurance. Soon after assuming office, McNall pushed a scheme whereby any resident desiring public insurance could pay into a specially created fire fund at a rate based on schedules determined by the insurance department. McNall pointed out numerous advantages: "Parties who receive benefits of insurance of this kind will obtain the same for at least half that they now pay, and it will compel insurance companies to furnish insurance at actual cost, or lose the entire business. . . . " He underscored the often mentioned notion that "it would retain the money at home instead of sending it abroad."[23]

The McNall-inspired bill for state fire insurance met defeat in the 1897 legislature, a body only nominally dominated by reform types and where the insurance lobby "pulled every wire at its command." Realizing that his plan probably would not pass in the next legislature either, McNall asked lawmakers to consider a greatly modified version, still with the goal of providing residents with cheap, dependable coverage. His new measure—actually a system of state fire rates—would create a board of fire commissioners, appointed for a two-year term by the superintendent of insurance. It would be their duty to survey the insurable property and to fix the maximum rates the companies could charge. These rates would then be furnished to firms at actual cost, and they could either use them or leave the state. The majority of the legislators, however, disapproved.[24]

The 1897 legislature failed to pass another bill suggested by McNall. This one required life insurance companies to invest fifty percent of their Kansas premiums in approved local real-estate securities and to deposit them in the state treasury for taxation. The superintendent saw this as a way to repay the public for the excessive profits that life firms had made for years. He was quick to point out to critics, "A fact not generally known is that in 1894 and 1895 foreign [out-of-state] life insurance companies took out of Kansas $1,725,000 more than they sent to the State in payment of losses."[25]

As superintendent, McNall suggested measures to curb high salaries of life insurance officials and to establish more equitable and uniform policies. The only proposal he successfully initiated was one passed at a special session of the legislature in 1899 that placed a two to four percent tax on the gross earnings of all insurance firms operating locally.[26]

In addition to enforcing state statutes and proposing new ones, Webb McNall, characteristic of others of the new breed, encouraged formation of mutual fire insurance companies and strengthening of fraternal life insurance organizations as a positive balance to stock firms. His penchant for mutuals is clearly revealed in his annual reports; in fact, McNall shared another typical new-breed trait by using this long-established and legally required published record as a forum to express reform notions. McNall's promutual bias is easily explained: he believed that such programs offered the public adequate insurance protection at a fair cost. Specifically, McNall discussed the merits of mutual fire insurance in this fashion:

> The organization of mutual fire insurance companies in Kansas and other states of the union has tended to reduce the cost of insurance. The difference between joint stock fire insurance companies and mutual fire insurance companies is this: The mutual company, without paying extravagant salaries, insures the property of its members at actual cost. The joint stock fire insurance companies are always organized, and always will be, for the purpose of making money, and, in addition in a great many cases, paying extravagant salaries to their officers, as well as making large dividends to their stockholders.[27]

McNall also viewed the mutual movement as an acceptable alternative to state insurance, since he realized that despite his proposals the odds for Kansas going into the insurance business were slim.

Webb McNall was a popular official, probably the best-liked member of the Leedy administration. As one Republican voter from Valley Falls said, "I am for [Leedy] because he appointed Webb McNall." But not all members of the Grand Old Party thought so highly of the superintendent. With Governor Leedy's reelection bid stopped in 1898, Republicans came to power. Led by the conservative governor-elect William E. Stanley and backed by the powerful insurance lobby, the new administration placed removal of McNall high on its list of priorities. But this posed two problems: McNall's term did not expire until July 1, 1899, and Republicans realized he was well liked. They very likely sensed the truth in the *Kansas City Times*'s observation that "to oust [McNall] on any trumped up charges will be another nail in the Republican coffin."[28]

Spurred on by an unrelenting insurance lobby (insurance men by now had translated McNall's surname into a noun, "McNallism," a word that sent fear and anger through their veins), Governor Stanley, shortly after his inauguration, began the process of removing the superintendent. The governor hoped to use a "reform" act passed in 1897, which empowered the chief executive to remove the insurance head whenever he "shall become satisfied that the superintendent is incompetent, corrupt or oppressive." Stanley asked Topeka newspaperman Arthur Capper to draw up charges that he could use in the ouster proceedings. The final list accused McNall of acting "corruptly in authorizing certain insurance companies to transact business in the state and refusing other companies such authority" and of having "directly and indirectly received gifts, gratuities and compensation from insurance companies other than allowed by law." While the Capper charges were both groundless and generally disbelieved, McNall realized that it would be futile to fight, since he had only a little more than three months left in his term of office. On March 15, 1899, Webb McNall, who had served as Kansas superintendent of insurance for two years and one month, resigned and boarded a train for his farm home near Gaylord.[29]

II

THE NEW-BREED LABEL is not always easy to apply. While the crusading activities of Webb McNall place him solidly in new-breed ranks—he was the quintessential reformer—some commissioners battled only intermittently for consumer protection. Even their public-spirited activities, however, might be overshadowed by self-serving motives. The career of W. D. Vandiver is one such case. This Missouri Insurance Department head, in fact, exhibits strong characteristics of both an old-breed type and a modernizer.

The first significant reaction outside New York to the "great insurance wrongs" of 1905 came from Missouri. That state's new superintendent, W. D. Vandiver, learning of the Armstrong Committee's findings in the New York Life case, demanded return of all company funds that President John A. McCall admitted giving the Republican party and called for resignation of McCall and other top-ranking company officials.

Superintendent Vandiver's highly publicized demands of October 7, 1905, stated in part:

> The public has been very properly taught by yourself [McCall] and other officials of great insurance companies that the funds of a mutual company constitute a fiduciary trust, held and administered for the sole use of those named as beneficiaries, many of whom are or will be widows and orphans, and many thousands of people have taken insurance in your company because of this very fact, and the assurance that every dollar of its assets belongs to the policy holders.
>
> That any portion of the policy holders' premiums or profits on premiums should be diverted to political purposes or other uses not contemplated when the premiums were paid in, and not consistent with the avowed purpose of a life insurance organization, must be considered by all right-thinking people as a gross violation of a sacred trust, if not embezzlement, as defined by the statutes.
>
> The department insists that all funds used by you, or by your order, and particularly the sum of $148,702.50, which amount you confess to having contributed out of the funds of the company to Republican National Campaign Committee for the years 1896, 1900, 1904, must be replaced in the treasury of said New York Life Company within the next thirty days.
>
> This department will insist that a new president and vice president and Finance Committee be put in charge of the affairs of the company as soon as its Board of Directors may be able to effect the change.

If these demands were not met within thirty days, the firm's license to operate in Missouri would be revoked.[30]

For his action of October 7 the Missouri superintendent became an instant national celebrity. William Jennings Bryan's newspaper, the *Commoner,* declared that Vandiver's attack on New York Life should be followed by every other insurance commissioner in the United States. Upon reading the Vandiver ultimatum, the *Montana Miner,* an organ of the Western Federation of Miners, asked the Montana commissioner of insurance to follow the "Missouri defender of the people." And the *Raleigh* (North Carolina) *Democrat* "thank[ed] God for . . . Vandiver." Who then was W. D. Vandiver, a man seen as a defender of the public interest against life insurance "grafters"?[31]

Willard Duncan Vandiver (1854–1932), a Virginian turned Missourian, taught collegiate mathematics and natural sciences and served as a college administrator before he embarked upon a political career in 1896. After capturing the Democratic nomination for Congress in Missouri's fourteenth district (roughly the southeastern portion of the state), Vandiver stumped this seventeen-county area, ardently espousing free silver and the candidacy of William Jennings Bryan, whom he described as the "greatest living man on this continent." As a novice in politics, Vandiver did surprisingly well; he won by a comfortable margin in a previously Republican stronghold.

The highly partisan freshman congressman proved popular; fourteenth district voters loved W. D. Vandiver's engaging personality and found him to be a colorful and dynamic speaker. They returned him to Washington in 1898, 1900, and again in 1902, where he wholeheartedly supported the Bryan wing of Democracy. He championed "soft money," attacked the growing wave of trust formation, and fought American involvement in the Philippines. Like all successful politicians, Congressman Vandiver secured pork barrel legislation for his district. His voter popularity soared with passage of a measure calling for construction of much needed flood control levees along the Mississippi River in two bootheel counties.[32]

Because of his popularity and steadfast party loyalty, key Missouri political forecasters considered W. D. Vandiver a logical candidate for the governorship in 1904. Feeling instead that he did not have a statewide following and lacking sufficient financial backing to wage such a campaign, Vandiver threw his support behind the candidacy of the widely known St. Louis attorney and reformer Joseph Wingate Folk. In January 1904, while still a member of Congress, Vandiver became Folk's campaign manager. Although he was criticized for spending the greater part of his time campaigning for Folk, voters seem to have forgotten this on election day. While a large number of Democrats were going down to defeat, Vandiver's man Folk swept the fourteenth district and the rest of the state.[33]

The election of Joseph W. Folk guaranteed Vandiver a position on the Missouri political scene. After taking office, the new governor appointed Vandiver to the insurance superintendency, a position generally considered to be a major political plum. In accepting the post, Vandiver, never overly modest, said, "I was not a candidate for this office, nor, indeed, for any other appointment under the Governor, but some time after Governor Folk was inaugurated, and after my term in Congress had expired, he offered me the position." And he added, "At first I told him I did not think I wanted it, but he put the matter to me in such a way that I could not very well decline, as he

Willard Duncan Vandiver, Missouri's superintendent of insurance from 1905 to 1909, demonstrated only limited interest in consumerism. A supreme egoist and publicity hound, he bore a striking facial resemblance to Mark Twain, a similarity he proudly cultivated. (Courtesy of Louis H. Vandiver, Columbia, Mo.)

said he felt that this was a very important office and he wanted some one [sic] to fill it that he knew he could rely on."[34]

Not long after Vandiver entered the superintendent's office, he became embroiled with New York Life over the issue of campaign contributions. Missouri's initial reaction to Vandiver's October 7 ultimatum proved generally enthusiastic. Consumers identified with a man who showed deep concern for their interests, for all too frequently the head of the insurance department in Jefferson City had taken the industry's side. In one of numerous Missouri newspaper editorials on the superintendent's bout with New York Life, Joseph Pulitzer's *St. Louis Post-Dispatch* commented, "But there can be no doubt in the minds of intelligent men that Mr. Vandiver's demands on the New York Life are reasonable. Nor can there be any difference of opinion with reference to the propriety of empowering an Insurance Commissioner to insist upon good management and the rectifying of wrongs to the policyholders as a condition of permission to do business in the state."[35]

Yet not all Missourians applauded the Vandiver ultimatum. The first widely publicized complaint against his handling of the New York Life affair came from Speaker of the Missouri House of Representatives David W. Hill, a Poplar Bluff Republican. On October 18, 1905, Hill requested a delay in the revocation of New York Life's license. He argued that Vandiver should allow the state's New York Life policyholders an opportunity to determine what could be done to remedy the situation.[36]

Speaker Hill's recommendation for delay apparently surprised Vandiver. The superintendent replied shortly. "Why [Hill] should come to me with a proposition for delay and postponement of action, I don't know. But I do know that the attorneys for the company are also urging delay, and pressure from various quarters is being brought to bear to have me hold the matter up until after the state authorities of New York have acted." He parenthetically added his hope that the whole insurance affair would not become a "political" issue.[37]

Two of the state's premier Republican newspapers, the *Missouri State Republican,* published in St. Louis with a statewide circulation, and the *Kansas City Journal* failed to grant Vandiver his wish. In a scathing editorial, the *Republican* accused Vandiver of attempting to create a public spectacle with his attack on the insurance "octopus," charging that McCall's contributions to the Grand Old Party were the least offensive of his revealed shortcomings. The paper believed that Vandiver's objection was not to the gifts, but "that the contribution was made to the wrong party," and therefore the superintendent was attacking the wrong thing. The *Journal* similarly felt that if the money given by McCall to the Republicans had "gone to the Bryan free silver committee instead of the sound money party, he [Vandiver] would not feel so indignant about it."[38]

In a later article the *Journal* attempted to discredit totally Vandiver's crusade. The paper claimed evidence disclosing that Reau Folk, brother of the governor and the Tennessee commissioner of insurance, had gone to New York during the 1904 campaign to solicit life insurance company monies for use in securing the nomination and election of Joseph Folk. Since Vandiver was campaign manager, the *Journal* reasoned, he must have sanctioned this act. Also, according to the paper, certain St. Louis insurance men had contributed substantially to the Folk campaign coffers. In the eyes of the partisan Republican press, Vandiver's attack on New York Life was a good example of the pot calling the kettle black. The *Journal* went so far as to suggest an appropriate cartoon: "The St. Louis Insurance agents who contributed to the Folk-Vandiver campaign are frightened; they are behind Vandiver begging him to let loose of the bear's tail he is holding but Vandiver can't let loose; he has gone too far and said too much. Folk stands at one side, looking with horrified face, and Vandiver cries to him to grab the bear's tail, and great reform governor is trying to figure it out whether he can safely do so or not."[39]

W. D. Vandiver vaguely answered his critics. In justifying his action in attacking New York Life first, he said, "Its disclosures came first [first mutual case] and with great boldness and defiance by its officials. . . . It should not be supposed," he added, "that the others are overlooked," and stated that the axiom of his administration was "Honest business or no business in Missouri."[40]

New York Life failed to meet the thirty-day ultimatum, and Vandiver suspended the company's license on November 8, 1905. New York Life immediately petitioned the federal district court in St. Louis to prevent Vandiver from enforcing the suspension notice. Judge G. T. Adams issued a temporary restraining order against the Missouri superintendent and directed him to show cause why the injunction should not be made permanent.[41]

Vandiver felt confident that the court would uphold his position. He based his optimism on the Armstrong Committee's findings that New York Life had been misusing funds for such a long time that its reserves had been impaired. Consequently, it would be "hazardous" to Missouri policyholders for the firm to continue operating in the state.[42]

A docket backlog twice postponed the New York Life case. Although the court finally set the third week in January 1906 as the hearing date, it never considered the matter. On December 30, 1905,

President McCall quit due to "poor health." His resignation had been preceded by George W. Perkins' "retirement" as the company's vice-president and chief fiscal officer.[43]

Officials of New York Life shortly thereafter informed Vandiver that an effort would be made to have the misused funds restored to the company treasury. The trustees went so far as to pledge their own property to this end and further stated that the firm would adopt additional safeguards to protect consumers. Vandiver considered his original demands fully met, and on January 12, 1906, he ordered the suspension notice officially dropped. The court likewise vacated its restraining order. In his annual report, Vandiver boastfully summed up the outcome of his nationally famous clash with New York Life: "It is not too much to say that this vigorous application of common sense and law to the largest and most powerful company doing business in the State has done more to bring about practical reform in the insurance business of the State than all other causes combined."[44]

Following the ultimatum to New York Life, Superintendent Vandiver launched his second reform offensive, this time against the small Mutual Reserve Life Insurance Company of New York. Since assuming the superintendency, Vandiver had received frequent complaints from Missouri policyholders alleging certain company abuses. A typical condemnation came from a Glasgow widow whose husband carried a $1,000 policy with Mutual Reserve. She charged the company with first delaying payment and then refusing it altogether. After several letters of protest, Mutual Reserve finally offered her $200. The widow decided to accept this amount rather than take her chances in trying to receive the full value of the policy, which might be achieved only after expensive and lengthy litigation.[45]

Complaint letters were not the only factors prompting Vandiver to question operations of Mutual Reserve. The Armstrong hearings disclosed that company officials scaled down claims of $1,925,000 to $906,656, so that beneficiaries like the Glasgow widow received only a portion of the face value of their policies. The investigation further showed that the company concealed on its books more than $180,000 in court judgments.[46]

In view of consumer charges and Armstrong revelations, Vandiver notified Mutual Reserve on November 14, 1905, that a joint state-company investigation must occur if the firm desired to continue its Missouri business. On December 6 Vandiver engaged S. H. Wolfe, a New York City attorney and former employee of the Armstrong Committee, to make a thorough investigation of the company's financial standings and its methods of dealing with individual policyholders and claimants.[47]

G. D. Eldridge, first vice-president of Mutual Reserve, objected bitterly to Vandiver's procedures on grounds of prejudice of the examiner and expense to the company. Eldridge made little headway with the Missouri superintendent, although he later received moral encouragement from the *Kansas City Journal* and several other state papers. The *Journal* contended that it was not fair for Mutual Reserve to have to conduct a full-scale investigation since the costs ultimately must be paid by policyholders. The general practice of allowing a state insurance commissioner the right to investigate companies, the *Journal* believed, afforded an opportunity to reward friends with lucrative jobs and extensive junkets. Furthermore, firms like Mutual Reserve would in time not dare complain for fear of incurring the wrath of the insurance commissioner, the newspaper claimed.[48]

Vandiver cogently argued that the cost of hiring Wolfe was low and his integrity and competence high. He therefore overruled Eldridge's objections. In a subsequent reply, Eldridge charged the Missouri examination to be both "unfair" and "senseless." After receiving this communiqué, Vandiver decided to revoke Mutual Reserve's Missouri license. While the order of revocation was being prepared, the insurance department received notice on February 26, 1906, that the company had decided to withdraw on March 1. Since the expiration date was only three days away, its license was allowed to expire. Five days later a New York grand jury indicted President Frederick Burnham, First Vice-president Eldridge, and another high-ranking official for embezzlement of company funds.[49]

The question arises as to how dedicated W. D. Vandiver was to his credo, "Honest business or no business in Missouri." Notwithstanding consumers' praise and Vandiver's own public pronouncement that "other irregularities are being eradicated," evidence minimizes the Missouri superintendent's role as a bona fide new-breed commissioner. One of the most damaging charges that can be leveled against him was his failure to attack other life insurance companies cited by the Armstrong Committee as betrayers of the public trust. Vandiver left office early in 1909 without issuing a single additional charge against any major life concern. The superintendent gave little encouragement to the reform-oriented International Policyholders' Committee—the group launched in 1906 to promote the candidacies of reform trustees in Mutual Life and New York Life. He even refused to respond positively to the scandalous activities of the Great Western Life Insurance Company of Kansas City, a firm that allegedly bilked unsuspecting individuals out of thousands of dollars.

Vandiver simply announced that a "reform element" within the firm appeared to be correcting the situation. Fortunately for Missourians, New York lawmakers enacted sweeping reforms following the Armstrong disclosures; as a result, most of the state's policyholders were protected, since nearly all companies operating in the Show Me State were also subject to the New York insurance code.[50]

In the field of fire insurance W. D. Vandiver did little. While other consumer-minded commissioners responded to public demands for reform by spearheading drives to regulate this industry, Vandiver commonly remarked, "By and large the Missouri anti-trust act, as amended, is working fine and I do not see any need for special action. . . . " As seen in Chapter 5, his two successors—Republican Frank Blake and Democrat Charles G. Revelle—became nationally recognized for their fire insurance reform efforts, specifically their push for state rates.[51]

To Vandiver's credit he did step in on several occasions to protect policyholders of mutual fire insurance and fraternal life insurance firms. His efforts centered on solvency rather than on rates or marketing shortcomings. Major life and fire concerns endorsed Vandiver's efforts, for they had long opposed the wildcatters and fly-by-nights that gave insurance bad publicity. But unlike the new breed, Vandiver did not seek to strengthen mutuals and fraternals as a counterforce against old-line stock companies.[52]

W. D. Vandiver's lack of enthusiasm for insurance reform outside the New York Life and Mutual Reserve cases caused his stock among recognized reformers to plummet sharply after 1906. In St. Louis, William Marion Reedy of the *Mirror* expressed this feeling of disappointment when he said in 1907, "Old W. D. started off with a bang, but this was about it. Surely our great superintendent of insurance could do much more for the public." New-breed commissioner Thomas B. Love also lamented that "Vandiver did not do more for Missouri policyholders." In a letter to a Springfield, Missouri, friend Love directly criticized him: "While I am a loyal Democrat, I cannot agree with Vandiver's seeming belief that life insurance reform is a partisan matter. He has raised the public's expectations only to fail them with his subsequent inaction." In a similar vein a Missouri country editor commented, "It should make no difference how the purchaser of a policy happens to vote or how a stock or even mutual company spends its rightful profits, but it does make a great deal of difference how the industry treats its policyholders. . . ." He concluded, "Vandiver, I'm afraid doesn't buy this philosophy and he is himself a roadblock to much needed reform, especially in the area of fire rates."[53]

Were the allegations issued by Missouri's leading Republican papers and other critics correct—that W. D. Vandiver attacked New York Life solely on political grounds? Answers must be viewed in light of the 1904 political milieu. Louis G. Geiger in his biography of Joseph W. Folk suggests that the 1904 gubernatorial election was one of the most bitterly fought in the annals of Missouri political history. Republicans would have their own prejudices against Folk's campaign manager.[54]

On the whole, charges made by Vandiver's critics have merit. Since little of his personal correspondence survives, one can only speculate that if McCall had given financial support to the Democrat party, Vandiver might never have issued his famous ultimatum. If the superintendent sincerely opposed the right of insurance companies to contribute to political parties, why did he accept industry money for Folk's campaign chest? There is more than Vandiver's seeming hypocrisy to suggest that political reasons motivated his attack on New York Life. Vandiver despised the Republican party. As a member of Congress, he voted consistently with the Democracy. Just as revealing as his voting record were his typically partisan remarks. "I am a Democrat, I will always be one," he told a Jefferson City political gathering in 1906. "The Republican party is the party of the privileged few. It must be overturned!" And the Missouri superintendent, always partial to mottoes, wrote a fellow insurance commissioner a thoroughly twisted version of Rutherford B. Hayes's well-known inaugural statement, saying, "He serves his country best who serves his party best."[55]

If political motivations explain the Vandiver attack on New York Life, what explains his actions against Mutual Reserve? Since the Reserve case coincided with the New York Life fracas, perhaps Vandiver believed that an assault on Mutual Reserve would add to his national fame. It did not, however, since there was minimal interest in the dispute outside Missouri; even the state's leading dailies failed to play up the story. The Mutual Reserve case may therefore have discouraged Vandiver from making additional attacks. Perhaps consumer outcries forced him to take some type of action against Mutual Reserve's sordid affairs. Admittedly, there was also pressure on Vandiver during the 1908 Great Western Life controversy, when he did nothing.

Thus Willard D. Vandiver, while initially demonstrating the hallmark of a new-breed commissioner, seems to have lapsed to the long-standing tradition of the old-breed type. For most of his years in office he even lacked the characteristics of a modernizer.

III

As WITNESSED in the administrative careers of Webb McNall and W. D. Vandiver, the head of a state insurance department could effect reform if he desired. The insurance commissioner had options. He could use the powers of his office to enforce existing statutes, as was frequently done; and he could initiate new legislation. Most did both. Moreover, threats alone might cause life and fire firms to behave. "Fear," argued McNall, "has an amazing impact on the insurance crowd. They are not used to uncertainties."[56]

Motivation became a crucial factor in the relationship of an insurance commissioner to reform. The new breed, as demonstrated in the case of Webb McNall, exhibited an overriding desire to protect the consumer. (McNall developed a record of public service prior to becoming superintendent, while Vandiver's philosophy of "Honest business or no business in Missouri" seemed to be more a function of his long-standing Democratic party loyalty than any dedication to consumerism.) Motivation probably also came from sources other than an individual commissioner's sense of fair play. Policyholder response to insurance injustices, together with the startling disclosures made by the Armstrong and other investigations, surely influenced the actions of these officials. Yet the reform impulse was not fundamentally radical, even though some (McNall is an example) did suggest the socialist alternative to state regulation—government-sponsored insurance.

The role of the state insurance commissioner should not be underestimated in explaining why reform of the insurance enterprise occurred during the progressive era. Unlike a pressure group, a motivated commissioner possessed unique opportunities to help the customer; he could marshal the powers of his office to effect change. But departure of one of the new breed could be troublesome. Not only did a reform milieu prove virtually impossible to "institutionalize"— the very nature of personality precluded this—but returning old-breed types, rather blatantly at times, weakened consumer protection. Indeed, the old relationship of political intimacy with the industry replaced the adversary one. The help given policyholders by the modernizers, while important, was hardly spectacular. Even their loyally supported organization, the National Convention of Insurance Commissioners, seemed at times more concerned with "professionalism" than with reform. Fortunately, statutory safeguards continued to shield the public, irrespective of who held the post of insurance commissioner.

7

Quest for Federal Regulation

THE HONEYMOON between reputable life and fire insurance companies and their clients showed signs of ending by the 1870s. When the structure of the life industry dramatically changed with the advent of tontine and industrial insurance, aggressive sales forces emerged to market these novel policies. Consumers soon were dismayed and angered by pushy lightning agents who commonly used twisting, rebating, and other nefarious techniques to obtain greater profits for themselves and their firms. Friction similarly developed between fire patrons and that industry when scores of companies in the wake of the great Chicago and Boston conflagrations either refused or hesitated to pay the full value of policies when losses occurred. These already taxed relations were placed under additional strain when the fire industry subsequently established tariff associations and fire rating bureaus that often fixed rates in a high and arbitrary manner.

The coming of depressed conditions in the early nineties further exacerbated the troubled relationship between companies and consumers. Some owners of life policies, as taxpayers, disapproved strongly of any acts of corporate and individual tax dodging during this difficult period. Policyholders and nonpolicyholders alike regularly demanded that the life industry's high cash reserves be taxed so that the financial burden of government might be more equitably distributed. The first rumblings could be heard in the West and South for forced investment of premium funds in local property and securities by the life enterprise; the crippling depression greatly intensified chronic shortages of capital in these regions. Economic reversals likewise affected fire policyholders. They were aggravated with the increased cost of protection and frequently charged that they were "at the mercy of an abusive trust."

Consumer agitation began to initiate change in both the life and fire industries. Starting in the 1890s, life officials began to feel the sting of policyholder anger through passage of stringent taxation measures, tighter licensing requirements, and proposals for mandatory investments in local securities by nonresident companies. Although the fire industry experienced consumer wrath earlier with the drive for valued-policy laws, the nineties witnessed a flurry of state antitrust acts. Designed to break up rate combination agreements and rating organizations, these measures sought true competition and hence lower costs.

Policyholder agitation for substantial changes did not flag with the return of prosperity after 1897. In the life field the startling disclosures in such muckraking exposés as Thomas Lawson's "Frenzied Finance" series fueled the fires of unrest. And when Joseph Pulitzer's crusading *New York World* exposed corruption in the august Equitable Life Assurance Society, the result was the famed New York State Armstrong Investigation—that milestone in the annals of insurance reform. This 1905 probe into the inner workings of life insurance produced tough regulatory statutes and sent shock waves throughout the nation. In other states the New York hearings spawned investigations and corrective measures.

From 1907 until World War I, adjustment to life insurance regulation produced still more reform, some of which badly frightened the industry. Passage of the Robertson Investment Act in Texas and Wisconsin's venture into public life insurance, in particular, prompted concern. And the increased activities of the new breed of insurance commissioner also caused alarm. Insurance men shuddered at the thought that "Pandora's Box has now been opened. . . . Cranks and visionaries, if left unchecked, will in time ruin our business."[1]

The fire insurance sector also felt the jabs of consumer discontent. Initiated by the legislatures of Kansas and Texas, by 1909 a spontaneous drive began to replace largely ineffective antitrust statutes with more satisfactory systems of state-made rates. J. Gordon Payne, president of the Southern Fire Insurance Company, aptly expressed industry sentiment when he remarked that government-controlled rates "could well be the beginning of state fire insurance and the end of private companies in the United States." Furthermore, the fire industry continued to face creation and expansion of mutuals, which traditionally offered low-cost protection.[2]

The life and fire businesses responded to what they initially considered to be the "inadequacies of the several states to regulate insurance" and then later the excesses of such legislation. At first, most willingly joined hands with consumers who demanded an end to the disruptive and dishonest activities of the wildcat and insolvent firms. Subsequently, the more conservative managers regularly pressed hard for marketing reforms. But with the shocking trend away from what insurance men regarded as "friendly" and "useful" state regulation, the industry employed extensive lobbying, threats of withdrawal, and court injunctions to combat passage and enforcement of "hostile" state insurance statutes.

I

AT AN EARLY DATE some company leaders favored federal over state supervision of insurance, just as businessmen in oil, airlines, and broadcasting would later seek the same objective. On the eve of the Civil War, James E. Lewis, spokesman for several eastern life companies, was one of the first to discuss federal regulation. "Chaos reigns throughout the land," he told St. Louis community leaders. "Most states lack any type of regulatory bodies . . . and insurance statutes. . . . Local politicians seem to be undisturbed at the problem; therefore the good name of insurance is being blackened and the public suffers." Lewis suggested that the federal government "establish a system for the licensing of all types of insurance companies."[3]

In 1865 a score of life insurance managers, joined by several of their colleagues from the fire field, petitioned Congress for a national incorporation act to end "the anarchy that presently exists in the States" and "to establish the insurance business on a safe and even keel." These seekers of order wanted insurance firms, like national banks, to become federal institutions. Three years later they succeeded in having the Senate consider a bill corresponding to their 1865 petition. Although this measure died, industry personnel who endorsed national regulation continued their quest.[4]

Like Congress, the United States Supreme Court stood as a roadblock in the drive for federal control. While companies consistently enjoyed cordial relations with state and inferior courts, the nation's highest tribunal ruled in the 1869 case of *Paul* vs. *Virginia* that the federal government lacked power to regulate the industry. According to Justice Stephen Field, an insurance policy was a contract of indemnity, not a transaction in commerce, and hence immune from federal supervision.[5]

During the 1870s and early 1880s the *Paul* decision, coupled with increased but largely friendly state regulation, lessened talk of federal supervision. Afterward, however, mounting local reform activities and consumer demands for valued-policy laws prompted some insurance leaders (mostly in the fire field) to denounce these statutes as wholly "unwarranted" and "hostile." As a result, they renewed their efforts to bring about federal control and thus circumvent state supervision. At the 1885 convention of the Fire Underwriters of the Northwest in Chicago J. C. Griffiths, an agent with the Home Fire Insurance Company, expressed a growing sentiment: "I believe Congress has power to legislate . . . ; and I further believe a proper effort could secure such legislation as would nullify most, if not all, [of] the obnoxious laws on the statute books of the several States."[6]

The Interstate Commerce Act in 1887 revived hope of federal controls, because it seemed to be a fundamental step toward national supervision over quasi-public corporations. Creation of the Interstate Commerce Commission, together with increased "unfriendly" state regulation, produced considerable industry backing for Max Cohen, a veteran life insurance journalist, in his efforts in 1889 to launch a trade journal dedicated to federal restraints. Cohen's *Views,* published in the most appropriate location, Washington, D.C., became the celebrated forum for those seeking escape from state regulation.[7]

Shortly after the debut of *Views,* there was a second major attempt to force Congress to enact a federal control measure. The strategy centered on first obtaining congressional approval and then worrying about a favorable court interpretation. In the summer of 1892 Ohio congressman John M. Pattison, president of the Cincinnati-based Union Central Life Insurance Company, called for creation of a National Bureau of Insurance to be attached to the Treasury Department. Under the Pattison plan a national commissioner of insurance would issue licenses to all firms; he would subject the industry to no requirements other than those enacted by Congress and by the state in which the companies were chartered. Annual reports would be made only to the national bureau and to the home insurance department. A final provision exempted companies from taxation except in the state granting their charters.[8]

Unhappily for advocates of federal control, the House Committee of Interstate and Foreign Commerce refused to report out Pattison's bill. Prudential president John F. Dryden, himself a leading proponent of this measure, later reflected on its failure: "The bill, in spite of many excellent provisions, was, unfortunately, weighted down with too many minor provisions and matters of detail, which gave rise to an opposition sufficiently strong to prevent a favorable report." A more plausible explanation is that Congress believed the measure to be both unconstitutional and unpopular with the nation's consumers. Commented one Kansas lawmaker, "Pattison's bill is more than of questionable constitutionality . . . it is a special interest piece which, if ever enacted, would in no way benefit the policyholder."[9]

Again defeat did not silence advocates of federal supervision. In December 1897 Senator Orville Hitchcock Platt of Connecticut, spokesman for the Hartford-based insurance companies, patterned a bill largely after Pattison's proposal. The Platt measure, however, permitted states to levy taxes on an insurance company's property even though the firm was chartered elsewhere. This made the bill more palatable to legislators who insisted that the insurance enterprise pay its fair share of the tax burden. Some objectionable details included in the earlier bill were omitted, and this also enhanced chances for passage.[10]

During congressional debate more officials supported the Platt proposal than had five years earlier. Increased state supervision in both the life and fire fields caused industry members to view federal regulation with sympathy and understanding. Similarly, additional trade papers backed federal supervision. Although commonly reflecting a particular company or regional position, even journals of an independent bent characterized state reform activities as "meddling, burdensome and harmful." In spite of general industry approbation the Platt bill died in committee. Efforts to force reconsideration proved futile; the mood of Congress had shown no appreciable signs of changing from its 1892 position.[11]

Large segments of the insurance business continued the quest for federal supervision. *Views* and sister publications, often in special "Federal Regulation" columns, repeatedly denounced state regulation and urged united industry action in behalf of federal control. The thrust of the arguments was the old fear that if local interference remained unchecked the insurance enterprise would surely face a bleak future. Individual company leaders concurred and continued to discuss the question, but many doubted if the movement would ever succeed.

II

INDUSTRY PESSIMISM about the prospect of federal control gave way to guarded optimism when the Theodore Roosevelt administration created the Bureau of Corporations in 1903. At the prodding of Senator John F. Dryden and such politically powerful insurance executives as John A. McCall of New York Life and Richard McCurdy of Mutual Life, both generous contributors to Republican campaign coffers, the bureau, as two of its early tasks, examined insurance regulatory problems and explored the feasibility of federal supervision. Agency investigators soon discovered a ground swell of support within industry ranks for central control. The president of the New

Hampshire Fire Company, U. C. Crosby, for example, reasoned that it would "end the present conditions in which State regulation is onerous to the operation of business. . . . We believe thoroughly in national supervision providing it will wipe out State supervision."[12]

The Crosby statement can be interpreted in two ways. Often the argument of corporate officialdom is merely the desire for order and efficiency. A hodgepodge of state and territorial laws, for example, caused confusion and waste. Undeniably, proponents of federal supervision of insurance who sought "certainty" in their work shared what became a long-standing and commonplace American business objective. Yet the root issue in this case was the longing of insurance managers to escape consumer triumphs in the various states.

The drive for federal supervision at last gained the public support of President Roosevelt when he endorsed a recommendation by James R. Garfield, commissioner of corporations, that Congress institute control. In his annual message sent to Capitol Hill on December 6, 1904, the president said, "The business of insurance vitally affects the great mass of people of the United States and is national and not local in its application. It involves a multitude of transactions among the people of the different States and between American companies and foreign governments." Roosevelt then urged Congress to consider "whether the power of the Bureau of Corporations cannot constitutionally be extended to cover inter-state transactions in insurance." Consultation with high-ranking industry representatives and the Armstrong disclosures in New York again prompted T. R. to incorporate an appeal for federal control in 1905.[13]

During the interim between the two Roosevelt messages John F. Dryden, New Jersey's junior senator and Prudential's president, introduced his pet federal control scheme. Like the earlier Pattison and Platt proposals Dryden's bill called for a national insurance department, headed by a federal superintendent who could issue licenses. Stipulations included filing of annual reports with the new bureau and the posting of a $100,000 guaranty bond—the latter being the type of antiwildcat control big firms had sought for decades. Under the Dryden plan, states could supervise only home companies. Local laws that taxed or harassed interstate operations were also sharply curtailed.[14]

During debate on the Dryden bill an important fissure developed within the ranks of the life insurance industry over the issue of federal supervison. While Dryden led forces favoring his bill, Morgan Bulkeley, senator from Connecticut and head of Aetna Life, scathingly attacked his colleague's proposal and questioned its overall concept. Bulkeley represented the sentiments of his home-state companies and several of the small, regional life insurance concerns that feared domination of the federal regulatory machinery by the giant and politically powerful New York-based firms. These companies, as Bulkeley and his supporters privately surmised, would surely exploit their advantage.[15]

The life scandals of 1905 drastically diminished industry dissension on the federal control issue. Pressure built steadily for prompt congressional action on the Dryden bill. A large number of life insurance people, including Bulkeley backers, began to worry about what New York lawmakers might do in the aftermath of the Armstrong revelations; they therefore labored vigorously for the Dryden proposal. Logically, these individuals welcomed all "outside" support for federal supervision. Industry leaders smiled in late 1905 when the Committee on Insurance Law of the American Bar Association (ABA) concluded that the only practical solution to regulatory problems involving insurance lay in federal action. The ABA, as a result, blessed Dryden's measure. Even the National Convention of Insurance Commissioners (NCIC), an organization that often sparred with the industry, collectively concluded that the Equitable and other insurance scandals made federal regulation necessary or perhaps inevitable. Yet some NCIC members vehemently opposed federal supervision in any form. (These diehards came principally from the ranks of the new breed, those actively committed to consumer interests.) Remarked one commissioner, "We want to maintain the meaningful reform which is possible only at the state level. . . . Federal supervision is an anathema to those who desire justice for the policy-holder."[16]

The Dryden measure failed to gain President Roosevelt's wholehearted approval. This perhaps occurred because the "White House has been deluged with anti-Dryden letters." Said T. R., "[It is] doubtful whether Congress will assert its power over the insurance business, and it is even doubtful whether it has the power to assert." This uncertainty conceivably led the often unpredictable Roosevelt to abandon the Dryden proposal. Instead of the Dryden format the chief executive suggested that Congress pass a set of model insurance laws for the District of Columbia, which other states and territories might then copy. Thus Roosevelt adopted the model code as the practical and "safe" method of insurance regulation.[17]

In April 1906 the president gave Congress the recommendations of a February conference in Chicago of state attorneys general, governors, and insurance commissioners, which discussed local responses to the Armstrong disclosures. Specifically, the meeting, through its Committee of Fifteen, had called for passage of the previously introduced Ames model code. Brainchild of Congressman Butler Ames of Massachusetts, this measure proposed to transfer the District of Columbia's Department of Insurance to the Department of Commerce and Labor. There it would be streamlined and its laws and procedures publicized to serve as a standard for existing insurance departments. Even though the bill received both White House and industry support, the model code proposal experienced trouble. In committee the Ames bill became so burdened with amendments that it never appeared before the House. Furthermore, the House and Senate judiciary committees concluded that Congress lacked authority to supervise insurance in any way. It is likely that these lawmakers merely reflected the lack of public interest in model insurance legislation.[18]

III

As THE DRIVE for federal regulation foundered on the rock of congressional inaction, previously garnered support for federal control weakened. Most industry spokesmen, while still desiring federal supervision, came to feel that it was unattainable; the ABA soon doubted the issue's constitutionality; and Roosevelt himself turned his attention to other more pressing national problems.[19]

Nevertheless, the rash of state life insurance reforms generated by the Armstrong investigation caused the industry, particularly the New York-based firms, to continue to seek some form of federal relief. As the influential trade journal, the *Spectator,* observed, "Legislation in a number of States during the past year or so has certainly caused many life insurance company officials to wish that national supervision was possible." However, only a temporary period of frustration prevented those who backed federal control from immediately inaugurating a new campaign.[20]

After 1910 the nucleus of federal supervision proponents began to regain a sizable following of industry leaders who for a variety of reasons had abandoned the cause. Those returning to the fold were in the fire insurance industry. Passage by Congress of the Hepburn Act in 1906, a measure that granted the federal government authority to determine railroad rates, initially sent panic through the ranks of the fire industry. But it quickly became apparent that the worst effects of federal rate control prophesied by some railroads failed to materialize. Soon, however, there was a special reason for fire people to seek federal supervision. Beginning in 1909 various legislatures embarked on state-made fire insurance rates. Such events convinced many to rethink their position on federal supervision. A pamphlet distributed by the Hartford Fire Insurance Company in 1911 argued that a federal rate board would be more "sympathetic" to the industry's problems. Ideally, the board would in time take the firms' point of view and would thus act as a shield between companies and policyholders in much the same way as the Interstate Commerce Commission came to protect rail carriers on a variety of matters.[21]

Solidarity among life insurance officials on the question of federal regulation also showed signs of returning. Just as state-controlled fire rates caused industry personnel to reassess their position on federal supervision, the clamor for state life insurance (beginning in Wisconsin and spreading to a number of other states by 1913) prompted a host of small, regional life insurance companies (Kansas City Life, Northwestern Mutual, Equitable of Iowa, and others) to reconsider their stance on the need for federal control. While not all firms apparently felt strongly enough to agitate for such legislation, considerable support existed for the cause of federal supervision.[22]

IV

THE INDUSTRY'S last serious quest for federal relief during the progressive era occurred between 1912 and 1915. A number of prominent insurance leaders, directed by New York Life President Darwin P. Kingsley, called by his peers "that militant knight of federal supervision," now thought a systematic program of legal action could achieve federal control. They formulated a twofold plan: first force the courts to test the legality of the 1869 *Paul* vs. *Virginia* decision; then if the *Paul* case could not be overturned, mount a rigorous campaign to amend the Constitution.[23]

After careful deliberation federal supervision proponents chose a Montana tax dispute as a test case. Their *New York Life Insurance Company* vs. *Deer Lodge County* came before the United States Supreme Court late in 1913. Much to the industry's consternation, the high court not only adhered to its previous decision in *Paul* vs. *Virginia* but extended the *Paul* rationale by saying that the manner in which a company conducted its business did not alter the fact that the issuance of an insurance policy was not a transaction of interstate commerce.[24]

Defeated by the *Deer Lodge County* decision, Kingsley and his followers started agitation for a constitutional amendment. While on the surface this stratagem seemed an exercise in futility, proponents thought an amendment would push Congress to act favorably on the industry's demands. The nation's lawmakers, however, showed little or no interest in helping the insurance men achieve federal supervision. As one congressman phrased it, "The public is solidly against the industry on this amendment question. Local reforms, especially in the progressive states, have worked to the great advantage of the policyholder." Politicians, furthermore, generally desired to preserve the status quo where states collected handsome license fees and tax revenues from the various companies. The constitutional amendment movement collapsed totally.[25]

Although most insurance officials wanted federal rather than state regulation, those who had effected local reforms almost universally opposed any change. The fiery Kansas consumer advocate Webb McNall succinctly expressed reformers' feelings in the 1890s toward the industry-sponsored drive for federal control. In a letter to a Fort Scott citizens' reform club, McNall wrote, "The recent move[s] on the part of Congressman Patison [*sic*] and Senator Platt to escape state reform statutes are dangerous. The public should not believe their talk about the industry's desire to be regulated. . . . If the insurance people get a special Washington department like the railroads got eleven years ago, then real reform is futile for I know any such depart[ment] will take the companys' [*sic*] point of view."[26]

Consumers' attitudes toward federal supervision, where known, duplicate those of McNall and his fellow reformers. One observer captured their views during the debate on the Dryden bill. "Strange as it may seem, the policyholder, who primarily is the one benefited most by supervision, has indicated no desire to have the present methods [of regulation] changed. The entire demand for the new order of things comes from the officers of the insurance companies, who seek in this way to escape the burdens and compliance with the dicta of state supervision."[27]

The only significant deviation from the stance taken by the public against federal supervision came with the proposal for a model code for the District of Columbia. Modernizers within commissioner ranks generally endorsed efforts to make state insurance statutes uniform. Regulation that varied "widely and wildly" from state to state annoyed them. But the new breed understandably questioned whether any model code could match the high standards already established by the New York and Wisconsin statutes.[28]

Varying dimensions of progressive era politics can be identified during the lengthy quest for federal supervision. The drive itself came in two distinct phases—initially a search for order spearheaded by industry's desires to remedy the inadequacies, "the anarchy," of state insurance regulation, and then a wish to escape stringent state control.

Unquestionably, insurance personnel echoed sentiments of contemporary corporate leaders who typically endorsed increased order and efficiency through benevolent legislation but, when a flood of "unfriendly" laws seemed inevitable, found federal meddling less objectionable than state and local actions. Reformers, insurance commissioners in particular, shared beliefs of most insurance people when they too sought predictability and efficiency with modernizing statutes. But when those totally dedicated to policyholder justice campaigned for tough consumer protection laws, the life and fire insurance enterprise balked and joined the bandwagon for federal supervision.

The battle for federal control further reveals the troublesome split within the larger reform ranks over how best to regulate society. Throughout the progressive era, efficiency drives collided with genuine efforts to protect the public interest. One example is municipal uplift. The more comfortable changes—ones the average businessman applauded—were the widespread and largely successful attempts to supplant the inefficiency, patronage, and bossism of nineteenth-century city governments with bureaucratic methods, most commonly represented in the commission and manager plans. But advanced reformers (workers, consumers, and the like) expressed much less interest in efficiency than in democratizing the structure of local government. They consistently fought for inclusion of initiative, referendum, and recall to protect the commonweal. A city run on sound business practices did not necessarily mean that social, political, and economic justice prevailed.

Whatever the objectives of progressive era reformers, an axiom might be that the most meaningful and even radical changes occurred in the states and municipalities rather than at the national level. The reason is easily explained. Citizens typically confronted on a continued and extremely personal basis a host of abusive and arrogant concerns, which nearly always included street railway, electric light, and other quasi-public corporations. When their grievances were compounded by hard times, the public frequently attacked operations thought to be unjust and a menace to the community. "Gas and water" socialism often resulted. In the insurance field this same consumer advocacy explains most reform. Policyholders' intimate contact with both the life and fire industries helps to account for such "radical" solutions as government life insurance and state rates. Overall, a policyholder had better luck venting his anger and concern on local lawmakers or the insurance commissioner in the state capital than on congressmen or the president in Washington, D.C.

Insurance reformers were thus more successful than most of their counterparts in controlling the new industrial state. The principal explanation is that they blocked the life and fire enterprises from replacing local reforms with less stringent federal ones. Writing on the eve of World War I, a former insurance department official nicely summed up the results of the industry's failure: "While there are perhaps merits to having uniform and systematic insurance statutes, there exists greater merit in having the states administer the insurance business. . . . They know what is best and there has been great policyholder satisfaction over the past years with local regulation in most states."[29]

8

Afterword

CONSUMER CONCERNS about insurance did not evaporate completely with the triumphs of the progressive era. Yet when viewed in historical perspective, they are less frequent today and fail to rival those directed toward the myriad wrongdoings that once confronted the policyholder. More vocal unrest has focused on life rather than fire matters, and only in recent years. The principal complaint is that firms are failing to provide complete information on the cost of their policies. Companies emphasize stability or attributes of their agents, not price. Buyers suffer through not knowing that different carriers charge vastly different rates for the same coverage. But other grievances exist in the form of commonly employed practices that reward the industry. Firms, for example, regularly do not pay interest on policies from the date of the insured's demise until the day they settle the claim; instead, companies compute interest only from the time they receive "due proof of death," which might be a month or more after the event itself.

Unhappiness with unfair financial practices similarly applies to fire insurance but to a more limited degree. Fortunately, the method of state-made rates worked well. Rapid urban deterioration since World War II, however, has produced conditions where policyholders in certain inner-city areas are unable to afford coverage or, more likely, to obtain it at all. The disastrous riots of the 1960s prompted the federal government to assist companies by guaranteeing through assigned-risk pools (so-called "fair plans") continued availability of property insurance to inner-city residents who had become "undesirables" because of their place of residence. Although Congress left to each state the details of how to set up the plan, it did say that protection should be available at "reasonable cost." But by the mid-1970s consumer groups maintained that rates in some fair-plan states, particularly New York, were many times higher than those charged for risks not in the pool.

Just as the new breed of commissioners emerged to direct consumer militancy more than sixty years ago, their heirs have just lately made their debut. Present-day counterparts use identical techniques in their fight for policyholder justice, including enforcement of existing statutes, proposals for new ones, and the old standby publicity. Commissioners in Wisconsin and New York, for instance, have returned to earlier consumer victories and are publicizing the availability of two inexpensive government insurance plans, Wisconsin State Life Fund and Savings Bank Life Insurance. Once again both the limitations and possibilities of reform are demonstrated. While reform is difficult to institutionalize, an official sensitive to policyholders' needs can contribute significantly to their welfare.

The best known of the modern new-breed commissioners is Herbert S. Denenberg, who ran a highly publicized consumerism campaign as head of the Pennsylvania Department of Insurance from 1971 to 1974. Frequently called the Ralph Nader of insurance, this former Harry J. Loman Professor of Insurance at the Wharton School of Finance and Commerce strove to aid the consumer. Denenberg's nationally famous *Shopper's Guide to Life Insurance,* first published in April 1972, helped combat the greatest single evil confronting the purchaser of life insurance. The book includes his ranking of the fifty largest companies selling life protection in the Keystone State by the "true costs of their policies." The facts astonished readers. Similar coverage from The Bankers Life of Iowa cost $61.97 annually but totaled $119.30 from Georgia International Life and $114.67 from State Life of Indiana.[1]

Commissioner Denenberg shared uncanny similarities with the earlier new-breed types. Like them, he alerted consumers to the possibilities of forcing insurance companies to act in the public interest. But there is more. For years industry leaders had been accustomed to bland political appointees who usually rubber-stamped company desires. But like Webb McNall, Denenberg badly upset and angered the carriers. Just as McNallism represented unjustified interference in the eyes of corporate officialdom, "Herb the Horrible" produced an equivalent effect. Reminiscent of W. D. Vandiver's catchy slogan of "Honest business or no business . . . ," Denenberg popularized a Latin motto, *Populus iamdudum defutatus est.* (His translation: The consumer has been screwed long enough!) And in typical fashion he employed every avenue to further his crusade. Duplicating McNall and Vandiver he turned his department's annual reports and even his biographical entry in *Who's Who in America* into vehicles for expounding his world view.[2]

The appearance of Herbert Denenberg in Pennsylvania or of his protégé James Stone in Massachusetts did not mean that all states obtained insurance heads eager to combat abuse. The old-breed type of commissioner dominates the regulation of insurance; many recently have triggered consumer anger. For instance, in January 1978 members of Cleveland's Buckeye-Woodland Community Congress blasted Harry V. Jump, Ohio's superintendent of insurance, for allowing fire insurance firms to redline inner-city neighborhoods and even to drop homeowners' policies. Local residents saw Jump as "a good example of one who caters to the industry."[3]

The postprogressive decades witnessed a general decline in consumerism and the virtual disappearance of new-breed commissioners. Insurance men liked this milieu. It is understandable then that they totally flip-flopped in their attitudes about federal control, rejecting this once cherished objective.

Life and fire executives ignored the judicial green light given them by the Supreme Court in 1944. In *U.S.* vs. *Southeastern Underwriters Association* the high court overturned the 1869 *Paul* decision, arguing that it was not the nature of an insurance contract but the entire chain of events that determined the character of the transaction. The court noted, however, that the existence of federal regulatory power did not deny any state the right to regulate aspects of the business relating to the local welfare.[4]

The revival of consumerism—the Nader phenomenon of the 1960s and 1970s—and the reappearance of the new breed of commissioners only reinforced the desire of insurance leaders to protect the status quo. They quote the old Arab proverb, "Let a camel's nose under your tent at night, and by morning the whole beast will be sleeping with you." Since many life firms have extended their insurance services to include health and automobile coverage, they have become extremely sensitive to consumer and legislative clamor for national health and no-fault auto protection and overall truth-in-insurance legislation. While some endorse the benefits to be gained by federal statutes that would establish uniform regulations and outlaw wildcatting (the age-old desire for efficiency and order), the majority fervently want insurance to remain the largest state-regulated business in the nation.

While the actuality of "what is past is prologue" is limited, the forces that long ago produced and sustained life and fire insurance reform still exist. Consumer conquests over an industry are never total or complete.

Note on Sources

THE BULK of the source material used in this study is located in the Papers of the Kansas Insurance Department. Unlike most states the Kansas State Historical Society in Topeka carefully preserved an extremely valuable collection of state agency records. The Kansas papers are especially significant because the reform efforts of various commissioners, particularly Webb McNall, generated an enormous amount of correspondence. Written material came not only from policyholders and the industry, but from a variety of interested parties and organizations. Out-of-state commissioners, for instance, commonly forwarded copies of their own correspondence, newspaper clippings, and pamphlets to Topeka. The Kansas Insurance Department, moreover, subscribed to several clipping services during the general period of this study. The collection contains various pamphlets, broadsides, and insurance-related publications.

The New York State Department of Insurance in Albany also owns useful correspondence, but not in the volume of the Kansas holdings. The New York department preserved various miscellaneous material, mostly pamphlets (unfortunately, employees destroyed some of this during a housecleaning in 1969–1970). The various official insurance department holdings in Wisconsin, Texas, and Missouri are minimal; but the voluminous Herman L. Ekern Papers in the State Historical Society of Wisconsin help to make the Wisconsin story more complete.

This study relied heavily on the insurance trade press. While the large national publications—especially the *Spectator*—give keen insights into a dimension of the reform story, smaller regional ones—especially the *Western Insurance Review, Texas Insurance,* and the *Insurance Radiator*—are extremely valuable. The trade press also publishes annual or semiannual supplements with some regularity. These often contain a digest of legislative happenings and overall comments on insurance reform affairs.

Finally, newspapers, corporate histories (virtually nonexistent for fire insurance firms), proceedings of insurance organizations, and department annual reports are at times helpful. The latter assume considerable value when new-breed commissioners review their year's work.

Notes

PREFACE

1. William R. Baker to Ben C. Hyde, May 12, 1923, Kansas Insurance Department Papers, Kansas State Historical Society, Topeka, hereafter cited as KIDP.
2. Robert S. Maxwell, *La Follette and the Rise of the Progressives in Wisconsin* (Madison, 1956); James Aubrey Tinsley, "The Progressive Movement in Texas," unpub. Ph.D. diss., Univ. Wisconsin, 1953.

CHAPTER 1

1. See, for example, Charles Kelley Knight, *The History of Life Insurance in the United States to 1870* (Philadelphia, 1920), 75-131.
2. "Insurance: Past and Present in New York" (Albany, n.d.), 4-5, pam., New York Insurance Department Papers, Albany, hereafter cited as NYIDP.
3. Knight, *Life Insurance,* ch. 4; Miles Menander Dawson, *The Business of Life Insurance* (New York, 1905), 186. State officials also sought to eliminate wildcatting. For instance, Attorney General James Stephen Hogg and Insurance Commissioner L. L. Foster of Texas "drove more than 40 'wildcats' from the State" in the late 1880s. See Robert C. Cotner, ed., *Addresses and State Papers of James Stephen Hogg* (Austin, 1951), 37-40.
4. Earl M. Lewis, "History of Public Regulation in New York State," unpub. Ph.D. diss., Univ. Chicago, 1951, 93; Knight, *Life Insurance,* 127-28; *New York Insurance Reports: Barnes' Condensed Edition* (Albany, n.d.), I, 652-60.
5. L. G. Fouse, "State Regulation of Insurance," *Annals, American Academy of Political and Social Science* 24(July 1904):70.
6. *New York Assembly Documents,* 1860, #90, 4, New York State Library, Albany.
7. "Massachusetts Department of Insurance: A History" (Boston, n.d.), 3-10, pam., NYIDP; Knight, *Life Insurance,* 156-58. There is debate over whether Massachusetts had the nation's first insurance department. In 1851 New Hampshire transferred the regulation of insurance companies from the legislative branch to an administrative agency when it established a board of insurance commissioners. This legislation authorized the governor to appoint three suitable persons for an annual term, whose duty it was to examine personally each year the affairs of all insurance firms and to report to the legislature. This board served until 1869 when the New Hampshire Insurance Department was created. Massachusetts became the first state to have an insurance department headed by a bona fide commissioner of insurance. See *Spectator,* New York, Oct. 2, 1913.
8. Harry Chase Brearley, *The History of the National Board of Fire Underwriters* (New York, 1916), 268-72; *First Annual Report of the Superintendent of the Insurance Department of the State of Missouri* (Jefferson City, 1870), 4-7; *Jefferson City Daily Tribune,* Aug. 23, 1893; James A. Waterworth, *My Memories of the St. Louis Board of*

Fire Underwriters, Its Members and Its Work (St. Louis, 1926), 36-37; *First Annual Report of the Superintendent of Insurance of the State of Kansas* (Topeka, 1872), 25.

9. See *Report of Commissioner of Agriculture, Insurance, Statistics, and History* (Austin, 1889), 3; *Spectator,* Nov. 17, 1887; *First Annual Report of the Insurance Department of the State of Wisconsin* (Madison, 1870), 6.

10. Douglass North, "Capital Accumulation in Life Insurance between the Civil War and the Investigation of 1905," in William Miller, ed., *Men in Business: Essays in the History of Entrepreneurship* (Cambridge, 1952), 238-40; John A. McCall, *A Review of Life Insurance from the Date of the First National Convention of Insurance Officials, 1871-1897* (New York, 1898), 36-37; Henry Wysham Lanier, "Great Questions in Life Insurance," *World's Work* 8(October 1904):5380; *Independent* 58(Feb. 16, 1905):396.

11. North, "Capital Accumulation," 239; "Insurance: Past and Present in New York," 16-19.

12. These overall conclusions are based on Viviana Zelizer, "The Development of Life Insurance in the United States: A Sociological Analysis," diss. abstr., Business History Conference, Columbus, Ohio, Feb. 25, 1977.

13. R. Carlyle Buley, *The Equitable Life Assurance Society of the United States, 1859-1964* (New York, 1965), I, 91-100; *Henry Baldwin Hyde: A Biographical Sketch* (New York, 1902), 44, 53-57; Terence O'Donnell, *History of Life Insurance in Its Formative Years* (Chicago, 1936), 549-51.

14. North, "Capital Accumulation," 241-42; William H. Price, "Life Insurance Reform in New York," *American Economic Association Quarterly,* 3rd ser., 10(Dec. 1909):79.

15. Shepard B. Clough, *A Century of American Life Insurance: A History of the Mutual Life Insurance Company of New York, 1843-1943* (New York, 1946), 127; Marquis James, *The Metropolitan Life: A Study in Business Growth* (New York, 1947); J. Owen Stalson, *Marketing Life Insurance: Its History in America* (Cambridge, 1942), 493.

16. Buley, *Equitable,* I, 89-293; Stalson, *Marketing,* 433-34.

17. James, *Metropolitan,* 73-90; Earl Chapin May and Will Oursler, *The Prudential: A Story of Human Security* (Garden City, 1950), 40-60; *Report . . . of the Metropolitan Life Insurance Company* (New York, 1911), 1.

18. James, *Metropolitan,* 73; North, "Capital Accumulation," 243-44.

19. *Spectator,* May 24, 1888.

20. Judson Knight Madison to the New York superintendent of insurance, May 1, 1880, NYIDP; *Index* (Boston), Jan. 1874.

21. *Western Insurance Review* (St. Louis), Spring 1882, suppl.

22. *Spectator,* Nov. 17, 1892.

23. Statement made by G. E. Tarbell in *Testimony Taken by the Joint Committee of Senate and Assembly of the State of New York Appointed to Investigate the Affairs of Life Insurance Companies* (Albany, 1906), IV, 3444.

24. Harris Proschansky, "The National Association of Life Underwriters: Its First 40 Years (1890-1930)," unpub. Ph.D. diss., New York Univ., 1954, 19-20.

25. *Milwaukee Sentinel,* Apr. 17, 1896; *Texas Insurance* (Dallas), Mar. 21, 1904.

26. Proschansky, "National Association," 22-23.

27. Harris Proschansky, "The Origins of the National Association of Life Underwriters," *Business History Review* 29(Sept. 1955):245.

28. Proschansky, "National Association," 25; *Proceedings of the Thirty-First Annual Convention of Insurance Commissioners of the United States* (1900), copy NYIDP.

29. Wisconsin Life Insurance Company, "Collected Speeches and Statements on the Nature of the Life Insurance Business," n.d., 18-19, pam., NYIDP.

30. Quotations in newspaper clippings, NYIDP.

31. See National Association of Life Underwriters, "Professional Standards" (New York, 1892), 3-34, pam., NYIDP.

32. Proschansky, "National Association," 100-105; *Thirty-First Annual Report of the Superintendent of the Insurance Department* [New York] (Albany, 1890), xxxii; James H. Hudnut, *Semi-Centennial History of the New York Life Insurance Company, 1845-1895* (New York, 1895), 250; *Western Insurance Review,* Feb. 25, 1903; *Spectator,* Sept. 29, 1892.

33. Spencer L. Kimball, *Insurance and Public Policy: A Study in the Legal Implementation of Social and Economic Public Policy, Based on Wisconsin Records, 1835-1959* (Madison, 1960), 123; *Milwaukee Sentinel,* Apr. 7, 1896.

34. Proschansky, "National Association," 118; *New York Daily Tribune,* Oct. 13, 1895.

35. *New York Times,* Oct. 13, 1895, Sept. 26, 1899; *New York Daily Tribune,* Oct. 19, 1899.

36. Proschansky, "National Association," 118.

37. Ibid., 155-56; *Standard* (Boston), May 1, 1903.

38. Harold F. Williamson and Orange A. Smalley, *Northwestern Mutual Life: A Century of Trusteeship* (Evanston, 1957), 110-11; *Spectator,* Oct. 13, 1892.

39. Zeno M. Host to Charles H. Luling, May 2, 1905, KIDP.

40. North, "Capital Accumulation," 250; Buley, *Equitable,* I, 294-348; Williamson and Smalley, *Northwestern,* 102-3.

41. See *Waukesha Freeman,* 1891; *Milwaukee Sentinel,* 1891; Albert R. Hall to John E. Hollingsworth, June 1, 1891, James Stephen Hogg Papers, Baker Library, University of Texas, Austin, hereafter cited as Hogg Papers; newspaper clippings, "Anti-Rebate Laws—Wisconsin, 1891," KIDP.

42. *Proceedings of the National Convention of Insurance Commissioners of the United States* (1891-1905), esp. 1891, 54-55, 67; W. H. Hart to William V. Church, June 6, 1899, KIDP; *Spectator,* Dec. 25, 1913.

43. For material on the 1890s depression, see Charles Hoffman, *The Depression of the Nineties: An Economic History* (Westport, Conn., 1970), esp. ch. 2; Gilbert C. Fite, *The Farmers' Frontier, 1865-1900* (New York, 1966), chs. 7, 11; Ray Ginger, *Altgeld's America* (New York, 1958), 20-21, 91-93, 149-51; Carlos C. Closson, Jr., "Unemployed in American Cities," *Quarterly Journal of Economics* 8(Jan., July 1894):168-217, 257-60, 453-77, 499-502; Samuel Rezneck, "Unemployment, Unrest, and Relief in the United States during the Depression of 1893-97," *Journal of Political Economy* 61(Aug. 1953):324-45; and Douglas W. Steeples, "Five Troubled Years: A History of the Depression of 1893-1897," unpub. Ph.D. diss., Univ. North Carolina, 1961.

44. *Palo Pinto County Star,* (Palo Pinto, Tex.), May 12, 1894.

45. *Spectator,* June 30, 1887.

46. Ibid., Feb. 24, May 19, June 16, June 30, 1887.

47. Newspaper clippings, NYIDP.

48. Ibid.; *Insurance Field* (Louisville, Ky.), Feb. 28, 1901. See also tax statute correspondence (bound vol., 1890-1910), NYIDP.

49. *Insurance Radiator* (Kansas City), 1897, 1899 suppl. on state legislative proposals.

50. George Curtis, Jr., "Life Insurance Taxation: Speech to the General Assembly, March 21, 1911," 10, NYIDP. See also David P. Thelen, *The New Citizenship: Origins of Progressivism in Wisconsin, 1885-1900,* (Columbia, Mo., 1972), 210.

51. *Waukesha Freeman,* Mar. 23, 1899; William A. Fricke to Webb McNall, Jan. 7, 1899, KIDP.

52. *Waukesha Freeman,* Mar. 16, 1893; *Beloit Free Press,* Mar.-May 1899; *Wisconsin Legislature: Acts of 1899,* (Madison, 1899), ch. 326.

53. A retaliatory or reciprocal tax is as follows: if the premium tax imposed by state A on life insurance companies domiciled in state B is greater than the corresponding tax imposed by state B on firms based in state A, state B will in retaliation increase its premium tax on companies from state A to the extent of the difference.

54. Curtis, "Taxation," 10–11; *Waukesha Freeman,* Feb. 21, 1901; Williamson and Smalley, *Northwestern,* 130; Kimball, *Insurance and Public Policy,* 265.

55. *Twenty-First Annual Report . . . Missouri* (St. Louis, 1890), xviii–xxi; *Twenty-Third Annual Report . . . Missouri* (St. Louis, 1892), xxi; *Western Insurance Review,* Apr. 25, 1903; *Spectator,* Dec. 22, 1892, Dec. 8, 1904.

56. *Fourteenth Annual Report . . . Kansas* (Topeka, 1884), 7; C. L. Holman to G. T. Anthony, Nov. 23, 1895, KIDP; E. F. Beddal to Judge C. E. Foote, Jan. 14, 1899, KIDP.

57. E. T. Miller, "The Historical Development of the Texas State Tax System," *Southwestern Historical Quarterly* 55(July 1951):4; E. T. Miller, *A Financial History of Texas* (Austin, 1916), 310; *Galveston Daily News,* Feb. 18, 1893.

58. The precedent for state investment came with New York's 1851 deposit law discussed earlier in this chapter; broadsides (1891–1895), KIDP; *Spectator,* Jan. 24, 1895.

59. William H. Chase to John Snider, ca. 1894, KIDP.

60. *Insurance Journal* (Hartford), Dec. 15, 1896.

61. *Kansas City Times,* Jan. 13, 1897; clippings, KIDP.

62. *Insurance Radiator,* New York, Feb. 1897.

63. Charles Clyde Mitchell, "The Robertson Insurance Law," unpub. M.A. thesis, Univ. Texas, 1939, 13–14.

64. *Houston Daily Post,* Jan. 24, 1905; Miller, "Texas Tax System," 10.

65. For the industry's response to state investment proposals, see Metropolitan Life Insurance Company, "Why Investment Laws Would Hurt Policyholders" (New York, 1898), 1–25, pam., NYIDP.

66. See Walter Prescott Webb, *Divided We Stand: The Crisis of a Frontierless Democracy* (New York, 1937); Gene M. Gressley, "Colonialism: A Western Complaint," *Pacific Northwest Quarterly* 54(Jan. 1963):1–8; Gregory M. Tobin, *The Making of a History: Walter Prescott Webb and The Great Plains* (Austin, 1976); and Necah Stewart Turmon, *Walter Prescott Webb: His Life and Impact* (Albuquerque, 1976).

67. K. G. King to Webb McNall, Oct. 12, 1897, KIDP.

68. *Insurance Radiator,* Feb. 1897; letters, 1897–1898, KIDP.

69. Charles S. Bishop to Webb McNall, Feb. 9, 1898, KIDP.

70. Elizabeth Watson to Webb McNall, Dec. 9, 1898, KIDP.

71. *Mirror* (St. Louis), Oct. 9, 1902. See also Amasa Thornton to Webb McNall, July 27, 1898, KIDP.

72. Ike Nathan to Webb McNall, May 4, 1897, KIDP.

73. Charles O. Littick to Webb McNall, Mar. 17, 1898, KIDP.

74. "A policyholder" to Webb McNall, Apr. 1, 1897, KIDP.

75. *Kansas City Times,* Nov. 13, 1898; *Insurance Radiator,* Dec. 1898; newspaper clippings, "1897—Mo.," KIDP.

76. *Spectator,* Sept. 8, 1904.

CHAPTER 2

1. *Arena, Collier's, Independent,* and *World's Work* are magazines particularly rich in their coverage of life insurance wrongdoings. New York City newspapers, including the *Herald, Journal-American,* and *Press,* similarly hammered away at the industry.

2. Lawson's "Frenzied Finance" articles not only were sellouts but *Everybody's Magazine* circulation soared from less than 150,000 before the Lawson issues to 750,000 by the end of the series. See Mark Sullivan, *Our Times* (New York, 1930), III, 89–90; C. C. Regier, "The Muck-Raking Campaign," *Historical Outlook* 15(Jan. 1904):8; *Era Magazine* 15(Apr. 1905):278, 15(May 1905):337, 16(July 1905):89; and Frank Luther Mott, *A History of American Magazines, 1885–1905* (Cambridge, 1957), 126.

3. Lawson's *Everybody's* articles later appeared in book form: Thomas W. Lawson, *Frenzied Finance: The Crime of Amalgamated* (New York, 1905); Albert Nelson Marquis, ed., *Who's Who in America* (Chicago, 1924), 1936; Alvin P. Harlow, "Thomas William Lawson," *Dictionary of American Biography* (New York, 1927-1928), XI (1933), 60.

4. Thomas W. Lawson, "Frenzied Finance," *Everybody's Magazine* 12(Oct-Dec. 1904):455-68, 65-74 (adv. sec.), 601-13, 65-72 (adv. sec.), 747-60, 65-78 (adv. sec.). Quotation appears in 12(Dec. 1904):69-70 (adv. sec.). Lawson made his intentions clear in other publications as well. In an *Era Magazine* feature story, he said, "I have no selfish motive save the desire to earn the gratitude of the people in whose interests I am working. I have an ambition too great to be satisfied by dollars." Edward Bruce Channing, "The Many-Sided Lawson," *Era Magazine* 15(Feb. 1905):111.

5. *American Underwriter* (New York), Oct. 1904; *Spectator,* Nov. 17, 1904; See ibid., Nov. 24, 1904; and Louis Filler, *Crusaders for American Liberalism: The Story of the Muckrakers* (New York, 1939), 186.

6. *Waukesha Freeman,* Jan. 26, 1905, May 18, 1905.

7. *Era Magazine* 14(Nov-Dec. 1904):401-16, 507-22; 15(Jan.-Feb., Apr-June 1905):1-16, 169-84, 277-98, 337-57, 425-44; 16(July-Oct. 1905):73-89, 163-73, 271-82, 394-410. The insurance series continued in *New England Magazine* 34(Apr.-May, July 1906):224-32, 336-42, 543-48. This publication absorbed *Era* in the fall of 1905.

8. *Era Magazine* 15(June 1905):431; ibid. 15(Jan. 1905):1.

9. Ibid., 16(July 1905):77.

10. "The Ringing Echo from the Public," *Era Magazine* 16(July 1905):97; ibid. 15(Apr. 1905):294.

11. Ibid. 15(Jan. 1905):14; *Spectator,* Apr. 27, 1905, suppl.

12. *New York World,* Jan. 31, Feb. 5, 1905. A marvelous account of the ball is found in J. C. Cartwright, "James Hazen Hyde's Costume Ball," *Metropolitan Magazine* 22(June 1905):305-19.

13. *New York World,* Feb. 15, 18, 1905, Mar. 5, 19, 1905. See also R. Carlyle Buley, *The Equitable Life Assurance Society of the United States, 1859-1964* (New York, 1965), I, 587-660. Some of the nation's most prominent businessmen became involved in the Equitable's internal squabbling, including J. P. Morgan, George Gould, Edward H. Harriman, and Thomas Fortune Ryan.

14. Ibid.; nationwide newspaper comments and cartoons were sampled in *Literary Digest* 30(Feb. 25, 1905):268, 30(Mar. 25, 1905):424-25, 30(Apr. 15, 1905):533-35, 30(Apr. 22, 1905):577-78. See also John L. Heaton, *The Story of a Page* (New York, 1913), 212-27.

15. *New York World,* Apr. 2, 1905.

16. *Report of the Investigating Committee of the Board of Directors of the Equitable Life Assurance Society of the United States* (New York, 1905), 1-50; *New York World,* May 31, June 3, 1905; *New York Times,* June 4, 1905; Buley, *Equitable,* I, 646-66; *Spectator,* June 15, July 27, 1905.

17. Herbert Hillel Rosenthal, "The Progressive Movement in New York State, 1906-1914," unpub. Ph.D. diss., Harvard Univ., 1955, 19.

18. *Preliminary Report on the Investigation into the Management of Equitable Life Assurance Society of the United States* (New York, 1905); *Spectator,* June 29, 1905; Sister Helen Dolores McDonald, "Hughes and the Armstrong Investigation of 1905," unpub. Ph.D. diss., Fordham Univ., 1957, 20-29.

19. Samuel R. McKeen to Francis Hendrick, June 19, 1905, NYIDP. A representative sample of the nation's concern over affairs in the Equitable can be found in the *Dallas Morning News,* June 4, 1905; *New York Tribune,* June 11, 1905; *St. Louis Post-Dispatch,* June 4, 1905; and *Literary Digest* 30(June 10, 1905):849-50.

20. *New York World,* June 25, 1905.

21. *Insurance Monitor* (New York), June 1905; *Outlook* 81(July 29, 1905):796; *Independent* 59(July 27, 1905):219; *Public Papers of Frank W. Higgins, Governor*

(Albany, 1906-1907), I, 176-80. This would not be the first state-sponsored probe of the life insurance enterprise. In 1877 policyholder agitation prompted the legislature to appoint an Assembly committee to investigate all phases of industry operation. Hampered by the companies and lacking overall direction, the examination produced nearly 600 pages of testimony but no major legislation. See *The Condition of the Life Insurance Companies of the State of New York: Revised Tabulated Edition of the Official Stenographer's Notes of the Investigation by the Assembly Committee* (Albany, 1877); *Spectator,* Apr. 1877; *Insurance Monitor,* June 1877. A similar investigation of tontine insurance came to naught in 1885. See *Spectator,* Apr. 9, 1885.

22. Shepard B. Clough, *A Century of American Life Insurance* (New York, 1946), 218-19.

23. Besides Chairman Armstrong the committee consisted of senators William J. Tully and Daniel J. Riordan and assemblymen James T. Rogers, Robert L. Cox, William W. Wemple, Ezra P. Prentice (secretary), and John McKeown. The *New York World* applauded the Republican appointees but severely criticized the two Democrats named to the committee. "The Democratic members revealed the poverty of talent to which the boss system reduces a great city's representatives in a great state." See Heaton, *Story,* 217; *New York Times,* Sept. 3, 1905. In addition to Armstrong's keen interest in political reform, he and his wife both enthusiastically backed the Society for the Prevention of Cruelty to Animals; *Outlook* 80(Aug. 19, 1905):950.

24. Historians have described in detail the committee's three-month probe of the inner workings of the life industry. Virtually every corporate history of a life company contains at least a chapter on the investigation. While all business histories contain some narrative passages, the major interpretation they present is that the hearings marked the close of the "abusive" era in the annals of the industry. Even the best of the corporate studies, Buley's *Equitable Life Assurance Society of the United States,* has serious weaknesses. For instance, Buley, a staunch supporter of the life enterprise, does not recognize the widespread popular disgust and distrust that infected the consumer. A much more interpretative and hence more valuable overview of the 1905 hearings is found in Morton Keller's *The Life-Insurance Enterprise, 1885-1910* (Cambridge, 1963), ch. 15. Menlo J. Pusey, *Charles Evans Hughes* (New York, 1951), and Robert Wessler, *Charles Evans Hughes: Politics and Reform in New York, 1905-1910* (Ithaca, 1967) are both useful. The two unpublished scholarly studies of the Armstrong Investigation (McDonald, "Hughes and the Armstrong Investigation"; and Robert Reppenhagen, "New York State Investigation of Life Insurance in 1905," unpub. M.A. thesis, Univ. Buffalo, 1946) are essentially narrative reports. *Spectator,* Sept. 14, 1905.

25. *Outlook* 81(Oct. 28, 1905):458; *McClure's Magazine* 26(Dec. 1905):220.

26. *Testimony Taken before the Joint Committee of the Senate and Assembly of the State of New York . . .* (Albany, 1906), I, 788, hereafter cited as *Testimony.*

27. Clough, *Century,* 221.

28. Keller, *Life Insurance,* 252; *Outlook* 81(Oct. 28, 1905):442; *Independent* 59(Dec. 7, 1905):1362.

29. *Testimony,* X, 9-155, 279-343.

30. Ibid., VII, 5863-73, III, 2062-74, 2080; *Outlook* 81(Sept. 30, 1905):238; ibid. 81(Oct. 7, 1905):286; ibid. 81(Oct. 14, 1905):342; *Independent* 59(Nov. 23, 1905):1233; Zeno M. Host to Charles H. Luling, Nov. 3, 1905, KIDP.

31. *Testimony,* X, 155-279; *Spectator,* Dec. 14, 1905.

32. *Testimony,* X, 362-446; *New York Times,* Jan. 5, 1906; William H. Price, "Life Insurance Reform in New York," *American Economic Association Quarterly,* 3rd ser., 10(Dec. 1909):10-11.

33. *Independent* 60(Apr. 19, 1906):943; *New York World,* Apr. 28, 1906.

34. *Independent* 59(Oct. 19, 1905):947; John T. Stephens to Herman L. Ekern, Oct. 1, 1905, in Ekern Papers, State Historical Society of Wisconsin, Madison, hereafter cited as Ekern Papers; Glenn Syman Jenkins to W. D. Vandiver, n.d. (day letter), Missouri Department of Insurance Papers, Office of the Missouri Secretary of State, Jefferson City, hereafter cited as MDIP; E. C. Manning to Charles H. Luling, Sept. 23,

1905, KIDP; Rev. Paul Falvey to ?, Oct. 19, 1905, in T. S. Henderson Papers, University of Texas, Austin, hereafter cited as Henderson Papers.

35. *Emporia Gazette,* clipping, ca. 1905, KIDP; *Outlook,* 81(Nov. 4, 1905):545; *St. Joseph Gazette,* Oct. 14, 1905.

36. The New York investigation sparked a number of internal reforms within the ranks of the life insurance industry, particularly within the Big Three. Top officials resigned and some, including John McCall of New York Life and Richard A. McCurdy of Mutual Life, not only quit but returned large sums of money.

37. *Spectator,* July–Dec. 1905; *Western Insurance Review* (St. Louis), Oct. 1905; *Insurance Field* (Louisville), Nov.–Dec. 1905; Charles A. Jenney to Charles H. Luling, Nov. 13, 1905, KIDP. (Jenney served as president of the *Weekly Underwriter* of New York City.)

38. W. D. Vandiver, "The Responsibility of Insurance Officials," *World To-Day,* 9(Dec. 6, 1905):1283–85; *Spectator,* Apr. 19, 1906. An excellent summary of the post-Armstrong state investigations appears in *Thirty-Eighth Annual Report of the Commissioner of Insurance of Wisconsin* (Madison, 1907), Life and Casualty vol., 18.

39. *Chicago Daily Tribune,* Feb. 1, 3, 190.

40. Ibid., Feb. 3, 1906; *Spectator,* Feb. 8, 1906. The Committee of Fifteen finished its work in November 1906.

41. *Report of the Joint Committee of Senate and Assembly on the Life Insurance Companies* (Madison, 1907), 1–2. See also Albert Erlebacher, "The Wisconsin Life Insurance Reform of 1907," *Wisconsin Magazine of History* 55(Spring 1972):213–30. For La Follette's attitudes toward reform and reformers, see David P. Thelen, *The Early Life of Robert M. La Follette, 1855–1884* (Chicago, 1966); Thelen, *Robert M. La Follette and the Insurgent Spirit* (Boston, 1976); and Stanley P. Caine, *The Myth of a Progressive Reform: Railroad Regulation in Wisconsin, 1903–1910* (Madison, 1970).

42. *New York Sun,* Dec. 9, 1905; *Spectator,* May 17, 1906; newspaper clippings, Ekern Papers; *Dictionary of Wisconsin Biography* (Madison, 1960), 116, 135. Other members of the investigating committee were senators Julius E. Roehr and Jacob Rummel and assemblymen W. S. Braddock, G. W. Beedle, and Barney Potter.

43. *Report of the Joint Committee,* 4.

44. Harold F. Williamson and Orange A. Smalley, *Northwestern Mutual Life* (Evanston, 1957), 137–43; *Spectator,* May 24, June 21, Dec. 13, 1906; *Report of the Joint Committee,* 11–15, 70, 105–12.

45. *Waukesha Freeman,* Jan. 1, 1907.

46. *Report of the Joint Committee,* 234–35; *Annual Report . . . Wisconsin* (Madison, 1908), Life and Casualty vol., 8–9.

47. W. Clyde Manns to Herman L. Ekern, Oct. 20, 1907, Ekern Papers; clippings from *Forest Leaves* and similar public response in ibid.

48. *Proceedings of the First Annual Meeting of the Association of Life Insurance Presidents* (1907), 31–35; *Milwaukee Sentinel,* Oct. 9, Nov. 30, Dec. 1, 1907); Robert S. Maxwell, *La Follette and the Rise of the Progressives in Wisconsin* (Madison, 1956), 117.

49. The literature is best typified by Burton J. Hendrick, *The Story of Life Insurance* (New York, 1907).

50. *Texas Insurance* (Dallas), Sept. 1, 1909; Robert Lyman Cox, "Statutory Direction of Life Insurance Companies Investments with Special Reference to the Robertson Law of Texas" (New York, 1924), 1, pam., NYIDP.

51. *Dallas Morning News,* Nov. 7, 1905; Alwyn Barr, *Reconstruction to Reform: Texas Politics, 1876–1906* (Austin, 1971), 237; Thomas B. Love to Charles H. Luling, July 5, 1906, KIDP.

52. Walter Prescott Webb, ed., *The Handbook of Texas* (Austin, 1952), II, 487; *House Journal* (Austin, 1907), 88; James Harvey Robertson to William Day, Nov. 7, 1910, Thomas B. Love Papers, Dallas Historical Society, Dallas, hereafter cited as Love Papers.

53. "Public United for Life Insurance Investment" (1907), 3-16, pam., Love Papers; T. S. Henderson to C. W. Nelson, June 15, 1907, Henderson Papers.

54. *Dallas Morning News,* Nov. 26, 1906, Mar. 10-11, 1907; *Spectator,* Aug. 8, 1907; *Texas Insurance,* Apr. 1, 1907.

55. *Spectator,* May 2, 1907; *Dallas Morning News,* Apr. 21, 26, 1907. It also appears that eastern life insurance forces instigated a bill designed to raise requirements of stock and mutual life companies to a point where Texas home firms could not possibly operate. Introduced by Representative Clay Briggs of Galveston, the measure was postponed on a legislative "suspension day" and was thus killed. See *Dallas Morning News,* Feb. 17, Mar. 4, 1907; *Texas Insurance,* Feb. 15, 1907; and James A. Tinsley, "Texas Progressives and Insurance Regulation," *Southwestern Social Science Quarterly* 36(Dec. 1955):242-43.

56. "The Life Insurance Investment Proposal" (Dallas, 1916), 1-5, pam., KIDP; clipping from *Kansas City Star,* ca. May 1907, KIDP.

57. *Spectator,* Nov. 22, 1906; *Proceedings of the National Convention of Insurance Commissioners of the United States* (1907-1908); A. I. Vorys to Otto Kelsey, Oct. 9, 1906, NYIDP: *Mirror* (St. Louis), July 18, 1907; *Forty-Second Annual Report of the Kansas Insurance Department* (Topeka, 1907), 7; *Dallas Morning News,* Mar. 15, 1907; *Thirty-First Annual Report of the Commissioner of Agriculture, Insurance, Statistics and History* (Houston, 1906), 14-15.

58. *Emporia Gazette,* Dec. 15, 1906; William Allen White to Charles Barnes, Feb. 2, Apr. 15, 1907, Jan. 17, 1908, KIDP. The groups that supported White and the Square Deal movement in Kansas were a varied lot, including railroad brotherhoods, the Socialist party, and the Municipal Reform League.

CHAPTER 3

1. *New York Times,* Feb. 10, 1906.

2. "Democracy in Life Insurance," *Outlook* 84(Nov. 10, 1906):601-3; "A Time for Reform" (New York, n.d.), 3, pam., published by IPC, NYIDP; *Spectator,* July 12, 1906; N. B. Broward to Charles H. Luling, June 6, 1906, KIDP.

3. "Closing of the Insurance Campaign," *Independent,* 61(Dec. 13, 1906):1441; *Mirror* (St. Louis), Oct. 18, 1906.

4. "The Mutual Ballots Counted," *Independent,* 62(Apr. 25, 1907):989. A third slate of candidates appeared in the Mutual Life election contest. Known as the "fusion ticket," this group of trustee candidates came in equal numbers from administration and IPC tickets. According to *Outlook* 84(Nov. 10, 1906):601, "The Fusion ticket is believed to be supported by responsible employees and managers of the Mutual Company, who desire to see some necessary reform effected."

5. *Mirror,* Apr. 25, 1907. See also various letters from IPC members and other interested parties in KIDP, 1906-1907, including Thomas B. Wanamaker to Charles W. Barnes, Apr. 2, 1907; Alton B. Parker to Charles W. Barnes, Apr. 14, 1907.

6. *Mirror,* Apr. 18, 1907. Superintendent Kelsey's fight with Governor Hughes is described in Robert Wesser, *Charles Evans Hughes* (Ithaca, 1967), 126-44; and *Spectator,* June 18, 1908, Feb. 11, 1909. As superintendent, Kelsey proved no better than his predecessor Francis Hendricks. "Kelsey [was] another friend of the [Republican] machine, whose incumbency meant that the cleaning up of the department would be postponed." See John L. Heaton, *The Story of a Page* (New York, 1913), 219.

7. *Spectator,* Nov. 8, 1906; *Western Insurance Review* (St. Louis), Spring 1907 suppl.

8. *Spectator,* Dec. 5, 1907; William H. Price, "Life Insurance Reform in New York," *American Economics Association Quarterly,* 3rd ser., 10(Dec. 1909):56-65.

9. *St. Louis Times,* May 29, 1909; R. Carlyle Buley, *The American Life Convention, 1906-1952: A Study in the History of Life Insurance* (New York, 1953), I, 319;

Spectator, Apr. 9, 1908; *Insurance Field* (Louisville, Ky.), July–Dec. 1907; Harris Proschansky, "The National Association of Life Underwriters," unpub. Ph.D. diss. New York Univ., 1954, 185; *Western Insurance Review,* Jan. 1909.

10. Clipping, *Buffalo Morning Express,* n.d., NYIDP; *Spectator,* Jan. 9, May 8, 1908.

11. *Western Insurance Review,* Apr., July 1909; *New York Times,* Jan. 16, 1909; *Chronicle* (New York), May 21, 1908.

12. See "Rulings, Sections 92–97," bound letters, NYIDP; *New York Sun,* Apr. 30, 1909.

13. *Spectator,* May 13, 1909; clipping, *Kansas City Star,* n.d., KIDP. The legislature also modified section 101 of the code. This particular Armstrong provision called for the use of compulsory standard policy forms. However, the 1909 revision required that all forms be approved by the New York superintendent of insurance and embody ten standard features for the consumer's protection; thus standard provisions were substituted for standard policy forms.

14. *New York Times,* Mar. 27, 1915; Lawrence Puddy to New York Insurance Department, Apr. 1, 1915, NYIDP.

15. The industry objected to this statute largely on grounds that liquidation of stocks and bonds in various corporations would cause a marked reduction in their value and policyholders would suffer accordingly. However, there was no general demand for repeal or modification of this provision. By 1911 companies had disposed of thirty-eight percent of their holdings as required by section 100. See *Spectator,* May 4, 1911; *Western Insurance Review,* May 1911.

16. Clipping, *New York Times,* ca. Mar. 1915, NYIDP.

17. Eugene J. McGivney to Charles Evans Hughes, June 29, 1909, NYIDP; Menlo J. Pusey, *Charles Evans Hughes* (New York, 1951), I, 167; George Sexton Pease, *Patriarch of the Prairie: The Story of Equitable of Iowa, 1867–1967* (New York, 1967), 129–30.

18. *Spectator,* Dec. 5, 1907; James A. Frear to Bruce Whitney, n.d., Ekern Papers; Miles M. Dawson to James O. Davidson, July 5, 1907, James O. Davidson Papers, State Historical Society of Wisconsin, Madison, hereafter cited as Davidson Papers; *Wisconsin State Journal* (Madison), July 14, 1907; Frederick C. Howe, *Wisconsin: An Experiment in Democracy* (New York, 1912), 119.

19. M. Johnson to Herman L. Ekern, n.d., Ekern Papers; note written by George R. Beedle, Ekern Papers. Popular reaction to the companies' withdrawal can be found in the *Waukesha Freeman, Milwaukee Free Press,* and *Milwaukee Sentinel,* Dec. 1907. Beedle's public statement favoring state life insurance infuriated the large eastern firms and prompted them in 1908 to back an unsuccessful attempt to oust Beedle as commissioner. See *Western Insurance Review,* "Review of 1908 Elections" suppl.

20. Typed manuscript written by Herman L. Ekern on the history of the Wisconsin State Life Fund, Ekern Papers, hereafter cited as State Life Fund MS; *Proceedings of the NCIC* (Helena, 1911), I, 58–59. See also Spencer L. Kimball, *Insurance and Public Policy* (Madison, 1960), 57; and Robert S. Maxwell, *La Follette and the Rise of the Progressives in Wisconsin* (Madison, 1956), 124–25.

21. Ekern's political career is carefully traced in Albert Erlebacher, "Herman L. Ekern, the Quiet Progressive," unpub. Ph.D. diss., Univ. Wisconsin, 1965. See also *Dictionary of Wisconsin Biography* (Madison, 1960), 116; and Robert M. La Follette, *La Follette's Autobiography* (Madison, 1913), 155–56.

22. State Life Fund MS.

23. Ibid.; *La Follette's Weekly Magazine* 4(May 25, 1912):7, 15.

24. Ibid. 5(Nov. 8, 1913):5; *Spectator,* July 13, 1911; David McCahan, *State Insurance in the United States* (Philadelphia, 1929), 240; *Insurance Advocate* (New York), Oct. 18, 1913; Benjamin S. Beecher, "State Insurance in Wisconsin," *American Review of Reviews* 47(Jan. 1914):79–82. While Wisconsin became the first state to offer its citizenry "true" government life insurance, Massachusetts three years earlier established its Savings Bank Life Insurance System. Its central concept was to have savings

banks (purely mutual institutions in the Bay State) organize departments to write life policies under state supervision.

25. "The Experiment in State Life Insurance," *Outlook* 105(Nov. 15, 1913): 565–66; *La Follette's Weekly Magazine* 5(Nov. 8, 1913):5, 7(June 1915):12; McCahan, *State Insurance*, 240; "The State Life Fund," *Wisconsin Blue Book* (Madison, 1927), 129. To promote the fund, Commissioner Ekern distributed hundreds of press releases and circulars advertising the state's new function. A typical advertisement said: "The state premiums range from $1.50 to $13 below the company premiums for the same kinds of insurance, and the savings and gains on the state policies will be returned to you annually in dividends. Health and life are uncertain. Act to-day and add that much to your own feelings of security and to your family's future happiness." Press release, Ekern Papers.

26. *Insurance Leader* (St. Louis), Jan. 1915; Robert S. Maxwell, *Emanuel L. Philipp: Wisconsin Stalwart* (Madison, 1959), 184; Clipping, *Western Insurance Review*, ca. 1916, KIDP. In 1915 the Wisconsin legislature, with conservative Republican approval, clarified the laws regulating the limitation of expenses and the total amount of premiums a life company could charge policyholders. These bills outlined what the industry could and could not do, but they did not significantly alter the effects of the 1907 reforms. See *Insurance Leader,* May 1915.

27. State Life Fund MS; Herman L. Ekern to Ike S. Lewis, Feb. 20, 1914; KIDP; Charles W. Barnes, typed speech, "A Reply to Ex-Superintendent William H. Hotchkiss's 'The Case against State Insurance,' " KIDP. Reform groups that staunchly backed Ekern and the state insurance fund included the Milwaukee Municipal League, the Wisconsin Rapids Business Men's Association, and the League of Wisconsin Municipalities.

28. Proposals for state life insurance were submitted in both Missouri and New York between 1907 and 1914, but none emerged from committee. See *Spectator,* Mar. 19, 1908; and *Western Insurance Review,* Aug. 1915 suppl. Florida, however, came close to enacting state life insurance in 1905, but the progressive Broward administration failed in an eleventh-hour attempt to push the proposal through the legislative chambers. See ibid.; and *Florida Assembly Journal* (Tallahassee, 1905), 43–45; see also note 24 for details on the Massachusetts Savings Bank Life Insurance System. *Emporia Gazette,* Feb. 26, 1913; *Spectator,* Feb. 6, 1913; *Western Insurance Review,* Feb. 1913; Ike S. Lewis to Prof. Reuben McKitrick, Feb. 27, 1913, KIDP. Evidence indicates that Representative Mahurin modeled his bill after the Wisconsin Life Fund.

29. *Insurance Leader,* Mar. 1913; the complete legislative history of the Mahurin bill is found in "Mahurin bill folder," KIDP.

30. Twenty out-of-state life insurance companies had withdrawn from Texas as of Sept. 1, 1907. Later the total reached twenty-two. See *Texas Insurance* (Dallas), Sept. 1, 1907; Charles Clyde Mitchell, "The Robertson Insurance Law," unpub. M.A. thesis, Univ. Texas, 1939, 6–7; and Mutual Benefit Life broadside, Henderson Papers.

31. *Spectator,* May 2, May 16, 1907, May 7, 1908; *Texas Insurance,* July 15, 1907; *Proceedings of the NCIC* (1911), 66; Hamilton Cooke to W. E. Merritt, n.d., Henderson Papers. In the decade following the passage of the Robertson Act more than a dozen states considered similar measures. In 1911 alone lawmakers in Montana, Missouri, North Dakota, and Oklahoma debated investment bills.

32. *Houston Chronicle and Herald,* June 2, 1907; "An Address by T. H. McGregor," pam., KIDP; "Notice from New York Life," Henderson Papers; *Texas Insurance,* Dec. 1, 1912.

33. *Dallas Morning News,* Feb. 20, 1908; *Spectator,* Apr. 2, 1908; Marquis James, *The Metropolitan Life* (New York, 1947), 424; *Texas Insurance,* Feb. 15, 1909; James Harvey Robertson to William Day, Nov. 7, 1910, Love Papers; Mitchell, "Robertson Insurance Law," 82.

34. *Spectator,* Mar. 27, 1913; "An Address to the People of Texas by T. H. McGregor," pam., Barker Library, Univ. Texas; *Thirty-Eighth Annual Report of the Commissioner of Insurance and Banking* (Austin, 1913), 7–9.

35. *Texas Insurance,* Mar. 15, 1915; *Insurance Leader,* Feb. 1915.

36. Mitchell, "Robertson Insurance Law," 34–35.

37. *Texas Insurance,* Feb. 15, May 1, 1915; Hugh Williamson, ed., *The Story of Insurance in Texas* (Dallas, 1954), 46–47; clipping, *Austin Statesman,* n.d., Love Papers; Powell Stamper, *The National Life Story* (New York, 1968), 74–75. Enthusiastically pushing for retention of the Robertson law were the small "on-the-make" companies, ones that feared competition from the life giants and viewed the Texas market as an excellent source of income.

38. Mitchell, "Robertson Insurance Law," 45–46; *Dallas Morning News,* June 22, 1915; Lewis L. Gould, *Progressives and Prohibitionists: Texas Democrats in the Wilson Era* (Austin, 1973), 156–57; Stamper, *National Life,* 75.

39. "The Movement for Model Life Insurance Reforms" (Milwaukee, 1916), 2–34, pam., NYIDP; *Insurance Leader,* Apr. 1913.

40. "Model Life Insurance," 22–24; C. Wilson to W. L. Brown, Feb. 27, 1913, KIDP; *Western Insurance Review,* June 1915.

41. D. P. Kingsley to L. G. Fouse, Love Papers; *Spectator,* Dec. 10, 1908; *Western Insurance Review,* Jan. 1910, Jan. 1911, June, Oct., Nov. 1915.

42. Ibid., Oct. 1915; *Spectator,* Nov. 12, 1908; *Proceedings of the Second Annual Meeting of the Association of Life Insurance Presidents* (1909); *Insurance Leader,* Sept. 1914; *Emporia Gazette,* Dec. 2, 1914.

43. Typed speech by Superintendent of Insurance Charles W. Barnes, n.d., KIDP.

44. *Spectator,* Jan. 17, 1907, Jan. 20, 1910; *Proceedings . . . Association of Life Insurance Presidents* (1910), 31–33; "Injustice and Inequality of Life Insurance Taxation" (NCIC, 1908), 1–16; newspaper clipping, Ekern Papers; Maxwell, *Emanuel L. Philipp,* 106.

CHAPTER 4

1. Harry Chase Brearley, *The History of the National Board of Fire Underwriters: Fifty Years a Civilizing Force* (New York, 1916); Lee McKenzie, *Fire Insurance: Its History and Functions* (Seattle, 1914); George H. Holt, *State Fire Insurance Board* (Chicago, 1912); *Western Insurance Review* (St. Louis), July 25, 1903; *Second Annual Report of the Commissioner of Insurance of the State of Wisconsin* (Madison, 1871), 4–5.

2. *Spectator,* Sept. 3, 1885.

3. *Proceedings of the National Convention of Insurance Commissioners* (Hartford, 1889), 35–36; "The Valued-Policy Law; A Brief History," pam., NYIDP.

4. Ibid.; *Fifth Annual Report . . . Wisconsin* (Madison, 1874), pt. 1, 18; Brearley, *National Board of Fire Underwriters,* 276; Spencer L. Kimball, *Insurance and Public Policy* (Madison, 1960), 241–42; R. D. West to Phillip Cheek, Jr., May 1, 1875, rpt. *Western Insurance Review* (St. Louis), legislative suppl., Summer 1875. One source suggests that Wisconsin's valued-policy law very likely grew out of the public's familiarity with northern European fire insurance. "The European practice of carefully valuing buildings, and of fixing the value through Municipal or State Surveyors, may have been in the background of the minds of those who insisted upon buildings being similarly valued in Wisconsin." See Brearley, *National Board of Fire Underwriters,* 276.

5. *Proceedings of the NCIC* (1889), 15–17, 30–33; *Tenth Annual Report . . . Wisconsin* (Madison, 1879), Fire and Marine vol., 16–17.

6. "Valued-Policy Law," 7–9; *Spectator,* Mar. 20, 1890.

7. Brearley, *National Board of Fire Underwriters,* 278; *Spectator,* Apr. 16, 1885; *Thirty-First Annual Report of the Superintendent of the Insurance Department of the State of New York* (Albany, 1890), pt. 1, xxvi–xxvii; "Valued-Policy Law," 18–22.

8. *Spectator,* Nov. 5, 1885; Brearley, *National Board of Fire Underwriters,* 74–76;

J. I. Wilson to "The Commissioners of the United States," Feb. 6, 1891, KIDP; *Insurance Radiator* (Kansas City), Dec. 1896.

9. *Proceedings of the Fire Underwriters' Association of the Northwest* (1885); *Spectator,* July 16, 1885, May 8, 1890; Continental Insurance Company flyer, Feb. 1904, KIDP.

10. *Spectator,* Apr. 22, 1885; "Valued-Policy Law," 14–16.

11. *New York Times,* Jan. 20, 1885; *New York Daily Tribune,* Jan. 21, 1885; *Dallas Morning News,* Oct. 4, 1885; *Spectator,* Jan. 29, Feb. 12, 19, 1885.

12. Brearley, *National Board of Fire Underwriters,* 20–21, 287–88.

13. Ibid., 12–13, 23–24.

14. Ibid., 288; *Proceedings . . . Northwest* (1873, 1874, 1880, 1890, 1893); *Report of the Wisconsin Legislative Fire Insurance Investigating Committee of the Senate and Assembly Made to the Governor . . .* (Madison, 1913), 24.

15. *Proceedings . . . Northwest* (Chicago, 1888), 26.

16. James A. Waterworth, *My Memories of the St. Louis Board of Fire Underwriters, Its Members and Its Work* (St. Louis, 1926), 48–74, 105–5; *Kansas City Times,* Aug. 8, 1897. A much earlier group of underwriters, although less formal, banded together in 1849 in the wake of the great St. Louis fire of that year, but for unknown reasons it quickly dissolved. See William S. Hereford to Solomon P. Sublette, July 4, 1849, in Sublette Papers, Missouri Historical Society, St. Louis.

17. James A. Waterworth, *The Cost of Fire Insurance in the City of St. Louis* (St. Louis, 1884); *Missouri Republican* (St. Louis), Jan. 13, 1884; Waterworth, *Memories,* 113–19. For biographical material relating to Waterworth, see Walter P. Tracy, ed., *Men Who Make Saint Louis the City of Opportunity* (n.p., n.d.), 219.

18. *Western Insurance Review,* spec. ann. suppl., 1890–1894; "The Fire Insurance Situation in Saint Louis," ca. 1894, pam., in KIDP.

19. *Spectator,* Dec. 31, 1891, Mar. 24, 1892; *Western Insurance Review,* 1892 suppl.

20. *Spectator,* Aug. 10, 1893; *Kansas City Times,* Oct. 31, 1893; *Lamar Democrat,* Oct. 19, 1893; *Slater Rustler,* Oct. 26, 1894; *Twenty-Sixth Annual Report of the Superintendent of the Insurance Department of the State of Missouri* (Jefferson City, 1895), viii.

21. *Kansas City Times,* Nov. 25, 27, 1893, Apr. 21, 1894.

22. Ibid., Oct. 31, 1893, Mar. 15, 1897; Evan Samuel Dix to E. Paul Sloan, ca. 1894, KIDP.

23. *Mexico Intelligencer,* Aug. 17, 31, 1893.

24. Ibid., June 1, Aug. 17, 1893.

25. Ibid., Aug. 31, 1893.

26. Ibid., Aug. 3, 1893; *Kansas City Times,* Oct. 1, 1893.

27. Waterworth, *Memories,* 134–45; *Hamilton News-Graphic,* Jan. 24, 1895; *Insurance Journal* (Hartford), Feb. 1, 1895.

28. Waterworth, *Memories,* 134–35, 138–39; *Kansas City Times,* Mar. 16, 1895, Aug. 1, 1897.

29. Ibid., July 25, 1897.

30. Ibid., July 23, 29, 31, 1897, Aug. 7, 10, 1897, Sept. 1, 1897; *Insurance Journal,* Aug. 12, 1897.

31. *Kansas City Times,* Sept. 4, 7, 1897.

32. Ibid., Oct. 12, 1897.

33. Ibid., Sept. 11, 1897; *Joplin Daily Globe,* Sept. 9, 1897; *Mexico Intelligencer,* Sept. 8, 1897; *Jefferson City Tribune,* Sept. 8, 1897.

34. *Kansas City Times,* Oct. 13, 1897; "Why Missouri Businessmen Do Not Support Mr. Fetter's Bureau," Oct. 21, 1897, 1–21, pam., KIDP; *Hannibal Gazette,* Oct. 16, 1897.

35. *Kansas City Times,* June 3, 1898; *Western Insurance Review,* July 1898; Brearley, *National Board of Fire Underwriters,* 293.

36. *Kansas City Times,* Feb. 16, 1899; *Insurance Journal,* June 8, 1899; R. H. Lindsay to Webb McNall, Mar. 6, 1899, KIDP; Waterworth, *Memories,* 146.

37. *Insurance Field* (Louisville, Ky.), Sept. 26, 1901; *Joplin Sunday News-Herald,* Sept. 29, 1901; *Western Insurance Review,* Dec. 25, 1902; *Mirror* (St. Louis), May 8, 1902; *Columbia* (Missouri) *Herald,* May 6, 1904; *Thirty-Sixth Annual Report . . . Missouri* (Jefferson City, 1905), xi.

38. *Insurance Journal,* July 6, 20, 1899; Brearley, *National Board of Fire Underwriters,* 294-95.

39. Edward C. Crow to Webb McNall, n.d., KIDP; *Western Insurance Review,* Winter 1901-1902 suppl.

40. *Session Laws of 1889* (Topeka, 1889), 389.

41. *Report of Investigation of Fire Insurance Rates and Rating Bureaus* (Topeka, 1919), 3-5; *Twenty-Eighth Annual Report of the Superintendent of Insurance of the State of Kansas* (Topeka, 1898), xv-xvi.

42. William Moore to George T. Anthony, June 21, 1895, KIDP. For additional examples of local consumer anger at the Clarkson rating organization, see Anna Potter to Webb McNall, Mar. 21, 1898; Board of Police Commissioners of Fort Scott to Webb McNall, Apr. 29, 1897; J. Hanna Vleo to Webb McNall, Apr. 9, 1898; C. T. Whittenhall to Webb McNall, Mar. 29, 1897; all in KIDP.

43. *Kansas City Times,* Sept. 3, 1897, July 30, 1898; *Emporia Gazette,* Oct. 6, 1897, Apr. 3, 1898; "Harrison Clarkson vs. Webb McNall, #18982, Opinion of the Honorable Z. T. Hazen in the District Court of Shawnee County, Kansas, 1897," Kansas State Historical Society Library, Topeka.

44. *Report . . . Fire Insurance Rates,* 5-6.

45. J. B. Case to William V. Church, July 7, 1902, KIDP. The incoming insurance department correspondence for 1900-1908 contains scores of complaint letters charging the Eldridge bureau with being a "trust." One especially revealing letter is from George K. Bideau to Charles Luling, Jan. 1, 1904, KIDP.

46. *Osage City Free Press,* Jan. 19, 1905.

47. *Emporia Gazette,* July 13, 1907; *Spectator,* Nov. 7, 1907; *Report . . . Fire Insurance Rates,* 6.

48. Williamson, *Insurance in Texas,* 39; "Texas Insurance Club, for Texas and the Nation" (n.p., n.d.), 2-5, pam., NYIDP. The rise of trusts in the Lone Star State during the 1880s and 1890s is described in Alwyn Barr, *Reconstruction to Reform: Texas Politics, 1876-1906* (Austin, 1971), 107-24. The pamphlet, "The Texas Fire-Insurance Problem" (Waco, 1899), 2-7, KIDP, includes numerous policyholder complaints about high and arbitrary rates. For instance, one Sherman policyholder charged, "Fire insurance rates are impossible. . . . I'm convinced that the fire combine is the most arrogant monopoly in our State."

49. Tom Finty, Jr., *Anti-Trust Legislation in Texas* (Galveston, 1916), 15, 63.

50. Ibid., 17; *Insurance Journal,* Sept. 15, 1895; James Stephen Hogg to Seymour Kisch, Apr. 7, 1896, Hogg Papers.

51. "Texas Fire-Insurance," 22-25.

52. Ibid. 28-29; clipping, *Southern Mercury* (Dallas), KIDP.

53. "Texas Fire-Insurance," 30-31; *Central Texan* (Franklin), Apr. 28, 1899; *Insurance Herald* (Louisville, Ky.), Sept. 14, 1899; *Insurance Journal,* June 1, 1899; James Stephen Hogg to Jeffer[son] Welborn, Apr. 17, 1899, Hogg Papers.

54. Finty, *Anti-Trust Legislation,* 18; *Insurance Herald,* May 3, 31, Aug. 9, 1900.

55. *Galveston Daily News,* June 3, 1900. Texas fire men disagreed strongly with the *New*'s assessment of the local situation. See, for example, J. T. Trezevant, "Public Prejudice against Fire Insurance Companies," 1900, pam., KIDP.

56. *Galveston Daily News,* June 28, 1900; *Insurance Field,* Sept. 12, 1901, Jan. 23, 1902; *Dallas Morning News,* Sept. 12, 1901.

57. Finty, *Anti-Trust Legislation,* 18.

58. *New York Times,* May 27, 28, 1903; *Western Insurance Review,* June 25, 1903; *State* vs. *Hartford Fire Insurance Company, et al.,* pam., KIDP.

59. *Insurance Field,* Feb. 1904; *Texas Insurance* (Dallas), 1906 ann. suppl., pt. 1.

60. "Fire Rates in New York," ca. 1907, 3–8, pam., NYIDP; *Spectator,* June 24, 1886; *New York Times,* Feb. 1, 26, June 25, Sept. 11, Oct. 8, 1886, Apr. 30, 1887, Jan. 25, Apr. 1, 14, 1888, Mar. 28, 1890, June 19, 1891; clipping, *New York Sun,* NYIDP.

61. "Fire Rates in New York," 2–3; *Western Insurance Review,* n.d., NYIDP.

62. *New York Daily Tribune,* Feb. 14, 1893; H. T. Yates to "Hon. Supt. of Insurance," May 7, 1893, NYIDP; clipping, *Buffalo Evening Times,* June 15, 1894, NYIDP.

63. Clipping, NYIDP; "Fire Rates in New York," 7–9.

64. Ibid, 28–29; *New York Daily Tribune,* July 28, 1897; *New York Times,* May 10, 1895.

65. *Insurance Journal,* Dec. 16, 1897; *New York Times,* Aug. 15, 1897, May 5, 19, 1898, Jan. 11, 1900; *New York Daily Tribune,* Dec. 1, 1897, Sept. 21, 1898; Brearley, *National Board of Fire Underwriters,* 84–85.

66. *New York Times,* June 14, 1900, Dec. 12, 1902; George W. Ellis to New York Insurance Department, May 3, 1902, NYIDP.

67. *New York Daily Tribune,* Jan. 1, 1903; *New York Times,* May 16, 1906; U. T. Avery to "Honorable Superintendent," July 2, 1905, NYIDP.

68. *Spectator,* Mar. 24, 1904, Jan. 18, Feb. 1, Apr. 19, 1906; legislative history of the Smith bill is traced in clippings from the *New York Herald* and *New York World,* NYIDP; Maurice Ailion to Superintendent of Insurance, Feb. 17, 1906, NYIDP.

69. *Rochester Post-Express,* Apr. 20, 1909; [President of Pilot Ribbon and Carbon Co.] to Senator W. A. Armstrong, Nov. 15, 1909, NYIDP; Howard H. Widener to William H. Hotchkiss, Nov. 11, 1909, NYIDP.

70. *Report of the Wisconsin Legislative Investigating Committee of the Senate and Assembly* . . . (Madison, 1913), 27; note probably written by Commissioner of Insurance Herman L. Ekern, Ekern Papers; *Waukesha Freeman,* Mar. 24, 1887; Kimball, *Insurance and Public Policy,* 96.

71. Albert R. Hall to Webb McNall, Feb. 23, 1897, KIDP; *Milwaukee Sentinel,* 1890–1894; *Superior Sunday Morning Forum,* Feb. 24, 1895.

72. Kimball, *Insurance and Public Policy,* 97; *Waukesha Freeman,* June 17, 1897; *Twenty-Eighth Annual Report* . . . *Wisconsin* (Madison, 1897), pt. 1, ix–x; W. H. Mylorea, "The Inconsistencies of Fire Insurance Legislation," in William A. Fricke, ed., *Insurance: A Text-Book* (Milwaukee, 1898), 870–71; *Report* . . . *Senate and Assembly,* 27.

73. Wisconsin was not the only state to have country, town, and industry mutuals. New York had dozens of rural mutuals, most of which dated from the time of the Civil War. Missouri, Kansas, and Texas had mutuals, but they were few in number and limited primarily to farmers. Nowhere in the nation did the mutual movement flourish as it did in Wisconsin.

74. Kimball, *Insurance and Public Policy,* 52; "History of State Insurance," typed MS, Ekern Papers.

75. Ibid.; *Western Insurance Review,* legislative suppl., 1905.

76. Kimball, *Insurance and Public Policy,* 54–55; Hall to McNall, Jan. 26, 1899, KIDP; *Thirty-Fourth Annual Report* . . . *Wisconsin* (Madison, 1903), Fire and Marine vol. iv; *Milwaukee Sentinel,* July 16, 1903.

77. Herman L. Ekern, "The Wisconsin State Fire Insurance Fund," *La Follette's Magazine,* 8(Dec. 1916):5; Zeno M. Host to "My Fellow Commissioner," Aug. 17, 1905, KIDP.

78. Kimball, *Insurance and Public Policy,* 45.

79. Ibid., 43.

80. Ibid., 43–44; *Western Insurance Review,* legislative suppl., 1903.

81. Kimball, *Insurance and Public Policy,* 47; *Waukesha Freeman,* Mar. 3, 24, 1887.

82. Ibid., Dec. 13, 1888, Feb. 11, 1897, Jan. 8, 17, 1903, Jan. 17, 1907.

83. *Appleton Weekly Post,* Feb. 16, 1893; *New York Daily Tribune,* Oct. 1, 1893; *Wausau Daily Record,* Mar. 17, 28, 1899; "Mutuals in Wisconsin," 1922, 29–30, pam., KIDP.

84. [?] Smith to John W. Breidenthal, n.d., KIDP.

CHAPTER 5

1. See "Legislative Review of State-Made Rates," 1921, 3–7, pam., NYIDP.
2. *Sterling Bulletin,* Nov. 23, 1922; correspondence, 1891–1893, KIDP; Peter H.
Argersinger, *Populism and Politics: William Alfred Peffer and the People's Party* (Lexington, 1974), 33–34.
3. W. H. McBride to editor, *Western Insurance Review* (St. Louis), June 12, 1892, KIDP. See also *Twenty-Second Annual Report of the Superintendent of Insurance of the State of Kansas* (Topeka, 1892), 9.
4. *Spectator,* June 9, 1892.
5. Percy Daniels to W. H. McBride, Jan. 7, 1893, KIDP.
6. Biographical sketch, KIDP; *Osage City Free Press,* 1904–1906: *Emporia Gazette,* Nov. 17, 1908; Charles W. Barnes to Barnesville Mercantile Company, Jan. 1, 1909, KIDP.
7. *Forty-Second Annual Report . . . Kansas* (Topeka, 1912), 6. See also *Spectator,* Mar. 11, 18, 1909.
8. Charles W. Barnes to Dallas C. Smith, Jan. 20, 1909, KIDP; *Western Insurance Review,* Dec. 1908.
9. Ibid., Jan. 1909; see also Robert Sherman La Forte, *Leaders of Reform: Progressive Republicans in Kansas, 1900–1916* (Lawrence, 1974), 75, 94–95, 125.
10. Newspaper clippings, KIDP.
11. *Spectator,* Mar. 11, 1909; *Weekly Underwriter* (New York), Mar. 1909; *Western Insurance Review,* Mar.–Apr. 1909.
12. See correspondence, 1909–1910, KIDP.
13. Newspaper clippings, KIDP.
14. See correspondence, 1909–1910, esp. June–July 1909, KIDP; *Spectator,* Sept. 2, 1909; *Emporia Gazette,* Aug. 20, 1909.
15. *Spectator,* Sept. 2, 23, 1909.
16. *Report of Investigation of Fire Insurance Rates and Rating Bureaus* (Topeka, 1919), 7; *Western Insurance Review,* Dec. 1909.
17. *Topeka Capital,* Dec. 16, 1909; Charles W. Barnes to *Kansas City Times,* Jan. 17, 1910, KIDP.
18. *Topeka Journal,* Feb. 19, 1910; correspondence, 1910, KIDP.
19. *Topeka Capital,* Feb. 24, 1910.
20. *Western Insurance Review,* Jan. 1910; [?] McJones to Charles W. Barnes, Nov. 7, 1909, KIDP.
21. As a "progressive" measure the office of superintendent of insurance became elective in 1901.
22. Biographical sketch, KIDP; *Spectator,* June 29, 1911.
23. Ike S. Lewis to Hunter Meriwether, Apr. 24, 1912, KIDP; Ike S. Lewis to D. E. Dunne, Sept. 9, 1912, KIDP.
24. *Western Insurance Review,* Apr. 1912.
25. *Forty-Fourth Annual Report . . . Kansas* (Topeka, 1914), 5–6.
26. *Spectator,* June 20, 1911; *Report . . . Fire Insurance Rates,* 7.
27. James Aubrey Tinsley, "The Progressive Movement in Texas," unpub. Ph.D. diss., Univ. Wisconsin, 1953, 117–18; *Thirty-Seventh Report of the Commissioner of Insurance and Banking Pertaining to Insurance* (Austin, 1912), 7–8; circular letter from Local Agents' Association of Texas, KIDP.
28. Ibid.; J. C. Hornberger to "Our Agents and Friends," Love Papers.
29. *New York Times,* Feb. 7, 1904; W. A. Traver to Thomas B. Love, Dec. 7, 1906, Love Papers.
30. *Texas Insurance* (Dallas), May 1, 1909; "Problem of Fire-Insurance Rates in Texas and the United States," pam., Love Papers.
31. Tinsley, "Progressive Movement," 118; *Texas Insurance,* legislative suppl., 1909.
32. Ibid.; W. J. Jones to Thomas B. Love, Apr. 1, 1909, Love Papers.

33. *Texas Insurance,* Apr. 15, May 1, 1909.

34. *Western Insurance Review,* May 1909; *Texas Insurance,* May 1, 1909.

35. William E. Hawkins to Charles W. Barnes, Sept. 9, 1909, KIDP; *San Antonio Express,* June 16, 1910.

36. *Texas Insurance,* Feb. 15, 1910; Tinsley, "Progressive Movement," 118-19; *Dallas Morning News,* June 13, 1910.

37. Thomas B. Love to Lee J. Wolfe, June 2[?], 1910, Love Papers.

38. Ibid.; *Spectator,* Sept. 1, 1910.

39. Ibid., Sept. 15, 1910; *Texas Insurance,* Sept. 15, 1910; *Western Insurance Review,* Oct. 1910.

40. *Spectator,* Jan. 11, Apr. 25, 1912; *Texas Insurance,* Feb. 15, 1915.

41. *Spectator,* Oct. 21, 28, Nov. 25, 1909; *Texas Insurance,* Nov. 1, 1911; *Western Insurance Review,* July 1909; clipping, *Western Insurance Review,* KIDP.

42. See *Texas Insurance,* 1913 legislative suppl.; summary of legislative history, Love Papers.

43. Thomas B. Love to editor, *St. Louis Post-Dispatch,* Aug. 1, 1913, Love Papers.

44. *Western Insurance Review,* Jan., May 1909.

45. Ibid., Jan. 1909.

46. Ibid., Dec. 1910.

47. *St. Louis Post-Dispatch,* Mar. 9, 1911; George D. Markham to E. Y. Mitchell, Apr. 10, 1909, E. Y. Mitchell Papers, Univ. Missouri-Columbia, hereafter cited as Mitchell Papers.

48. "Newsletter of the Missouri Association of Local Fire Insurance Agents, July 8, 1909," NYIDP; clippings, *Kansas City Times,* 1909, KIDP.

49. *Western Insurance Review,* May 1909.

50. Ibid.

51. "Why Missouri Needs a Fire-Rating Law," 1910, pam., KIDP.

52. *Western Insurance Review,* Mar. 1911, Nov. 1912.

53. *St. Louis Post-Dispatch,* Mar. 9, 1911.

54. *Western Insurance Review,* Mar. 1911; Markham to Mitchell, Mitchell Papers.

55. *Western Insurance Review,* Mar. 1911; newspaper clippings, KIDP.

56. *Journal of the Senate of the Forty-Sixth General Assembly* (Jefferson City, 1911), 270, 597, 902; *Journal of the House of Representatives of the Forty-Sixth General Assembly* (Jefferson City, 1911), 749; *Forty-Second Annual Report of the Superintendent of the Insurance Department of the State of Missouri* (Jefferson City, 1911); *Western Insurance Review,* 1911 legislative suppl.

57. Ibid., Jan., Nov. 1912.

58. Ibid., Nov. 1911; M. D. Aber to Frank Blake, Sept. 2, 1911, Frank Blake Papers, Missouri State Archives, Jefferson City, hereafter cited as Blake Papers.

59. *Western Insurance Review,* Nov. 1912.

60. Ibid.; Frank Blake to Elliot W. Major, various letters, 1911, Blake Papers.

61. Various letters and telegrams, Sept. 1-26, 1911, Blake Papers.

62. Miscellaneous memoranda, Blake Papers. See also *Insurance Leader* (St. Louis), Aug. 1913.

63. Miscellaneous memoranda, Blake Papers; *Western Insurance Review,* Aug., Nov. 1912.

64. Miscellaneous memoranda, Blake Papers; Samuel D. Capen to Frank Blake, Dec. 28, 1912, Blake Papers; *Insurance Leader,* Aug. 1913.

65. *St. Louis Post-Dispatch,* Mar. 3, 1913.

66. Ibid., Mar. 9, 1913.

67. Ibid.

68. *Chillicothe Constitution,* Jan. 21, 1913; *Journal . . . Forty-Seventh General Assembly* (Jefferson City, 1913), 76.

69. Ibid.; E. G. Orr to Charles G. Revelle, Feb. 2, 1913, Charles G. Revelle Papers, Missouri State Archives, Jefferson City, hereafter cited as Revelle Papers.

70. Thomas Lysaght to Charles G. Revelle, Mar. 1, 1913, Revelle Papers; Solomon E. Bronson to Charles G. Revelle, Mar. 6, 1913, Revelle Papers.

71. *St. Louis Post-Dispatch,* Mar. 19, 1913.

72. *Journal of the Senate of the Forty-Seventh General Assembly* (Jefferson City, 1913), 1079, 1264–66; *Journal . . . Forty-Seventh General Assembly,* 1708; clipping, *Kansas City Star,* KIDP.

73. *Philadelphia Public Ledger,* Apr. 11, 1913; *Spectator,* Apr. 10, 1913.

74. *St. Louis Post-Dispatch,* Apr. 10, 1913.

75. Ibid.

76. Ibid., Apr. 25, 1913.

77. Ibid., Apr. 26, 28, 1913.

78. *Spectator,* May 1, 1913; *State of Missouri ex. rel. John T. Barker, Attorney General* vs. *Assurance Company of America and One Hundred and Eighty-One Others,* May 1913, pam., State Historical Society of Missouri, Columbia; *Bolivar Free Press,* May 1, 1913; *Liberty Tribune,* May 2, 1913; *Worth County Times* (Grant City), May 1, 1913) *Mirror* (St. Louis), July 18, 1913.

79. John T. Barker, *Missouri Lawyer* (Philadelphia, 1949), 119; *Spectator,* Apr. 24, 1913.

80. *St. Louis Post-Dispatch,* Apr. 17, 18, 1913; *St. Louis Republic,* Apr. 18, 1913.

81. *St. Louis Post-Dispatch,* Apr. 25, 1913.

82. *Sedalia Democrat,* Apr. 27, 1913; S. D. Hodgdon to Charles G. Revelle, Apr. 29, 1913, Revelle Papers.

83. *Howard County Advertiser* (Fayette), May 1, 1913; *Mirror,* May 2, 1913.

84. *Howard County Advertiser,* Apr. 24, 1913; Charles G. Revelle to George Cates, Apr. 20, 1913, Revelle Papers. See also *Advertiser-Courier* (Hermann), June 25, 1913. Missouri communities considering fire mutuals included Bolivar, Cameron, Center, and Hermann.

85. *Insurance Leader,* Jan. 1913; *Spectator,* Apr. 10, 1913; *St. Louis Post-Dispatch,* Apr. 17, 26, 1913.

86. *Spectator,* Aug. 7, 14, 1913; James A. Waterworth to Edward F. Goltra, Aug. 8, 1913, Edward F. Goltra Papers, Missouri Historical Society, St. Louis, hereafter cited as Goltra Papers.

87. Ibid.; miscellaneous memoranda, Revelle Papers.

88. Ibid.

89. *Spectator,* Aug. 14, 1913; *Jefferson City Daily Democrat Tribune,* Dec. 6, 1913; *Forty-Sixth Annual Report of the Insurance Department of the State of Missouri* (Jefferson City, 1915), v–viii; *Forty-Seventh Annual Report . . . Missouri* (Jefferson City, 1916), vii–ix.

90. Miscellaneous memoranda, Walter K. Chorn Papers, Missouri State Archives, Jefferson City, hereafter cited as Chorn Papers; clipping from *Kansas City Star,* KIDP.

91. *Insurance Leader,* Mar. 1915.

92. See, for example, William H. Hotchkiss to Henry Evans, Jan. 14, 1910, NYIDP; William H. Hotchkiss to Lester W. Zartman, June 7, 1909, NYIDP; Morris Park Citizens' Association to William H. Hotchkiss, Nov. 25, 1910, NYIDP.

93. President of the Pilot Ribbon and Carbon Company to William A. Armstrong, Nov. 15, 1909, NYIDP.

94. Correspondence, 1905–1910, especially to W. W. Miller to William H. Hotchkiss, Dec. 12, 1909, NYIDP.

95. Ibid.; William H. Hotchkiss to Charles W. Barnes, Feb. 7, 1910, KIDP.

96. Newspaper clipping, ca. 1909, NYIDP.

97. *Western Insurance Review,* Feb. 1910; *Spectator,* Apr. 7, 1910; Charles Edward Russell, "What Are You Going to Do about It? Legislative Graft and the Albany Scandal," *Cosmopolitan Magazine* 49(July 1910):147–60; "Message from the Governor Transmitting Report of Superintendent of Insurance and Recommending Investigation into Legislative Practices and Procedures," 1910, NYIDP: various newspaper clippings, esp. *New York Times,* Mar. 19, 1910, NYIDP.

98. See *Spectator*, Dec. 12, 1911; *Report on the Joint Committee of the Senate and Assembly of the State of New York Appointed to Investigate Corrupt Practices in Connection with Legislation, and the Affairs of Insurance Companies Other Than Those Doing Life Insurance Business* (Albany, 1911), I, esp. 30–54; II, 1759, NYIDP; *Western Insurance Review*, Feb. 1911; *Proceedings*, 1915, 124–27.

99. William H. Hotchkiss to A. J. Carroll, Dec. 4, 1911, NYIDP; Harry Chase Brearley, *The History of the National Board of Fire Underwriters* (New York, 1916), 112–26; *Albany Times-Union*, Dec. 1, 1910. For material on the Page-Merritt Utility Act see Robert Wesser, *Charles Evans Hughes* (Ithaca, 1967), 155–71.

100. *Report . . . Corrupt Practices . . .* , I, 125; William H. Hotchkiss to Isidor J. Trubin, Oct. 27, 1911, NYIDP: *New York Times,* Apr. 30, 1915; Edwin W. Patterson, *The Insurance Commissioner in the United States: A Study in Administrative Law and Practice* (Cambridge, 1927), 274.

101. Correspondence, 1911–1915, NYIDP; *Fifty-Fourth Annual Report of the Superintendent of Insurance of the State of New York* (Albany, 1913) pt. 1, 23–24; *New York Times,* May 10, 1914; Apr. 30, 1915; letter to E. G. Griffin, May 18, 1923, NYIDP.

102. *Spectator,* May 4, 1911; "The Rate Making Question," n.d., MS, Ekern Papers; *La Follette's Weekly Magazine* 4(July 8, 1911):13; Brearley, *Fire Underwriters,* 115.

103. "Rate Making Question," Ekern Papers.

104. Miscellaneous memoranda, see especially news release from New London, Wis., Ekern Papers.

105. See *Report of the Wisconsin Legislative Fire Insurance Investigating Committee of the Senate and Assembly Made to the Governor* (Madison, 1913); *Forty-Third Annual Report of the Commissioner of Insurance* (Madison, 1912), xxi.

106. See *Report . . . Investigating Committee; Spectator,* Nov. 14, 1912.

107. Ibid.

108. Miscellaneous memoranda, Ekern Papers; trade journal clippings, KIDP: *NCIC Proceedings* (1915), 184–87.

109. *Waukesha Freeman,* July 31, 1913; Spencer L. Kimball, *Insurance and Public Policy* (Madison 1960), 201–2; Herbert L. Margulies, *The Decline of the Progressive Movement in Wisconsin, 1890–1920* (Madison, 1968), 121; Herman L. Ekern to Ike S. Lewis, Sept. 22, 1913, KIDP.

110. See Robert S. Maxwell, *Emanuel L. Philipp: Wisconsin Stalwart* (Madison, 1959).

111. *Madison Democrat,* Oct. 18, Nov. 3, 1914; *Milwaukee Sentinel,* Nov. 4, 1914; *Insurance Field* (Louisville, Ky.), May 27, 1915; *Western Insurance Review,* June–Aug. 1915.

112. Maxwell, *Emanuel L. Philipp,* 129; notes, Ekern Papers; Insurance Department correspondence, 1917–1925, State Historical Society of Wisconsin.

113. Kimball, *Insurance and Public Policy,* 100–101.

114. *Spectator,* June 20, 1911.

115. *Western Insurance Review,* ann. rev., 1911, May 1915.

CHAPTER 6

1. "Report on the Office of Insurance Commissioner" (New York, 1916), 2–3, pam., NYIDP. Morton Keller in his study, *The Life Insurance Enterprise, 1885–1910* (Cambridge, 1963), makes the first modern mention of the new breed of insurance commissioner. Yet the strength of Keller's work is not the chapter on state supervision, pp. 194–213; for instance, "Webster" McNall rather than Webb McNall, W. D. Vandiver identified as a "true-blue" new breed, and the general absence of the impact of consumer protest on reform.

2. "A Brief Account of the New York Insurance Department" (n.p., n.d.), pam., NYIDP.

3. See Philip Green Wright and Elizabeth Quincy Wright, *Elizur Wright: The Father of Life Insurance* (Chicago, 1937); broadside, ca. 1890, KIDP. See also *Twentieth Annual Report of the Superintendent of Insurance of the State of Kansas* (Topeka, 1890), 47-53; *Topeka Daily Capital,* Mar. 27, 1891; *Kansas Co-Operator* (Topeka), June 1900; "To Policyholders," William A. Fricke Papers, State Historical Society of Wisconsin, Madison, hereafter cited as Fricke Papers; W. A. Fricke, "Uniform Laws" (n.p., n.d.), pam., Fricke Papers.

4. "The Problems of Insurance" (Topeka, 1891), pam., KIDP.

5. More material on the overall subject of "modernizers" and reform during the populist-progressive era is found in Melvin G. Holli, *Reform in Detroit: Hazen S. Pingree and Urban Politics* (New York, 1969), ch. 8; and James Weinstein, *The Corporate Ideal in the Liberal State, 1900-1918* (Boston, 1968), esp. ch. 4.

6. A. T. Andreas, *History of Kansas* (Chicago, 1883); Preston E. McNall to author, Dec. 18, 1968 (Preston McNall is the late son of Webb McNall); Vera Edith Crosby Pletcher, "A History of Smith County, Kansas to 1860," unpub. M.A. thesis, Kansas State Univ., 1960, 189-70.

7. *Gaylord Herald,* Apr. 29, 1880, Sept. 7, 1882, Sept. 6, 1883; Preston McNall to author; Hill P. Wilson, *A Biographical History of Eminent Men of the State of Kansas* (Topeka, 1901), 493; newspaper clippings, KIDP.

8. *Gaylord Sentinel,* June 30, 1910; *Kansas City Times,* Jan. 21, 1897. See also O. Gene Glanton, *Kansas Populism: Ideas and Men* (Lawrence, 1969), ch. 11.

9. *Spectator,* Mar. 8, 1888; *Twenty-Eighth Annual Report . . . Kansas* (Topeka, 1898), viii; *Kansas City Times,* Mar. 24, 1897.

10. See, for example, Webb McNall to John W. Leedy, Apr. 2, 1897, KIDP.

11. *Kansas City Times,* Mar. 18, Apr. 18, Apr. 20, 1897; newspaper clipping, ca. 1897, KIDP.

12. Clipping, *Gaylord Herald,* ca. 1897, KIDP; "A Policyholder" to Webb McNall, Apr. 11, 1897, KIDP.

13. *Twenty-Eighth Annual Report . . . Kansas,* xii-xiii; *Kansas City Times,* May 27, 1897. See also "Report of the Examination of the Metropolitan Life Insurance Company" (Albany, 1911), pam., NYIDP.

14. *Kansas City Times,* June 2, 1897.

15. Ibid., June 30, 1897; "*Metropolitan Life Insurance Company* vs. *Webb McNall,* Oral Arguments" (Topeka, 1897), Kansas State Historical Society, Topeka; *Western Insurance Review,* Oct. 1909.

16. *Kansas City Times,* Dec. 24, 1897, Jan. 13, 1898.

17. *Twenty-Eighth Annual Report . . . Kansas,* xvi-xix; *Kansas City Times,* Dec. 22, 1897.

18. See correspondence, 1897-1899, KIDP; *Kansas City Times,* Aug. 12, 1898, Feb. 7, Mar. 10, 16, 1899; *Twenty-Eighth Annual Report . . . Kansas,* xxxi-xxxiii.

19. *Kansas City Times,* Sept. 3, Nov. 9, 1897, Jan. 12, July 30, 1898; *Emporia Gazette,* Apr. 3, 1897.

20. John C. Berry to Webb McNall, Apr. 1, 1897, KIDP.

21. *Twenty-Eighth Annual Report . . . Kansas,* xx.

22. Ibid., xxi.

23. Ibid., xxxiv.

24. *Insurance Journal* (Hartford), Feb. 2, 1899; "Plan for Fire Insurance Equity" (1899) pam., KIDP.

25. *Kansas City Times,* Feb. 8, 1897.

26. *Insurance Radiator* (Kansas City), Nov. 1897; *Twenty-Eighth Annual Report . . . Kansas,* xxxi-xxxiii.

27. Newspaper clipping, 1897, KIDP.

28. *Kansas City Times,* Aug. 12, 1898, Feb. 22, Mar. 7, 1899.

29. Ibid., Mar. 10, 16, 1899.

30. *St. Louis Republic,* Oct. 8, 1905.

31. See *Cole County Democrat* (Jefferson City), Jan. 26, 1906. See also *Independent* 60(Feb. 1, 1906):258.

32. William Hyde and Howard L. Conard, eds., *Encyclopedia of the History of Missouri* (St. Louis, 1901), VI, 282-83; Floyd C. Shoemaker, *Missouri: Mother of the West* (Chicago, 1930), III, 93; "Autobiography of Willard Duncan Vandiver," State Historical Society of Missouri, Columbia, 8-14, 23-26, hereafter cited as Vandiver Autobiography; *Congressional Record,* Fifty-Fifth through Fifty-Seventh Congresses. While in Congress Vandiver gained fame for his statement, "I'm from Missouri, you've got to show me." Even though he claimed to have coined this famous phrase, it is doubtful that it can be attributed to him; yet he helped to give the "show me" phrase nationwide currency.

33. Shoemaker, *Missouri,* III, 93-94; *Official Manual of the State of Missouri, 1905-1906* (Jefferson City, 1906), 446-502.

34. W. D. Vandiver, "What Governor Folk Has Done," *Independent* 60(Feb. 1, 1906):260.

35. *St. Louis Post-Dispatch,* Oct. 12, 1905.

36. Ibid., Oct. 18, 1905.

37. *Kansas City Journal,* Oct. 20, 1905.

38. *Missouri State Republican,* Oct. 27, 1905; *Kansas City Journal,* Oct. 27, 1905.

39. Ibid., Nov. 1, 1905.

40. Ibid., Nov. 20, 1905; Vandiver, "Governor Folk," 261.

41. *Jefferson City Tribune,* Nov. 9, 10, 1905.

42. W. D. Vandiver to Charles Luling, Dec. 3, 1905, KIDP.

43. *Independent* 59(Nov. 16, 1905):1187, 60(Jan. 4, 1906):49; *Jefferson City Tribune,* Nov. 10, 1905; *Kansas City World,* Jan. 1, 1906; *Thirty-Seventh Annual Report of the Superintendent of the Insurance Department of Missouri* (Jefferson City, 1906), viii.

44. Ibid., viii.

45. *Jefferson City Tribune,* Mar. 1, 1906; *St. Louis Republic,* Mar. 10, 1906.

46. *Thirty-Seventh Annual Report . . . Missouri,* ix.

47. *Kansas City Journal,* Dec. 6, 1905; *Spectator,* Apr. 1906.

48. *Thirty-Seventh Annual Report . . . Missouri,* ix; *Kansas City Journal,* Mar. 1, 1906.

49. *Spectator,* Apr. 1906.

50. Vandiver, "Governor Folk," 260; "International Policyholders Committee's Report to Policyholders," n.d., 16-17, pam., KIDP; *Thirty-Ninth* and *Fortieth Annual Reports . . . , Missouri; Insurance Advocate* (New York), Jan. 1907-Feb. 1909.

51. W. D. Vandiver to Thomas B. Love, Feb. 24, 1908, Love Papers.

52. *St. Louis Republic,* Aug. 8, 1908; W. D. Vandiver to Herbert S. Hadley, Aug. 3, 1907 (letter in possession of Louis H. Vandiver, Columbia, Mo.); W. D. Vandiver to Charles W. Barnes, Dec. 29, 1908, KIDP.

53. Clipping attached to letter from William Marion Reedy to the "Kansas superintendent of insurance," Nov. 30, 1907, KIDP; Thomas B. Love to William C. Scott, Oct. 22, 1908, Love Papers.

54. Louis G. Geiger, *Joseph W. Folk of Missouri* (Columbia, 1953), ch. 6; Vandiver, "Governor Folk," 258.

55. "Remarks of the Hon. W. D. Vandiver, Jefferson City Democratic Club, January 25, 1906," pam., KIDP.

56. Newspaper clipping, ca. 1898, KIDP.

CHAPTER 7

1. Darwin P. Kingsley to Ike S. Lewis, Oct. 22, 1913, KIDP.

2. J. Gordon Payne to Charles W. Barnes, Dec. 11, 1909, KIDP.

3. *Western Insurance Review* (St. Louis), Summer 1887 suppl.

4. Ibid.; Harry Chase Brearley, *The History of the National Board of Fire Under-writers* (New York, 1916), 5; *Proceedings of the Seventh Annual Meeting of the Association of Life Insurance Presidents* (1913) 62–63. Gabriel Kolko in *The Triumph of Conservatism* (New York, 1963) suggests that the initial reason why insurance leaders sought federal regulation was "to save the insurance companies from state regulation" (p. 90). The historical evidence fails to support such an interpretation.

5. S. H. Wolfe, "State Supervision of Insurance Companies," *Annals of the American Academy of Political and Social Science* 26(Sept. 1905):147–48; John William Wallace, reporter, *Cases Argued and Adjusted in the Supreme Court of the United States* (Washington, D.C., 1870), VIII, 168–85. Students of American insurance, with few exceptions, have cited the *Paul* case as having been decided by the U.S. Supreme Court in 1868, yet the correct date is 1869. See, for example, Joseph Ragland Long, *Cases on Constitutional Law*, 3rd ed. (Rochester, N.Y., 1938), 100–103, 835–36.

6. *Proceedings of the Sixteenth Regular Meeting of the Fire Underwriters' Association of the Northwest* (Chicago, 1885), 49.

7. *Spectator,* Jan. 27, 1887; *New York Daily Tribune,* Oct. 28, 1889; John F. Dryden, "The Regulation of Insurance by Congress," (address delivered to Boston Underwriters' Association, Nov. 24, 1904), 21, pam., NYIDP.

8. Ibid., 20–22; *Spectator,* Aug. 11, 1892.

9. Dryden, "Regulation of Insurance," 21–22; Jeremiah (Jerry) Simpson to "the superintendent of insurance," Dec. 30, 1892, KIDP.

10. Dryden, "Regulation of Insurance," 25–26; *Views* (Washington, D.C.), Dec. 1897.

11. Ibid.; Max Cohen to Webb McNall, Sept. 21, 1898, KIDP.

12. R. Carlyle Buley, *The American Life Convention, 1906–1952* (New York, 1953), I, 145; *Spectator,* 1903–1904; *Western Insurance Review,* 1904 annual.

13. James D. Richardson, ed., *A Compilation of the Messages and Papers of the Presidents* (New York, n.d.), XVI, 6901, 6986–87.

14. *Spectator,* Mar. 2, Mar. 9, 1905.

15. Morton Keller, *The Life Insurance Enterprise, 1885–1910* (Cambridge, 1963), 240: Frederick Marion Hubbell to Charles L. Luling, Aug. 1, 1905, KIDP.

16. *Views,* Aug.-Dec. 1905; *Spectator,* Aug. 24, 1905; "The National Convention of Insurance Commissioners Examines the Question of Federal Supervision" (Washington, D.C., 1906), 3–21, pam., NYIDP; Charles W. Barnes to William E. Smith, Nov. 5, 1907, KIDP; Keller, *Life Insurance,* 241.

17. Ibid.; "Question of Federal Supervision," 22–25.

18. Ibid.; "Speech of Hon. Butler Ames of Massachusetts in the House of Representatives," Dec. 18, 1905, 3–4, pam., NYIDP; *Chicago Daily Tribune,* Feb. 1, 3, 1906; *Emporia Gazette,* Feb. 1, 1906.

19. *Spectator,* Jan.-Nov. 1906; Jan.-Apr. 1907.

20. Ibid., Aug. 1, 1907. See also John F. Dryden, "Uniform Law and Legislation on Life Insurance" (Newark, 1910), 3–20, pam., NYIDP.

21. "The Dangers of the Fire Rate Laws" (Hartford, 1911), 1–17, pam., NYIDP.

22. *Western Insurance Review,* 1913–1914; *Insurance Leader,* Jan. 1914.

23. Buley, *American Life Convention,* I, 430; *Insurance Leader,* Apr. 1914.

24. Charles Henry Butler, reporter, *United States Reports* (New York, 1914), 495–512.

25. *Western Insurance Review,* Jan. 1914; Congressman John R. Connelly to the Governor of Kansas, Nov. 20, 1914, KIDP.

26. Webb McNall to the "Good Citizens of Fort Scott," May 4, 1898, KIDP.

27. Wolfe, "State Supervision," 146.

28. *Proceedings of the National Convention of Insurance Commissioners of the United States* (1906–1916).

29. Typed address, ca. 1915, Ekern Papers.

CHAPTER 8

1. See Daniel Grotta, "The Ralph Nader of Insurance," *Saturday Review* 55(July 1, 1972):34–41; Herbert S. Denenberg, *The Shopper's Guide to Life Insurance* . . . (Washington, D.C., 1974).

2. *Time* 100(July 10, 1972):80.

3. *Cleveland Plain Dealer,* Jan. 13, 1978.

4. *U.S.* vs. *Southeastern Underwriters Association,* 322 U.S 533 (1944), rehearing denied, 323 U.S. 811 (1944).

Index